I0095056

Revulsion

The Paradox of Disgust
in the Rape-Revenge Narrative

Brandon West

Embry-Riddle Aeronautical University

Series in Critical Media Studies

![Vernon Press logo] **VERNON PRESS**

Copyright © 2025 Vernon Press, an imprint of Vernon Art and Science Inc, on behalf of the author.

All rights reserved. No part of this publication may be reproduced, stored in a retrieval system, or transmitted in any form or by any means, electronic, mechanical, photocopying, recording, or otherwise, without the prior permission of Vernon Art and Science Inc.

www.vernonpress.com

In the Americas:	*In the rest of the world:*
Vernon Press	Vernon Press
1000 N West Street, Suite 1200	C/Sancti Espiritu 17,
Wilmington, Delaware, 19801	Malaga, 29006
United States	Spain

Series in Critical Media Studies

Library of Congress Control Number: 2025933290

ISBN: 979-8-8819-0304-6

Also available: 979-8-8819-0257-5 [Hardback]; 979-8-8819-0303-9 [PDF, E-Book]

Product and company names mentioned in this work are the trademarks of their respective owners. While every care has been taken in preparing this work, neither the authors nor Vernon Art and Science Inc. may be held responsible for any loss or damage caused or alleged to be caused directly or indirectly by the information contained in it.

Cover design by Vernon Press. Background image by freestockcenter on Freepik.

Every effort has been made to trace all copyright holders, but if any have been inadvertently overlooked the publisher will be pleased to include any necessary credits in any subsequent reprint or edition.

To Georgie,
Gone too soon

Table of Contents

Acknowledgments

I would like to thank Drs. Katherine Cleland, Shoshana Milgram Knapp, Sharon Johnson, Lisa Zunshine, and Jonathan Adams for their contributions to this project. Further thanks to Victoria West, Kirsten Powell, Ryan West, and Kimaya Thakur for their assistance along the way. I would also like to thank the various conference attendees and panelists who listened to (and offered advice about) this project at different stages of its development, as well as the excellent staffs at the libraries of Virginia Tech, the University of Kentucky, and Embry-Riddle Aeronautical University for making available the vast trove of sources without which this book would not exist. And, finally, I would like to thank Vernon Press for their patience and support throughout this process and the anonymous peer reviewers whose insightful feedback helped this volume take shape.

Foreword

This project started its life as a response paper for a Renaissance revenge tragedy course I took as a graduate student with Dr. Katherine Cleland. The sexualization of murder in *The Maid's Tragedy* troubled me so much that I felt compelled to ask what narrative function the sexualization and, by extension, sexual violence can fulfill. Since I was already familiar with the rape-revenge film's existence as well as acquainted with scholarship of those singularly alienating works, the connection between the two disparate media, Renaissance plays and 1970s horror films, felt natural to me. And, still feeling unsatisfied with my response paper's exploration of the morally treacherous topic, I undertook a longer study in a seminar paper that forms the basis for this manuscript's first major chapter.

My work on rape-revenge, then, started with a short, two-page paper about a scene with which I could not quite reconcile myself. The sexualization of violence raised, for me, too many ethical, affective, and narratological questions to overlook. My continued reckoning with these issues has owed largely to my continued desire to address these questions insofar as I am able. These stories have held me firm for several years now, that grip rooted in my disgust and discomfort with them. Perhaps both these responses, however, stem partially from my personal history. Like many involved in the production, analysis, and/or spectatorship of rape-revenge works, I have been a victim of sexual abuse.[1] Writing this book has, therefore, taken on a somewhat therapeutic role for me, as the occasion has forced me to confront finally that demon from my past.

It is possible, however, this demon will never be laid to rest. Indeed, it has dogged me this far, throughout the original two papers, into the conference presentations forming the basis for further chapters here, and into a second seminar paper I wrote during my doctoral studies, which also forms a chapter in this volume. I have, the reader may notice, been circling back to these same questions and this same type of story for some time and in different forms.

---

[1] Alexandra Heller-Nicholas, *Rape-Revenge Films: A Critical Study* 2nd edition. (Jefferson, NC: McFarland & Company, Inc., 2021), 5-6. Like Heller-Nicholas herself, I choose not to delve into the details of my personal experience. Nevertheless, I identify its existence in this volume because it forms an important part of my history and engagement with rape-revenge texts.

Introduction

Among film's most maligned yet resilient narrative forms lies the rape-revenge film, existing readings of which, I argue in this book, are too dichotomous. To date, readings of these films have tended to argue for rape-revenge's feminist bonafides (Clover) or dismiss these texts as misogynistic (Creed). Both of these camps would benefit from considering the rape-revenge narrative's inherent ambivalence. In this book, I argue contra feminist readings of rape-revenge films that this narrative form is, in fact, less redemptive than this camp construes it to be. Simultaneously, I argue contra readings of rape-revenge as misogynistic that these texts do often contain overt and latent feminist messaging, that the weight of the evidence for the stories I discuss tends to lean toward meanings more feminist than not.

Key to rape-revenge's ambivalence and the enduring difficulty I and so many other scholars have had in interpreting these texts is the paradox of disgust. That is, I argue these texts' reliance on evoking disgust through their narratives and imagery largely dooms the texts to ambivalence and the inability for one to deem them wholly feminist or wholly misogynist.

Aside from my personal investment in these stories, there is clear societal exigence for further scholarly work on rape-revenge. Today, past the #MeToo era, the problems of rape culture remain. Thus, much work remains as well. By continuing to engage in critical discussions of the crime of rape, I hope this volume and other works in this area may continue contributing to this cause. And while the texts I discuss in this book are works of fiction, I nevertheless maintain that examining our fiction helps tell us about ourselves. Films, after all, do not merely reflect our values; they also help determine them.[1] And movies help give us a sense of order and meaning.[2]

That established, allow me to delineate the texts I am considering. One of the major obstacles facing a work such as mine is the sheer number and variety of rape-revenge narratives. Rape, as Sarah Projansky observes, is narratively versatile.[3] Further, the rape-revenge narrative has existed at least since

---

[1] Elizabeth Cowie, "Woman as Sign." In *Feminism and Film*, edited by E. Ann Kaplan. (Oxford University Press, 2000), 64.

[2] Vivian C. Sobchack, "The Violent Dance: A Personal Memoir of Death in the Movies." In *Screening Violence*, edited by Stephen Prince. (Rutgers University Press, 2000), 117.

[3] Sarah Projansky, *Watching Rape: Film and Television in Postfeminist Culture*. (New York University Press, 2001), 3.

medieval ballads, has an established lineage through literature, and exists across a large range of film genres and in a variety of cultures. As such, considering the entire breadth of rape-revenge fiction in a single book is infeasible. To focus my argument and analysis, I have chosen, therefore, to hone in on rape-revenge films that originate from the Western world (but especially the United States) between 1970 and 2021.[4]

Focusing on this period not only allows me to control my study's scope but also identifies a place and time in which rape-revenge films proliferated. The start date of 1970 sets the oldest films in this volume during the decade of *I Spit on Your Grave*'s release. *I Spit on Your Grave* is not only (possibly) the most infamous rape-revenge film, but it is also the first I discuss in this volume. Its influence is profound, and it (and its sequels) will occupy a significant portion of my discussion. Meanwhile, the end date of 2021 marks when I began writing this volume in earnest and could not continue adding new rape-revenge releases.[5]

At times, however, I will reference works from rape-revenge's literary past where they provide useful counterpoints and so that I can offer some insight into rape-revenge more broadly while nevertheless leaving my analysis mostly grounded in a specific medium and time period. By referring to a couple of literary works (*The Maid's Tragedy* and *Clarissa*), I hope to demonstrate how much Western conceptions of rape and consequent revenge have changed while also showing some of the rape-revenge narrative's variety and, moreover, how deep its troubles run. Furthermore, in favor of keeping my analysis at least somewhat concise, I have curtailed the number of texts I consider. As such, some highly influential rape-revenge texts (e.g., *The Last House on the Left*) will not receive substantial discussion in this volume.[6] Instead, I have tried to pick a smaller selection of texts upon which to focus.

I am, however, going to narrow my focus even more by only considering rape-revenge in two film genres: horror and thriller.[7] This approach allows me to

---

[4] As such, discussion of, for example, rape-revenge in Japanese cinema (e.g., *Rashomon* and *Lady Snowblood*) will fall outside my scope in this volume.

[5] Numerous factors allowed for American films in the 1970s to become more graphically violent. Thus, the stage of 1970's America was one set for a film like *I Spit on Your Grave*. 1970 is, ergo, a natural starting point for a study of rape-revenge films. That said, studies on rape-revenge in cinema before 1970 could be fruitful even though they fall outside my scope here. Likewise, studies of rape-revenge films released after this volume began (or is published) could also prove fruitful.

[6] I plan to write about my thoughts on *The Last House on the Left* at another time and in another project.

[7] Rape-revenge does appear in other genres (e.g., in the crime film *Thelma & Louise*).

avoid devoting this volume to delimiting where, exactly, the rape-revenge "genre" lies. Doing so is its own can of worms since Jacinda Reed has argued rape-revenge is not a genre at all, but rather a narrative structure that various artists have adapted for use in a large number of different genres.[8] Contrariwise, Claire Henry has asserted the value of deeming rape-revenge a genre and thereby applying the insights of genre theory to studies of rape-revenge.[9] My goal is not to settle this debate. As such, I am focusing on rape revenge where it exists as a particular sub-genre of horror and thriller films. Such an approach allows my project greater specificity and a clearer agenda. To this end, I take pains in this volume to forego referring to rape-revenge as a genre unto itself.

So, what is the rape-revenge sub-genre of horror and the thriller? These texts are largely similar in that they follow a female protagonist who, typically while on a journey, is raped and left for dead only to then kill her rapists one-by-one. To be sure, this sub-genre shares significant overlap with other sub-genres of horror and the thriller. Even sexual violence is not unique to the rape-revenge film, as Nick Groom has noted how frequently the American gothic contains or is about sexual violence.[10] This is not, however, a book on the gothic. Nor is this a book on the road horror film. Finn Ballard has cataloged the aspects of the road horror film, which do resemble those of the rape-revenge movie to a remarkable degree.

Films from both these sub-genres tend to feature white, middle-class protagonists, to take place on journeys, and to have strong female leads.[11] Nevertheless, rape is not always a key feature of the road horror film, whereas it is essential to the rape-revenge film. The rape-revenge's dual focus on, first, rape and, second, revenge, do distinguish it from road horror, even though the two will often overlap, meaning some of the works I examine could easily fit into a volume on road horror films.

Similarly, rape-revenge films often resemble slasher movies (e.g., *Friday the 13th*) in that both show a character killing a group of people one-by-one. Like the road horror, however, the slasher does not always foreground the issues of sexual assault and revenge, meaning that, while the sub-genres of slasher and

---

[8] Jacinda Read, *The New Avengers: Feminism, Femininity, and the Rape-Revenge Cycle.* (Manchester University Press, 2000), 11.

[9] Claire Henry, *Revisionist Rape-revenge Redefining a Film Genre.* (Basingstoke: Palgrave Macmillan, 2014), 8.

[10] Nick Groom, *The Gothic: A Very Short Introduction.* (Oxford University Press, 2012), 11.

[11] Finn Ballard, "No Trespassing: The post-millennial road-horror movie," *The Irish Journal of Gothic and Horror Studies* 4 (2008): 22-24, https://irishgothicjournal.net/wp-content/uploads/2018/03/finn-ballard.pdf.

rape-revenge may overlap, they are not identical. And I can say the same for the rape-revenge and the western movie, both of which feature what Bernice Murphy has called regeneration through violence.[12]

Finally, as I have been revising this book, Barbara Creed has released a follow-up on her seminal *The Monstrous-Feminine* in which she discusses a new genre she christens the Feminist New Wave. Given that Creed devotes a chapter in her new book, *Return of the Monstrous-Feminine*, to contemporary rape-revenge films, it is unsurprising that the Feminist New Wave and the rape-revenge film overlap at times. Examining the list of films Creed includes, we can see that some Feminist New Wave movies (e.g., *Revenge*) are rape-revenge narratives and that others are not.

These matters established, allow me to turn to my methodology. To examine my key texts, I primarily use narratological analysis, focusing on matters of plot and character. To this end, I have made the conscious, albeit possibly controversial, decision to (largely) eschew historical analysis. That is to say, I will not spend as much time connecting these films to their differing historical and cultural contexts as I could. I have made this decision not out of disdain for historicism but for pragmatic reasons. Namely, part way through drafting this volume, I realized my historicist analyses were too disparate from my focus on disgust and were too lengthy to fit tidily alongside my examination of disgust in a single volume. I plan, therefore, to write a later volume that picks up the historicist thread for these movies.[13]

There is some critical backing for my decision to eschew a focus on historical analysis. Peter Brooks, for example, notes that plot reveals narrative intention.[14] Plus, David Bordwell has argued narrative has primacy in cinema.[15] And Andrew Tudor writes: "Narrative, then, has to be a central focus for any socially sensitive approach to a popular genre..."[16] Thus, the plot is

---

[12] Bernice M. Murphy, *The Highway Horror Film*. (Palgrave Macmillan, 2014), 10.

[13] In the meantime, see Robin Wood and Adam Lowenstein for historicist readings of horror films, including rape-revenge films in the horror genre.

[14] Peter Brooks, *Reading for the Plot: Design and Intention in Narrative*. (Harvard University Press, 1984), 37.

[15] Julian Hanich, *Cinematic Emotion in Horror Films and Thrillers: The Aesthetic Paradox of Pleasurable Fear*. (Routledge, 2010), 168. Hans Robert Jauss has argued that focus on historicist analysis often comes at the detriment of considering aesthetic matters (33). While my own analysis is more narratological than aesthetic, Jauss's point nevertheless stands: To focus my analysis, I must also narrow its lens.

[16] Andrew Tudor, *Monsters And Mad Scientists: A Cultural History of the Horror Movie*. (1989), 81.

important, and in this book, I look to the stories these films tell so I can discern their messages and discuss their impacts.

I will, however, move beyond plot to connect these films' stories to issues of disgust and feminist film theory. I will argue that careful analysis of rape-revenge texts, in fact, disrupts existing understandings of gender in film. Nevertheless, I do so with the following caveat in mind: some of the feminist scholarship I consider and offer to complicate concerns not rape-revenge but classical cinema, meaning some of the challenges I offer to the extant theories will be historically-conditioned.[17] That is, rape-revenge films, I argue, differ from feminist film theories, sometimes, because these texts are newer than the theories are.[18] Thus, when I argue one of these texts challenges or complicates existing theory, I am not arguing my perspicacious predecessors were wrong but, rather, that we need to alter how we apply their ideas moving forward. And because I am entering the realm of feminist film theory, my discussion contains references to psychoanalysis, which has had a profound influence on much seminal work in this area.

And now, I turn to one final matter: some disclaimers. First, I wish to follow in the steps of Douglas Cowan by noting that my book is not supposed to offer *the* way of discussing rape-revenge but, instead, is offering *a* way to understand the works I discuss.[19] I have to acknowledge up front that while the scholars I cite and I have particular ways of responding to my key texts, others might respond differently.[20] Again, my analysis offers one way of viewing these texts, not the only way, as my discussion of historicism shows. Second, and finally, I offer now a content warning. This book discusses rape and disgust in-depth and at length. Many readers may find this material objectionable or deeply disturbing, and I urge such readers to seek different films and (as much as I hate to state it) a different book.

---

[17] That said, tracing the exact line of *how* these sensibilities and theories have changed is outside my purview in this volume, where I focus on the tension between feminist messaging and the evocation of disgust in these works.

[18] This is, however, not always the case. Not only does some of the feminist scholarship I consider directly address rape-revenge, including some of the texts I discuss at length, but some of the scholarship also rose well after the modern rape-revenge cycle began in the 1970s.

[19] Douglas E. Cowan, *The Forbidden Body: Sex, Horror, and the Religious Imagination.* (New York: New York University Press, 2022), 10.

[20] Stephen Prince, "Graphic Violence in the Cinema: Origins, Aesthetic Design, and Social Effects." In *Screening Violence*, edited by Stephen Prince. (Rutgers University Press, 2000), 23.

Chapter 1

Rape as an Assertion of Masculine Identity: Problematizing Sexualized Revenge in Rape Narratives

Despite criticism and even condemnation through the ages, the rape-revenge narrative has persisted both through cult followings and remakes of films such as *Straw Dogs* and *I Spit on Your Grave*, which update these stories for modern audiences and make sure rape-revenge does not fall into obscurity. Rape-revenge stories are here to stay, meaning it would be irresponsible to ignore them. This chapter will briefly describe these stories' structures before examining two texts in particular, *The Maid's Tragedy* (1612) and *I Spit on Your Grave* (1978).[1] In the three centuries between our texts, much has changed. And yet, much has stayed the same. It is my contention that our societies have been wrestling with the issues of sexual violence and agency all this time.

Thus, after examining the rapes of Evadne, The King, and Jennifer in these two works, I will explore how the heroines' choice to sexualize their revenge ultimately renders their agency problematic and ambiguous. That is, I will argue that the sexualized nature of their revenges makes it unclear whether killing their assailants allows them to recapture the agency they lost when they were raped.[2]

---

[1] Because the rape-revenge segment is merely a sub-plot in *The Maid's Tragedy*, I will focus my analysis more on *I Spit on Your Grave*, though I will attempt to weave both works throughout.

[2] I assume most readers will take for granted that rape robs one of agency. As such, I relegate my argument about this to a footnote. Luce Irigaray notes in *This Sex Which Is Not One* that penetration is a forceful, violent act in that it separates the vaginal lips, which otherwise exist in a constant state of contact with one another (24). In other words, penetration separates a woman from herself, penetrates her being. Rape, then, is but a more violent form of this separation, whereby one's being is violated at its core. Of course, consent also factors in here, as rape violates, overrides even, one's ability to choose, thereby casting his or her agency into doubt. Thus, heroines in rape-revenge works have to try to reclaim their agency because they have been robbed of their ability to choose. Revenge becomes a way for them to make themselves whole again and regain choice. That rape robs its survivors of agency also crops up more directly in the scholarship of and critical discourse about this issue. See: Bowdler 147.

Throughout this chapter, I will attempt to defend the study of rape-revenge while nevertheless acknowledging the ambiguity at its core.[3]

Rape-revenge tales tend to follow a largely predictable pattern. The heroine is raped, often by a group of men, early in the work. She then recovers and murders her rapists. Moreover, the heroine's revenge usually mirrors the sexualized nature of her rape. That is, she chooses to punish sexual violence with sexual violence. Castration is a recurring element. Since it is often regarded as the archetypal rape-revenge narrative, I will now show this pattern at work in *I Spit on Your Grave* (1978) (henceforth *I Spit*).

I Spit follows Jennifer Hills, a writer from New York City, who rents a summer cabin in rural Connecticut. Jennifer is young, beautiful, and sexually active, all of which the local men notice. Four of them soon assault her, subjecting her and the audience to not one, not two, but three rape scenes. One need not wonder why this film was banned in the U.K. Jennifer recovers from her assault and then kills all four of the men. And, yes, she castrates one of them, the ringleader, Johnny.

Some critics have argued against the wholesale classification of rape-revenge as a sub-genre of horror. Alexandra Heller-Nicholas writes: "Despite its common association with the horror film in the United States during the 1970s in particular, [the rape-revenge tale] spans genres, time, and national borders."[4] It is, therefore, reductive to say that all rape-revenge stories are necessarily horror. For its reliance on graphic violence, however, *I Spit* is clearly a horror film. And thus, while not all rape-revenge is horror, there is, nonetheless, a sub-genre of rape-revenge within the horror genre.

I will focus my attention here. This sub-genre cuts its teeth on graphic, often sexual, violence. This thread, moreover, unites our two central texts: *The Maid's Tragedy* and *I Spit*.[5] Regicide, as in Evadne's murder of the King in *The Maid's Tragedy*, would have been shocking and heretical to an early modern audience. Meanwhile, graphic rape scenes like *I Spit*'s are shocking even to modern audiences. Indeed, *I Spit*'s reputation is based largely on the cult following it

---

[3] Graphic fiction, which rape-revenge certainly is, is often dismissed out of hand. I will attempt to show that rape-revenge, while potentially problematic, has more depth than may at first seem apparent.

[4] Alexandra Heller-Nicholas, *Rape-Revenge Films*. (Jefferson, NC: McFarland, 2011), 5. Throughout this volume I shall make frequent references to and use of Alexandra Heller-Nicholas's work on rape-revenge cinema, as her work is, so far as I can tell, the most exhaustive to date. Her book *Rape-Revenge Films*, a survey of these films, is the most definitive text available on the subject.

[5] While *The Maid's Tragedy* is not a horror work in itself, it is useful for developing my points about *I Spit*, which merits its inclusion here.

gained because of the backlash against its graphic nature. Even today, this film can be difficult to watch, and I, the jaded horror fan that I am, had to psych myself up for the task.

In her book *The Horror Sensorium*, Angela Ndalianis notes: "At the core of New Horror Cinema is the aesthetic of disgust."[6] Such a statement surely also applies to these two works, which shock the audience with the actions done to and by the women. Audiences recoil from Evadne's sexualized murder of the King (I certainly did) and from the three rapes Jennifer suffers through. They may also recoil from her murders of the men, however, and I will pick up this thread again later in this chapter. For now, one needs to merely note that these works dovetail because of disgust and revulsion, which ties back into the horror genre.[7]

Stevie Simkin has also made these sorts of comparisons, arguing for the connection between early modern plays such as *The Duchess of Malfi* and modern films like *Straw Dogs*. Both of them, Simkin points out, question the same subject matter, including, but not limited to, male proprietariness over the female body and negotiating women's space in society.[8] Thus, these works, separated by three and a half centuries, are still navigating the same troubled waters. Comparing them despite their disparate timeframes is therefore helpful for demonstrating both what has changed and what has not.

In particular, I chose to keep *The Maid's Tragedy* in this volume because it so clearly illustrates the longstanding (though now legally lapsed) view of rape as a property crime.[9] Unfortunately, it seems humans are wired to view power as a zero-sum game, and so we still struggle with violence against women and, as

---

[6] Angela Ndalianis, *The Horror Sensorium: Media and the Senses.* (Jefferson, NC: McFarland, 2012), 6. New Horror Cinema refers to a sub-genre of horror films released post 9/11. Ndalianis's point about disgust is useful, however, for understanding the level on which these rape-revenge narratives operate: disgust instead of terror. See Stephen King's *Danse Macabre* for an in-depth discussion of this hierarchy of horror.

[7] For more on this topic of audience response to horror, I direct the audience to Annette Hill's *Shocking Entertainment*, in which she describes research that has shown how horror cinema is a collective experience.

[8] Stevie Simkin, *Early Modern Tragedy and the Cinema of Violence.* (Basingstoke: Palgrave Macmillan, 2006), 98-99 & 111.

[9] Projansky 4; Robyn Doolittle, *Had It Coming. Rape Culture Meets #MeToo: Now What?* (Truth to Power, Steerforth Press, 2021), 43; Here would also be a good time to note Susan Brownmiller's argument that rape is about power rather than sex (49). Property, power, and so many other issues can all arise when rape appears in a fictional work or in real life.

Simkin points out, are still figuring out women's place in society. [10&11] Yet, whereas Evadne's unstable and precarious place in *The Maid's Tragedy* lies in her status as the property of the men in her life, Jennifer's troubled position stems from the question of her agency in an ostensibly more liberated society (1970s United States). Thus, taken together, these two works demonstrate in tandem how the Western world is still wrestling with this question despite casting off some of its legal trappings. Definitions may change, but misogynistic attitudes remain disconcertingly resilient.

Evadne and Jennifer are victimized largely because they exist in spaces that are decidedly male. Of the five major characters in *I Spit*, Jennifer is the only female, and, as Carol J. Clover emphasizes, Jennifer is the city-girl among rednecks, the outsider who disrupts the men's social dynamic. [12] Meanwhile, Evadne is not the only female character in *The Maid's Tragedy*, but she is nevertheless the pawn of others, important only insofar as she relates to their ongoing power struggles. The men around these women violate them in more ways than one.

Thus, this idea of comparing early modern dramas with modern horror films is not as far-fetched as one might expect. Returning to *Straw Dogs* for a moment, one should note that this film is often considered a rape-revenge work, though Simkin does not agree with this categorization. [13] We should also note the overlaps between *The Maid's Tragedy* and the horror film. Mark Jancovich has, for example, observed how horror films often sexualize their violent content, [14] a criticism which certainly holds true for *The Maid's Tragedy*. And Linda Williams has similarly argued horror features a "displacement of sex onto violence." [15] Having made this connection, though, I now turn my attention to this chapter's crux, the texts' rapes, revenges, and the question of agency hanging over both.

The Maid's Tragedy follows a group of citizens in the Kingdom of Rhodes. Melantius, a general, has returned victorious from war. To his surprise, he finds that his friend Amintor will no longer be marrying his original intended,

---

[10] Eugenie Brinkema, "The Lady Van(qu)ishes: Interiority, Abjection, and the Function of Rape in Horror Films," *Paradoxa: Studies in World Literary Genres* 20 (2006): 50.

[11] Simkin. *Early Modern Tragedy*. 111.

[12] Carol J. Clover, *Men Women and Chainsaws: Gender in the Modern Horror Film*. (London: BFI, 1992), 121.

[13] Simkin. *Early Modern* Tragedy. 127.

[14] Mark Jancovich, "Introduction." In *Horror, The Film Reader*, edited by Mark Jancovich. (Routledge, 2002), 57.

[15] Linda Williams, "Film Bodies: Gender, Genre, and Excess." In *Feminist Film Theory: A Reader*, edited by Sue Thornham. (NYU Press, 1999), 268.

Aspatia, but will rather be marrying Melantius's sister, Evadne, at the King's behest. Melantius and Amintor discover that the King has forced this marriage on Evadne and Amintor to cover for his, the King's, affair with her.

Melantius plots revenge against the King and coerces Evadne into murdering the tyrant. After Evadne murders the King, she makes overtures to become a real, rather than pretend, couple with Amintor, who rejects her. Evadne then commits suicide. In the meantime, Amintor has also mortally wounded a disguised Aspatia. After seeing what he has done when Aspatia reveals herself, Amintor commits suicide. Melantius attempts suicide as well when he sees his friend dead, but he is restrained, and a new king takes over the leadership of Rhodes.

As this summary may imply, the question of agency hounds Evadne's actions throughout the play. Indeed, her agency as a woman is necessarily more limited than that of her male companions. By societal conventions, she is a piece of property, and, as a citizen of a monarchy (i.e., Rhodes), she is subject to the King's will. Thus, she has little choice but to obey him. As if to drive this point home himself, the King threatens her when he believes she has slept with her husband, Amintor, saying "it is in me/To punish thee."[16&17] That he says this after she warns him that her ambition outweighs whatever feelings she has for him at once reveals both his power and the empty threat of her ambition.

That is to say, though she is ambitious, she can do little to save herself from throwing at the most powerful men around. The only recourse she has to threaten the King is to woo a stronger king. In what sense, then, does she have a relevant choice? Moreover, her ability to choose is questionable even in her retributive act: her murder of the King. After all, Melantius essentially forces her into it, threatening both her honor and herself: "swear to help me...or...thou shalt not live/To breathe a full hour longer."[18] Thus, one gets the sense that Evadne has little choice in either taking the King as a lover or killing him. In either case, a man with more power than her (and the power to do her harm) coerces her into a course of action.

As I stated earlier, Evadne's murder of the King is a partially retributive act, returning some sense of agency to a woman others have threatened. This return

[16] Francis Beaumont and John Fletcher, "The Maid's Tragedy." *English Renaissance Drama: A Norton Anthology*, edited by David M. Bevington et al. (New York: W.W. Norton, 2002), 3.1, 192-193.

[17] The King arranged Amintor and Evadne's marriage to hide his, the King's, own affair with her. And, though he has married her to another man, he is sexually possessive of her and becomes enraged when he fears that she has had sex with her lawful husband (she had not).

[18] Beaumont and Fletcher 4.1. 162-165.

of agency, though, becomes complicated both because of her questionable role in choosing to murder and because of her chosen method, for her murder of the King is decidedly sexual in nature and closely resembles a rape. First, Evadne kills the King in his bed, likely the spot of their sexual rendezvouses, in which, as previously noted, she had little choice.

This move is two-fold. It at once establishes the murder's sexualized nature and reverses the victimhood in their relationship. Evadne may have experienced sexual abuse, but she is about to murder the King, that is, reverse the abuse. The King himself notes this sexuality, as he treats Evadne's preparation as foreplay.[19] Here, one gets the image of Evadne straddling the bound King, preparing to kill him as he makes sexual overtures.

Finally, her choice of murder weapon, a knife, is sexual. She evokes penetration by stabbing him multiple times. This action further reinforces the metaphor of the murder as a rape, as most characters in Renaissance tragedies do not require multiple stab wounds to die (see, for example, Aspatia). But, though this returns some agency to Evadne in that she is no longer the King's victim and has gained agency in her sexuality (she tries to unite with Amintor later), rape, in this case, is ultimately a masculine act. Note, for instance, that Amintor threatens to rape Evadne when she refuses to yield to him on their wedding night.[20]

Note, also, how her choice of weapon is more phallic than yonic in its imagery. In other words, Evadne, likely raped by the King, sexualizes her revenge against him and essentially rapes her rapist, albeit symbolically, with her knife standing in for his penis. Here, we should also observe Evadne's sheer lack of agency. Indeed, were it not for the King's possessiveness of Evadne's sexuality, there would have been little recourse for her against Amintor if he had decided to rape her. Marital rape was not a crime in Renaissance England, after all.[21]

Jumping over to *I Spit*, we can see how, much like Evadne's, Jennifer's rape and revenge raise questions about her agency. *I Spit* is a useful comparison here largely because it shows aspects of the rape-revenge narrative that would have been impossible or outright dangerous to depict on the early modern stage. The Master of Revels would have had a heart attack. If Evadne's rape is implied and her rape of the King symbolic, Jennifer's rape and her revenge are starkly literal. This modern take on rape-revenge allows us to see it in a different light. Karen Bamford notes that Jacobean drama was usually critical of rape victims

---

[19] Ibid. 5.1. 47-50.

[20] Ibid. 2.1. 274-279.

[21] Indeed, audiences of the time would probably have questioned the very premise of whether a husband could rape his wife.

seeking revenge. Bamford points to John Fletcher's *Bonduca*, which concerns, in part, the eponymous queen's daughters, who seek revenge for their rapes.

The play, however, is critical of this quest, as it begins after the rapes, meaning it displaces the violence onto the women. In other words, we see the women act violently but never see the violence they experienced.[22] We have to rely on their word, and, as we still see today, many often dismiss the rape survivor's word. So the women seeking revenge for having been raped come across as the monsters, the rapists merely victims of female violence. Bamford phrases this perception thus: "The rapes were the women's own fault and they have no right to revenge."[23] One should be careful to note that Bamford is arguing not for rape apologia but rather for how this play portrays rape as if female survivors have no right to revenge. That is, she asserts, early modern drama tacitly frowns upon revenge against rape.

And her analysis fits *The Maid's Tragedy*. After all, the audience catches the tail-end of Evadne's affair with the King and never sees their actual rendezvouses. This narrative structure means the play leaves us, the readers, with mostly one side of the violence. While we see the King make threats, we do not see him sexually abuse Evadne, but we do see her sexually abuse and murder him. *The Maid's Tragedy*, then, seems to fall into this same pattern of condemning the woman who would avenge herself against her rapist. Such is, I regret to say, the pattern for the literary works of rape-revenge I consider in this volume, coming as they do from time periods in which women were legal property of men.[24]

If our modern film is useful in making Evadne's symbolic revenge literal, though, it is also useful in showing us the violence the heroine experiences (i.e., the motivation for her revenge) and for showing a refreshing view of women's independence. Further, whatever question we may have of Francis Beaumont and John Fletcher's attitude toward women revenging their rapes, Meir Zarchi, *I Spit*'s screenwriter and director, is clearly on Jennifer's side.[25] On its surface, *I*

---

[22] Karen Bamford, *Sexual Violence on the Jacobean Stage.* (New York: St. Martin's, 2000), 116-117.

[23] Bamford 118.

[24] The two literary works I consider in this book are *The Maid's Tragedy* and *Clarissa.* These two texts serve as useful comparison points so we can see how the rape-revenge text has changed over the intervening centuries between these literary works and the cinematic works upon which I focus most of my analysis.

[25] The film's cinematography forces us to view the rapes from Jennifer's perspective and make it seems as if God is endorsing Jennifer's actions. Thus, it seems, Zarchi approves of her revenge. When I argue that Jennifer's agency is questionable, I will argue not about Zarchi's intentions but rather about his product, which is more mixed.

Spit on Your Grave is not a subtle film. Indeed, critics like Clover and Allison Young have described the film as lex talionis embodied, and the former describes it as oddly simple and straightforward.[26&27] *I Spit on Your Grave*, Clover argues, is nothing new. Rather, it is just blunter than we are used to.[28]

And, on the surface, she is right. The movie's construction is minimalistic, with the only background music coming from a harmonica one of the men plays shortly before raping Jennifer and from a record Jennifer plays to drown out, or perhaps make more enjoyable, Johnny's screams of pain after she castrates him and leaves him to die of exsanguination. Obviously, such a scene would never have passed the censor in the early modern period. Evadne has to revenge herself symbolically, but Jennifer updates this common narrative by performing the same act, sexual revenge for a sexual offense, more graphically.

But this simplicity, this stark and unrelenting violence, belies the film's brilliant cinematographic choices. On this point, many have dismissed the film as sexist or even misogynistic. It does, after all, show a beautiful woman raped on three different occasions, all within the first half of the film. But the film, I argue, is not actually sexist and instead contains clear feminist messaging. For such a graphic, simply made film, it is surprisingly deep. In his two-part review of the movie, internet personality Jack Shen, whose screen name is Count Jackula, notes that the film was originally entitled *Day of the Woman* and was inspired by the director's brief encounter with law enforcement's utter indifference in the face of sexual violence.[29&30] Shen further points out that the film's recurring yonic imagery and Jennifer's foray into a church just prior to her

---

[26] Clover 115-116.

[27] Alison Young, *The Scene of Violence: Cinema, Crime, Affect.* (Abingdon: Routledge-Cavendish, 2010), 46. "Lex Talionis" refers to the "eye for an eye" attitude toward violence, whereby people have a right to seek revenge.

[28] Clover 120.

[29] "I Spit on Your Grave (part 1) – Count Jackula Horror Review." Uploaded by The Count Jackula Show, *YouTube*, September 21, 2015, https://www.youtube.com/watch?v=CQcDLLnKuhM.

[30] The title change was motivated by the film's marketing problems. That is, as Jackula and Peter Hutchings point out, the movie was not very popular when it was first released. Jackula notes that the title was therefore changed from the more accurate "Day of the Woman" to the more sensational "I Spit on Your Grave." The change worked, even though, according to Jackula, Meir Zarchi never liked it (Part Two); Laura Mee also notes the title change (76).

first murder seem to indicate, when coupled with the title, approval of Jennifer's actions.[31]

That is to say, the film aligns us not with the rapists but with Jennifer. And Clover agrees on this point. She cites Martin Starr in asserting that *I Spit* forces the viewer into the victim's perspective.[32] When the men rape Jennifer, the camera frequently gives us point-of-view shots from her position, looking up into what Shen describes as the men's disgusting expressions.[33] In other words, the film forces us to see the rapists as Jennifer does, and thereby forcibly aligns us with her position.

We view the rapes not from the outside as sexual acts, but from the inside as horrifically violent ones, meaning *I Spit* eschews the common tendency to downplay the violence of rape.[34] This twist of perspective is supposed to make the viewer empathize with Jennifer, condemn rape, and tacitly, or even explicitly, condone her actions in the last half of the film. None of this, however, prevents criticisms that the movie might fail to convey the anti-rape message its director clearly intends. Indeed, Projansky observes that anti-rape messages can backfire.[35]

There are still those, however, who will claim that the film endorses rape, that Jennifer "enjoyed it."[36] Well, the movie actually answers this charge. When confronting Johnny, the ring leader of the gang who assaulted her, she prepares to shoot him, probably in the genitals, since she forces him to strip at gunpoint. But after he says, "You coax a man into it," thus trotting out the "you were asking for it" argument we still see today, Jennifer ratchets up her revenge.[37] Instead of shooting him, she acts as if he has swayed her, and she invites him back to her place for a warm bath.

---

[31] "I Spit on Your Grave (part 2) – Count Jackula Horror Review." Uploaded by The Count Jackula Show, *YouTube*, September 22, 2015, https://www.youtube.com/watch?v=ZRlbB-jDS5U.

[32] Clover 139.

[33] Count Jackula Part 2.

[34] Michelle Bowdler, *Is Rape a Crime? A Memoir, an Investigation, and a Manifesto.* (Flatiron Books, 2020), 6-7.

[35] Projansky 95.

[36] Amy Greenstadt compares the "asked for it" defense to mis-readings in her book *Rape and the Rise of the Author.* While this chapter does not have time to treat this book in-depth, it is nevertheless helpful to understand how this defense is a common misreading. Of course, in the film, it is unclear whether Johnny actually believes this or not. He does not bring it up until Jennifer has him at gunpoint.

[37] *I Spit on Your Grave.* Directed by Meir Zarchi, performance by Camille Keaton. Cinemagic Pictures, 1978.

Only she then castrates him with a knife, which, one should note, is far more personal and graphic than a shooting.[38] And so Jennifer herself answers this charge, forcibly, with a sharp instrument. And, honestly, anyone who watches this film and tries to claim Jennifer, who gets bloodied and bruised, all while trying to run, trying to fight, and saying "stop it" repeatedly, actually wanted or enjoyed what happened to her is either obtuse or disingenuous.[39] Simkin notes that, unlike in some revenge films, the rapes in *I Spit* are decidedly unerotic.[40]

If the film is not outright misogynistic, then, one might ask, why is it so violent? Indeed, Alison Young raises this question in her book, *The Scene of Violence*, in which she concludes her chapter on rape-revenge films by arguing that these stories need not be so graphic and that audiences should stop watching them.[41] And Tea Fredriksson observes that graphic violence in rape-revenge is a longstanding moral issue.[42] One might also point to *The Maid's Tragedy* as an example of a less violent rape-revenge narrative, albeit one which robs its avenger of agency at every turn, especially since we can question whether it is even *her* revenge at all.

On this point, I once more defer to Shen, who declares this largely a non-criticism. He points out that horror functions by making its topics as stark and visceral as possible.[43] In other words, horror relies on being overt and violent. It reduces our fears and attitudes to their basest, most obvious and grotesque forms and then confronts us with them. According to Shen, not only is the film not misogynistic, but it confronts us with misogyny in our culture.[44] Jacinda Read seems to agree when she declares that rape-revenge texts are feminist stories.[45]

Here, we should also note that rape-revenge works present two very different types of violence: rape and revenge. And whereas revenge takes the form of violence to achieve an end, rape emerges as a form of torture, meaning rape appears particularly immoral, particularly gratuitous.[46] Rape-revenge fiction hereby pushes its audiences to reflect on the morality of violence in some of its

---

[38] Clover 32.

[39] *I Spit on Your Grave* 1978.

[40] Simkin. *Early Modern Tragedy*. 144.

[41] Young 72-73.

[42] Tea Fredriksson, "Avenger in distress: a semiotic study of Lisbeth Salander, rape-revenge and ideology," *Nordic Journal of Criminology* 22, no. 1 (2021): 65.

[43] Count Jackula Part 2.

[44] Count Jackula Part 2.

[45] Read 12.

[46] On this point, I credit one of this volume's peer reviewers, who pointed this difference out.

various iterations. And, by pushing audiences to examine violence moralistically, rape-revenge texts make violence a topic worthy of consideration. Indeed, Timo Airaksinen argues that violence only becomes an interesting topic when examined moralistically.[47]

In *I Spit*, we see four men with low opinions of women brutalize a woman and then get punished for it, during which time the men reveal their true colors as cowards.[48] In other words, the film punishes the misogynists, and it uses violence to do so because violence makes its condemnatory stance as stark as possible and makes the audience reflect on said stance. So, while I understand Young's assertion that the violence is unnecessary, I disagree. As Shen asks, how can one treat rape, such a horrific subject, without horror?[49&50] Horror gives us the language to treat this subject matter, and it shows rape for the violent, horrific act it is. Remember, *I Spit* is often explicit and straightforward.

Yet, one of the overarching questions about the violence in *I Spit* is whether it is moral. Perhaps the most interesting point I have heard someone make on this topic came in the documentary *The Found Footage Phenomenon*, wherein James Cullen Bressack, director of graphic horror film *Hate Crime* (2013), discusses his decision to include graphic violence in his movie. Bressack notes that the titular hate crimes in his film are the sorts of crimes he worries about as a Jewish man in what he perceives as an increasingly antisemitic society.[51] He further elaborates that, for him, fear is a way for a film to get into its audience's conscience and that, moreover, going too far allows the movie to stick in the audience's mind.[52] According to Bressack, the key to including such horrific violence in one's movie is knowing in advance why one is doing so.[53] And Meir Zarchi certainly knew why he was including this violence in *I Spit on Your Grave*.

---

[47] Timo Airaksinen, *The Philosophy of H.P. Lovecraft: The Route to Horror*. (Peter Lang, Inc., 1999), 145.

[48] Read 12.

[49] Count Jackula Parts 1 & 2.

[50] Brinkema argues that the violence of rape has to be made external for us to truly perceive it, and that this violence is therefore enacted, externalized, via the revenges. That is, we understand the violence of rape largely through the violence of the avenger's actions (39). This violence and *I Spit*'s brutal, daytime rape scenes allow us to understand rape's internal harm in a way we could not otherwise (45).

[51] *The Found Footage Phenomenon*. Directed by Sarah Appleton and Phillip Escott, Caprisar Productions, 2021.

[52] Ibid; On this topic, Stephen Prince observes that disturbing images can make the audience reflect on the filmmakers' intention (26).

[53] *The Found Footage Phenomenon*.

Notice how we are encountering issues with *I Spit*'s ability to treat the subject of rape-revenge. Notice, also, how we are encountering these issues even though *I Spit* avoids many of the issues plaguing *The Maid's Tragedy*. This means, and we shall see this issue continuously throughout this volume, that rape-revenge is a very difficult subject, one which seems doomed to issues no matter how one tells its stories. Indeed, here we also encounter some other criticisms of *I Spit* and rape-revenge films. Ferreday argues that rape-revenge normalizes sexual violence,[54] and Projansky worries that violent depictions of rape normalize the view of women as victims.[55]

Ferreday gets the causal chain backward, however, as rape in fiction is a reaction to the sexual violence we encounter in real-life, and it is unclear how these films normalize sexual violence when they are stemming from rape culture, meaning the issue preexists them. More problematic for these texts is the implication, buried in Ferreday's point, that these films perpetuate rape culture. That criticism, however, elides the anti-rape messaging we see in a movie like *I Spit*. And yet, I will shortly point to some shortcomings in *I Spit*'s messaging. As such, I do think Ferreday's criticism carries some water.

Projansky's argument, on the other hand, risks erasing how rape-revenge texts also show women as avengers. Jennifer is a rape victim, sure, but she is also a rape survivor who tracks down and systematically punishes her rapists. She is cunning and powerful, meaning it is too simplistic for us to box Jennifer into the category of "victim." Her role is far more complicated and powerful than that. The case is more muddled with Evadne, but even she does not come across as a mere victim since she violently murders the King.

This next point, however, is subtler. *I Spit*'s cinematography takes us on a journey along with Jennifer, as this is very much her story.[56] Her clothing through the film reflects her mood and identity. In the beginning, she wears revealing clothing, often in bright colors. She is free and comfortable with her body, as shown when she goes skinny dipping immediately after arriving at her cabin. She often dresses in red, orange, and yellow, and even her more muted

---

[54] Debra Ferreday, "'Only the Bad Gyal could do this': Rihanna, rape-revenge narratives and the cultural politics of white feminism," *Feminist Theory*, 18, no. 3 (2017): 271; Tamborini and Salomonson note a perceived correlation whereby viewers of sexual violence in fiction view sexual violence less putatively (185). Such a correlation is, indeed, very disconcerting. And yet, I question the causality here; correlation is not causation, after all.

[55] Projansky 95.

[56] Clover 138.

white and blue outfit is still revealing.[57] After her rape, she dresses primarily in black, unrevealing clothing, covering the body she was once unashamed of.[58] And yet, as she begins her revenges, she begins to take ownership of her body once more, wearing revealing clothing, albeit in often duller shades, and using her sexuality as a weapon. The men treat her as a sexual object, and she uses this to lure them in. She seduces and has sex with Matthew before hanging him, seduces and fondles Johnny before castrating him, and nearly kisses Stanley before pushing him in the river and killing him with a boat propeller while parroting his command to her during the third rape scene to "Suck it, bitch."[59]

Thus, Jennifer regains her identity throughout the movie, gradually moving back toward her typical style of clothing and her free, unashamed sexuality. And yet, her choices of weapons are decidedly phallic. As Shen notes, Jennifer's canoe, where the men find her just before the first rape, is yonic with its red interior and white exterior.[60] Meanwhile, the men's boat becomes phallic with its uplifted angle. Jennifer, though, kills Stanley and Andy not with the canoe but rather while in the boat. And, in doing so, not only is she adopting a phallus, but she is also repeating the violence she suffered. Stanley and Andy are the first two men to attack Jennifer, and they do so by circling her in their boat, harassing her, before towing her to shore and initiating the first rape. Here, in Jennifer's final revenge, she circles Stanley with the boat, and his terror is not unlike hers from the first rape scene. In a way, Zarchi punctuates the movie with horrific bookends.

We might, therefore, have an idea that Jennifer has completed a journey: from writer to victim, victim to avenger. At the end of the film, her attackers are mutilated and deceased. She is no longer a victim, and she has revenged herself. Since she no longer has violence inflicted upon her but rather is now inflicting violence, it is possible to get a sense that she has regained her agency. She wields the power in her relationships with the four men, as she no longer fears them; they fear her. This is most obvious with Matthew, but the other men clearly fear for their lives when Jennifer attacks. And yet, our notion that

---

[57] The first rape sees Jennifer in a bright orange and yellow bikini. The "more muted" outfit is a white buttoned shirt and jean shorts, which nevertheless fits the comfortable, revealing nature of her clothing prior to the rapes. Her clothing during the murders is usually less revealing (ankle-length dress and long skirt) or duller (green bikini).

[58] Jackula notes this in part 2 of his review, but he does not push the subject, moving instead to his theory about the triple goddess. Put briefly, he argues that *I Spit on Your Grave* evokes mythological concepts and connects Jennifer with goddess figures. On this point, he and I depart less because I disagree and more because this reading is not a topic my book is delving into and because I lack knowledge of the subject matter.

[59] *I Spit on Your Grave* 1978.

[60] Count Jackula Part 1.

Jennifer and Evadne may have recaptured their agency becomes more muddled when we consider the method of their revenge.

That Evadne and Jennifer both have to opt for phallic methods of revenge, that they have to appropriate masculine actions, would seem to indicate that they fail to really (or fully) regain their lost agency. Evadne struggles throughout the play to have any control over her own life. The King forces her into a sham marriage, after possibly forcing her into a relationship with him. He then forces her to remain in that relationship. And then her brother forces her to kill the King. The fact that she decides to do so through a simulated rape with a phallic object, the knife, puts the impetus of revenge and agency necessarily into masculine language that she assimilates.

That is to say, she has to act masculine to revenge herself. Whether she regains agency is, therefore, questionable. Meanwhile, Jennifer's clothing, which I have shown to be a mirror for her journey, never quite returns to its original vivacity. Her orange bikini gives way to a dull green one, and her red dress to a flowing white one. She recaptures her sexuality, but does so as a means of revenge, meaning she actually becomes, in some ways, the sexual object the men already considered her. That she does so for an end, just like Evadne kills the King for an end, remains problematic. Is she not just co-opting the identity they cast upon her to lure them? Also, note that her murder weapons, knife and boat, are largely phallic. Jennifer's actions are, therefore, coded as male when she is theoretically recapturing her female agency.

Nevertheless, as is becoming a trend in this chapter, I think it would be easy to overstate this criticism and how it undermines *I Spit*'s capacity as an anti-rape text. While Jennifer does use her body to lure her rapists and victims, her bikinis do not seem to fit this dynamic. At the end of the film, Jennifer wears a dull green bikini, apparently not for the benefits of the male gaze but, rather, for her own comfort. Mary Ann Doane has argued that femininity is a masquerade, a performance society pushes women into maintaining.[61] I argue Jennifer Hills pushes against this notion of femininity, even if only partially and for a moment.

Since Jennifer wears bikinis even when she has no audience to see her,[62] if her bikinis (her femininity) are a performance, then they are at least sometimes a performance only for herself. More crucially, if this performance is only for

---

[61] Mary Ann Doane, "Film and the Masquerade: Theorising the Female Spectator." In *Feminist Film Theory: A Reader*, edited by Sue Thornham. (Edinburgh University Press, 1999), 138-139.

[62] Jennifer is not a meta-aware character, meaning she does not, in-universe, know movie viewers are watching her.

herself, then Jennifer is owning and embracing her femininity, not as a masquerade, but as an identity. And while one might object that Jennifer only wears these revealing clothes because society has taught her to objectify and display herself, such an objection fails to consider how children revel in their nakedness before they (as Adam and Eve before them) are taught to feel shame about being nude, their barest selves. The masquerade is powerful but not quite inevitable, and Jennifer does seem to have an authenticity in her comfort with her own body.

In a somewhat related critical vein, Read observes how movies like *I Spit* often eroticize their avenging heroines, a depiction she sees as problematic.[63] There is definitely a risk here whereby those telling rape-revenge stories can fall into the trap of titillating their audiences when, if they were being morally conscious, they would eschew such portrayals. For *I Spit*, we can ask whether it was necessary to have Jennifer seduce two of her four rapists.[64] And, on this point, I think Read does raise an important objection, one which undermines (but does not erase) the film's potential feminist messaging.[65] Laura Mee concurs, arguing the original *I Spit* is more problematic than its 2010 remake because the original sexualizes Jennifer and her revenge.[66] And while I agree that the film's sexualized revenge is problematic, I find the sexualization of Jennifer far less troubling, given how her sartorial choices reflect her comfort with her own body, that is, her power and confidence.

This idea that Jennifer and Evadne fail to recapture their agency, that their revenges leave them incomplete or even unsympathetic, recurs in the critical discourse. Claire Henry argues that the audience stops identifying with Jennifer, as she and other raped women in these works become avenging figures.[67] After all, how can we say a woman regains her agency when she loses her identity in seeking revenge? Henry is not the only one who has made this argument. Eugenie Brinkema argues that women in these works (i.e., rape-revenge films such as *I Spit*) construct their identities through language.[68] More accurately, language in these films is a feminine enterprise. Jennifer, for

---

[63] Read 39-40.

[64] Clarie Henry views this aspect of *I Spit* as problematic ("Challenging" 141).

[65] I think there may be a redemptive reading of Jennifer's seducing her rapists if we consider *I Spit* as a folkloric text. To make such a reading here, however, would be to go too far afield of this project's analysis.

[66] Laura Mee, "The re-rape and revenge of Jennifer Hills: Gender and genre in *I Spit on Your Grave* (2010)," *Horror Studies* 4, no. 1 (2013): 76-77.

[67] Claire Henry, *Revisionist Rape-revenge Redefining a Film Genre.* (Basingstoke: Palgrave Macmillan, 2014), 49.

[68] Brinkema 49.

instance, is a writer, and she clearly has a greater command of language than the comparatively uneducated men around her do.[69]

But Jennifer seems to lose her control of language after being raped. After the second assault, she barely makes any sounds as she limps through the woods back toward her cabin. And, while recuperating from the rapes, she hardly speaks a word. Entire minutes of screen time go by without a line of dialogue. In this way, then, Jennifer does seem to lose the power of words because of her trauma, which Brinkema points out is usually connected to language for women in these works. I pair these charges together because they both make essentially the same argument: that the women lose their identity when they quest after vengeance either by becoming figures of vengeance or by losing access to language (a symptom of the rape).[70]

This criticism is not, however, as clear as Henry and Brinkema make it sound. Henry's argument rests on the supposition that audiences lose sympathy for Jennifer. However, as I have noted, this is not the case for every viewer. Shen and I both identify with her.[71] And, as I have argued, she seems to hold onto aspects of her agency throughout her revenge. Jennifer, I contend, does not lose all of her identity, though she does seem changed. Meanwhile, she also does not lose full access to language. Indeed, we see her piecing her torn manuscript back together and writing once again before embarking on her revenge. Thus, though she momentarily loses access to language, she regains it.

A more interesting charge, I think, is that Jennifer loses her biological identity, that is, her sex. Brinkema argues that the rape-revenge heroine "is more aggressive, more phallic, more *male* than any other type of female character. Rape ironically masculinizes the Final figure."[72] In other words, Jennifer adopts the aggressive, violent acts the film codes solely as masculine. On this topic,

---

[69] Ibid. 54.

[70] Evadne's role here is less clear. And, one should note, neither Brinkema nor Henry is discussing early modern drama, let alone *The Maid's Tragedy*. Evadne never does lose her access to language and does not take on the cold, detached, dehumanized avenger form that Jennifer and other straight rape-revenge heroines do. But I consider it poor form to use her to counter these arguments because she comes from a text that is not, at its heart, a full rape-revenge story. Evadne must therefore be held to different, albeit related, standards. She does not go through the full journey that Jennifer does because her abuse and the story she exists in are different. Jennifer is useful precisely because she fleshes out Evadne's story and updates it for a modern audience. One should, however, note that Evadne certainly engages in wordplay and is no slower than the men around her. This is, however, a conceit of the revenge tragedy genre. Male characters in plays, especially early modern ones, have to be good at wordplay.

[71] Count Jackula Part 2.

[72] Brinkema 60.

Frederiksson argues that avenging heroines (like Jennifer) incorporate patriarchal ideals.[73] This criticism is harder to counter. After all, as I have noted, Jennifer and Evadne both appropriate masculine modes of violence through their use of decidedly phallic murder weapons, be they knives or boats. And, though Jennifer uses her sexuality as a weapon, that is her feminine form, this does not override the preceding concern. It may, however, qualify it since Jennifer's weaponry is not solely masculine but rather a combination of masculine and feminine.

And so, the above would seem to indicate that neither Evadne nor Jennifer manage to recapture their lost agency. But I do not think this is so clear-cut. Evadne changes throughout the play, and, in the end, she appears genuinely contrite and seeks to reconnect with Amintor. Her utter indifference gives way, perhaps, to a sort of affection and penance unknown to her previously. Evadne, therefore, has a choice for the first time in the play, and she chooses Amintor, maybe.[74] Jennifer, meanwhile, becomes comfortable in her sexuality again and forgoes the long sleeves and concealing clothes she favored immediately after her rape but before her revenge.

So could their appropriations of masculine acts not, therefore, be an assertion of self? Just as groups often try to reclaim words others use to disparage them, it is possible that Jennifer and Evadne try to reclaim the weapons others use against them. They seize the phallus, sometimes not so symbolically speaking, and turn it against those who would have them subjugated to it. Jennifer's use of Stanley's own line against him could be her way of reclaiming the language. Those words, after she kills him, are hers. Indeed, as I have noted, Jennifer and Evadne both seem to regain at least some of the agency they lost through their rapes.

Other critics support my point here. Going back to the argument that rape-revenge stories are misogynistic, several critics, including Shen, Clover, Bamford, and Jocelyn Catty, have noted that male social structures, and indeed

---

[73] Frederiksson 70.

[74] It is also possible that she feels she has no other recourse but to try to make amends with him. She is, after all, a woman who killed a king and had an affair out of wedlock, both actions which would make her a pariah in early modern culture.

male agency, are often key players in these works.[75&76] These last two both concern early modern drama specifically, and they show how rape in these plays (e.g., in *The Maid's Tragedy*) is typically male-centric. In other words, these plays usually frame rape as a crime by one man (or tyrant) toward another man. Meanwhile, *I Spit on Your Grave* helps subvert this dynamic.

So, *The Maid's Tragedy* is useful for allowing us to understand how the rape-revenge tale has evolved. As more a proto-rape-revenge than a straight example, *The Maid's Tragedy*, when we compare it to films like *I Spit*, illustrates how rape-revenge has evolved to portray rape as a female-centered crime. That is, *I Spit* makes the rape about Jennifer and her suffering. But, and Shen is especially helpful here, the male dynamic is still very much at play, and the film is unable to shake its role.

Here, we have an ambivalent point. On the one hand, we get the rape from Jennifer's point of view. On the other, Shen points out that the men are very much treating Jennifer as a text to pass between one another. In other words, to use Bamford's language, Jennifer's violated body is the medium through which the men communicate.[77] Shen argues that the group's leader, Johnny, instigates the gang-rape because he feels his position as group leader, head of the male pack, is under threat from this outsider, this woman.[78]

Clover comments that Jennifer is very much the outsider, and that the men's rapes of her confirm their social pecking order.[79] Indeed, the men rape Jennifer roughly in the order of their social standing within their group. Johnny, the strongest member and clear leader, rapes her first. Matthew, the meek, virginal, and mentally handicapped man, rapes her last. Shen and Clover both read this as the rape reaffirming the male social dynamic. In other words, we have a contested point here. Are the rapes about Jennifer, or are they about the men?

Jennifer, and not a man in her life, is the rapes' victim. There is no man for us to put the crime onto and no man to take revenge for her. She has to do it. She has to make the choice and adopt the mantel of avenger for herself. She takes charge of her own destiny and makes her decision. And, in partial contrast to

---

[75] Bamford writes in *Sexual Violence on the Jacobean Stage* that fictional rapes during this time period often took the form of either a tyrant forcing his will on others or of men using "The female body [as] the medium for a message…[to] other men" (156). Both of these, one should note, are at play in *The Maid's Tragedy*, wherein Evadne is at once the victim of a tyrant and the pawn of the various men in her life.

[76] Catty writes in *Writing Rape, Writing Women in Early Modern England* that rape was often an expression of political tyranny or a crime against other men (10).

[77] Bamford 156.

[78] Count Jackula Part 2.

[79] Clover 121-122.

the point of Jennifer becoming masculinized, she seems to make her decision when her canoe returns to her.[80] That is, the yonic symbol returns to her, and she chooses to revenge. This feminizes her revenge. So, if we follow this thread, the revenge is by a woman for a woman.

And yet, on the other hand, the rapes themselves are about the men reaffirming their group dynamic with the ostensible excuse of getting Matthew to lose his virginity.[81] In this way, it seems *I Spit* still falls into the trap of making rapes about men, as Johnny seems to be sending a message to the rest of the group, and each of the men tries to show off for one another.[82] But, as noted before, *I Spit* brutally subverts this dynamic by, well, having Jennifer brutally murder the men. One can therefore read this reaffirmation of existing rape tropes as mere adherence to reality.

What we have here is a problem of interpretation and emphasis. Ultimately, *I Spit* shows rape from both the male and female perspectives. The rapes are not just about the male's social order, and they are not just about Jennifer regaining her agency. Rather, both threads exist at once. The rape-revenge tale is, therefore, difficult to read partially because it is itself ambivalent, failing to take single hard stances on the issues even when its directors have the intention to do so. If the reader has gotten a sense that I am ambivalent on the subject, it is because I am. I have tried to give both arguments, showing how they both have a leg to stand on, albeit to varying degrees.

The film's last shot, I believe, illustrates this ambivalence in the film itself, and both its placement at the end of the film and its ambivalence are crucial.[83] While I do not question Zarchi's intention (I believe he meant to give Jennifer full agency), I think the movie's relationship with Jennifer's agency is conflicted. The final shot is not, as Brinkema argues, of Jennifer's gaze.[84] I find this statement odd, as the final shot shows the space behind Jennifer, where she is

---

[80] Count Jackula Part 2.

[81] Jackula argues in part two of his review that Johnny feels his leadership and power over the group being threatened by Jennifer, as she, as a woman and outsider, has the power to disrupt the group's dynamic and is able to give Matthew a generous tip that Johnny himself could not provide. Jackula believes that Johnny pushes the men to rape Jennifer so as to reassert his power over the group. Getting Matthew to lose his virginity is therefore an excuse, a flimsy justification thrown over their acts to mask Johnny's underlying motive (Jackula Part 2).

[82] Matthew makes a show of it when he finally rapes Jennifer, having been too timid during the first assaults. He makes a triumphant, trumpet-like sound and then assaults her as the other men clap. The rapes are performative.

[83] Brooks argues for the importance of endings in understanding and interpreting narratives (22).

[84] Brinkema 56.

not looking. Rather, the final shots are of Jennifer subtly smiling while riding off in the men's boat and then, after a cut, Jennifer's arm steering the boat downriver. This shot at once returns agency to and removes agency from Jennifer. Augmenting the former view, Shen argues that the film depicts water as feminine.[85]

This reading, coupled with the shot's momentary linger on Jennifer's slight smile and bikini-clad body, returns agency insofar as it makes her seem triumphant. She has revenged herself, and she can finally smile once again, not for the sake of luring in her attackers but rather for herself. And she is no longer ashamed of revealing her body. This cut creates a synecdoche whereby Jennifer's arm stands in for her, and we therefore see her guiding herself and her destiny down river, leaving her trauma behind in her (literal) wake.[86]

And yet, while this shot clearly shows Jennifer guiding herself, that is driving her agency, we must also remember that she is doing so in Stanley and Andy's boat. Though this last shot gives us a feminine body and feminine waters, it also gives us another instance of phallic appropriation. Jennifer may be driving herself, but she is doing so in a masculine vehicle, appropriating the apparatus the men used to attack her, both in the literal and metaphorical senses. And so we get yet another moment of ambivalence. While the final shot clearly intends to return agency, there is still this nagging question of appropriation. Even in these last moments, the film fails to deliver an unambiguous answer to our overarching question of agency. The waters remain murky with blood and with doubt.

That doubt, however, is, as I have argued, not as strong as some scholars maintain. In her influential book *The Monstrous-Feminine: Film, Feminism, Psychoanalysis*, Barbara Creed, for example, advances a negative view of *I Spit* as misogynistic.[87] And her (mis)reading of this film has found support from such scholars as Simkin.[88] Despite her significant contributions to feminist

---

[85] In part two, Jackula points out how the film's river is feminized. It carries the yonic canoe, and Jennifer embraces the water in a way the men do not. Stanley cannot swim well, and Jennifer kills him partially by submerging herself to sneak up on him while he is in the boat. She is also the only character we see swimming of her own volition. Note also that the men first attack her while she is lounging in the river. But they bring her ashore to rape her; For the feminine coding of water, see also: Bottigheimer, Ruth B. *Grimms' Bad Girls and Bold Boys: the Moral and Social Vision of the Tales.* Yale University Press, 1987. Drawing on psychoanalysis, Clifton Snider also argues for water representing the feminine (and the unconscious) (22).

[86] On this point, I credit Dr. Sharon Johnson for helping me read the scene.

[87] Barbara Creed, *The Monstrous-Feminine: Film, Feminism, Psychoanalysis*. (New York, Routledge, 1993), 129.

[88] Stevie Simkin, *Straw Dogs*. (Palgrave Macmillan, 2011), 122.

understandings of horror films, though, Creed's analysis of *I Spit* misconstrues several of the film's aspects. Aside from the minor mistake of calling Jennifer "a teacher" (Jennifer is a writer for women's magazines), Creed also declares that Jennifer has apparently obtained superhuman powers, a critique which, in light of some other rape-revenge films, appears ill-founded.[89] Then Creed claims Jennifer's revenge entails erotic pleasure for the audience despite the abject violence in these scenes.[90]

Next, Creed asserts without evidence (and without considering the film's history and the director's intentions) that *I Spit's* "ideological purpose" is "to represent woman as monstrous because she castrates."[91] She makes this argument even though Jennifer is the film's clear protagonist, its final girl, not its monster. Finally, Creed criticizes the film for, as she sees it, reducing Jennifer to "a battered, bleeding wound," a reduction that reveals the men's desire to see women dead.[92] This reading once more misses crucial details in favor of making sweeping assertions the film directly counters. Jennifer emerges from the film cool-headed, patient, and powerful, hardly a walking injury. And the men show no affinity for dead women but rather prove incensed when a woman disrupts their patriarchal status quo. Note, for example, how the men grow hostile toward Jennifer but not toward Johnny's wife.

I have offered two different readings of Evadne and Jennifer's revenges. Whether we read their use of masculine modes to revenge their rapes (i.e., their use of sex to punish a sexual crime) as unrelenting victimhood (i.e., using the only mode they can) or as an assertion of ownership (i.e., turning one's own weapon against him or her) will determine our own individual answers to this question. The issue is clearly problematic in that both readings seem valid. Ultimately, the truth is ambiguous.

While they are able to use their sexuality, it is unclear if it is really their choice to do so or if they must work with what they have. Whether they have a meaningful choice is up for debate. Thus, at the core of the rape-revenge text is an ambivalence, whereby its approach to its subject matter remains unclear on the question of agency, as these works do not deliver a single, unified answer. Worse than an ambivalence, though, in this book, I argue rape-revenge offers a paradox.

---

[89] Creed. *The Monstrous-Feminine*. 129. Many rape-revenge works see their heroines actually gain supernatural powers that aid them as they seek revenge.
[90] Ibid. 130.
[91] Ibid.
[92] Ibid. 131.

Before getting to the paradox, however, I want to consider the alternatives. Much of the trouble in this chapter arose from the graphic depiction of rape. And even though I have discussed *The Maid's Tragedy*, in which rapes are mostly implied or symbolic, the reader may still question whether a text could advance an anti-rape message without depicting rape itself. To this end, we turn now to films that follow the rape-revenge pattern but largely eschew actual rape within their narratives.

Chapter 2

Hiding the Rape:
A Contemporary Outlook

To now, we have seen that vivid depictions of rape and sexualized violence can undermine rape-revenge works. Naturally, the consequent question becomes what happens when the texts hide the rape. To show how texts which do this can also run afoul of the issues I have described, in this chapter I discuss a very different sort of text. The films in this chapter take an often nigh-allegorical approach to the issue of how to portray sexual violence's nature without also showing sexual violence on screen. These films suggest sexual violence, mimic the set-up of rape-revenge films, and yet never show rape. Indeed, none of the films I discuss in part one of this chapter contains a completed rape.[1]

Put another way, I devote the bulk of this chapter to films which mimic the rape-revenge film's set up but do not show completed rapes. I dub these films non-rape, rape-revenge films.[2] Then, in part two, I end the chapter by considering a film which is unmistakably a rape-revenge film, but that flips the narrative by starting with the revenge and never explicitly showing the rapes the protagonist survived. This way, I aim to show how showing rape, not showing rape, and partially showing rape can all run into issues as narrative structures when we consider the rape-revenge texts' anti-rape messaging.

Part One: Hiding Rape

The first film I want to discuss that presents a rape-revenge narrative without showing rape is Katie Aselton's 2012 movie *Black Rock*, which follows a group of female friends, Sarah (Kate Bosworth), Abby (Aselton), and Lou (Lake Bell), vacationing on an island near their hometown. Sarah, we learn, is trying to reconcile Abby and Lou, who have been estranged since Lou seduced Abby's

---

[1] For my purposes here, I am using "rape" to mean a sexual assault involving penetration. In *I Spit on Your Grave*, Jennifer has multiple men penetrate her while sexually assaulting her, meaning she has multiple men rape her. Conversely, the films in part one of this chapter do not include this type of sexual assault. Rather, the films in part one of this chapter either show other types of sexual assault (e.g., groping or attempted rape) or mirror the rape-revenge narrative's structure, whereas the film in part 2 avoids graphically portraying the rapes that occurred within its narrative.

[2] I admit this name is not the catchiest.

now ex-boyfriend. Sarah, however, convinces them to join her on the excursion to the island. They do; and that night, the three women encounter a group of three male hunters, all veterans. Still resentful of Lou, Abby intercedes in her rival's flirtations with one of the hunters, Henry, and lures him into the woods. There, she and Henry make-out, but when the intoxicated Abby attempts to break it off, Henry grows aggressive and attempts to rape her. Fighting back, Abby hits Henry over the head with a rock, accidentally killing him.

When the rest of the campers find this scene, the other two hunters, Derek and Alex, grow angry and subdue the women. After awaking on the beach, the women manage to escape from the men, and a cat-and-mouse game ensues across the island. Sarah is gunned down, but Abby and Lou manage to kill Alex and Derek before starting their swim home.

The first aspect of this film that should stick out is the lack of an explicit rape scene. Rather than the hideous implication of *Bound to Vengeance* (see part two of this chapter) or the visceral detail of *I Spit*, *Black Rock* features only an attempted rape, and only one instance of it at that. Gone are the pervasive implications or explications of sexual violence from those other texts; instead, we have but one episode, which then shapes the rest of the plot. Aselton, the film's director and the actor for Abby, Henry's intended victim, is sure to portray the attempted rape as a reprehensible act.

The shot's low-key lighting (set in the woods on a remote, uninhabited island), the lack of nudity, and the women's immediate belief in Abby all reaffirm that *Black Rock* is not playing the scene for titillation. And because the attempted rape sets off the rest of the film's plot, one can hardly accuse it of being unimportant. Moreover, the scene (and, consequently, the film) hereby affirms a woman's right to say "no" in the middle of an intimate encounter, an important message rape-revenge overlooks when it focuses on forcible rape by (near) strangers rather than the more date-rape oriented approach we find in *Black Rock*.[3]

Once this scene ends, the film is done with sexual violence. Indeed, the film itself asserts that it will not stoop to sexualizing its characters. When they awaken after Alex and Derek first attack them, Abby, Lou, and Sarah find themselves on the beach, their wrists bound. Alex and Derek are debating what to do with them, with Derek insistent they must kill the women out of vengeance for Henry, their fellow veteran and fallen comrade.

Bound, heads reeling from the men's assault, and unarmed, the women are (ostensibly) at the men's mercy. And then Abby starts speaking to Derek. But rather than begging, Abby challenges him to fight. It is this challenge that allows

---

[3] Heller-Nicholas. 2nd edition. 161.

the women to escape. Notice how, here, *Black Rock* separates its heroines' capacity for violence from their sexuality. Rather than sexualizing their violent acts, the film shows its heroines attacking with pragmatic brutality: tackling, throwing sand, and sneaking up on their attackers. And so *Black Rock* avoids the pitfall we discussed in chapter one. By not sexualizing its violence, *Black Rock* not only remains realistic (one of Aselton's stated goals with the film) but also avoids reducing its heroines to their sexuality.[4] It furthermore pushes back against the tendency of women in American culture to be particularly adverse to their own rage.[5] Rather, feminine wrath in this film is both powerful and well-justified.

And yet, so, too, does *Black Rock* avoid separating the women themselves from their sexuality and their bodies. Sarah dies when the three women try to sneak back to their boat under cover of night, only to find that Alex and Derek have untethered it, setting it adrift into the frigid waters. Unsure of what to do, the three argue about whether they will be able to safely swim to the boat, with Sarah insisting the water is far too cold for them to make it, and Lou and Abby resolving to try anyway. The three begin making their way toward the water, only for Sarah to change her mind, again declaring they will not be able to make it. And, as she stands up, one of the men shoots her dead. Lou and Abby then attempt to flee across the water only to find Sarah was correct; the water is far too cold for them to make it to the boat.

Shivering, Lou and Abby abandon their swim and head back to the island, where they seek refuge in the forest, at their old childhood clubhouse (really a collapsed section of wood in the forest). Facing the imminent threat of hypothermia, Lou and Abby have to strip naked and huddle together for warmth. Thus begins an extended part of the film in which Aselton and Bell, the actresses playing Abby and Lou respectively, are entirely nude. Once again, however, Aselton avoids sexualizing the scene.

The women shiver realistically, and the camera avoids lingering on the actresses' bodies, meaning these scenes do not become titillating. Here, nudity becomes, ironically, a source of feminine power. I specify "ironically" because, on the one hand, the women are clearly vulnerable. They shiver dramatically

---

[4] Jay A. Fernandez, "Katie Aselton to Star in and Direct Thriller 'Black Rock' (Cannes)," *The Hollywood Reporter*, May 11, 2011. https://www.hollywoodreporter.com/movies/movie-news/katie-aselton-star-direct-thriller-187336/. This article includes a brief interview with Aselton in which she remarks how she wanted to make the film realistic, the women relatable.

[5] Harriet G. Lerner, *Women in Therapy*. (Harper & Row, 1998), 54; This moment also meshes with Clemens' observation that protagonists' struggles often reflect larger societal woes (6).

and huddle together at the edge of hypothermia. At this moment, they are unarmed and visibly ill-equipped to deal with the unhinged, trained soldiers dogging them across the island. Were the men to find them at this moment, Abby and Lou would be at their weakest, their least capable of defeating their better-armed foes.

And yet, despite this obvious vulnerability, their nudity, their doffing of clothes, symbolize their doffing of civility and their return to primal instincts. This becomes clearest in the film when Abby finds the normally stalwart Lou's confidence wavering. Abby responds by slapping Lou in the face repeatedly until Lou snaps; Lou growls at Abby, warning the latter that she will rip Abby's throat out if Abby hits her again. Rather than panic, Abby acknowledges that Lou's fighting spirit has returned. And, indeed, it has, for the two friends reconcile and resolve to take the fight to the men. Thereafter, they, still in the nude, recover the time capsule they and Sarah left on the island, and, salvaging an old Swiss Army knife from the capsule, they sharpen sticks and set out to ambush Alex and Derek.

Thus, in the film, the women's vulnerability ironically becomes a source of their power. Instead of opening them to assault, their return to primal nudity allows them to gain some control over their situation and, moreover, to reforge their shattered bonds of friendship. Far from powerlessness or openness to assault, then, *Black Rock* portrays the female body as a source of strength. When Abby and Lou strip off their wet clothes, they must reconnect with their bodies, attune to them, if only to stave off the cold. And once they have done this, they are able to become hunters rather than hunted and to kill their assailants, avenging Sarah's death in the process.

Of course, this discussion of nudity and empowerment in *Black Rock* is reminiscent of *I Spit on Your Grave* (2010), in which Jennifer's nudity before swan diving into the river also symbolizes her return to power. Thus, despite not featuring rape to the same extent as the traditional rape-revenge film, *Black Rock* is able to treat some of the same themes and, I assert, with their due gravity. The film does, however, also suffer a tad from its fealty to a realist mode. At the end of *Black Rock*, Abby and Lou face the prospect of trying to swim to shore, a task they already failed once and that may well kill them. As such, *Black Rock* appears to retreat right at the edge of liberating its surviving heroines. Thus, the film suggests there may be no winning in a culture still reliant on a he said/she said dynamic.

Black Rock also marks an important departure for the films I discuss in this volume. Whereas *I Spit on Your Grave* is a horror movie, *Black Rock* is a thriller with very little horror in it. Hence, as we have moved from films that outright show rape as horrifying, we have also moved away from the horror genre. And while *Black Rock* certainly makes rape significant both for its narrative and its characters, it does not make rape as viscerally horrifying as *I Spit on Your Grave* does. Nor does it make the revenge as unsettling as both *I Spit* and *The Maid's Tragedy* do.

On this topic, we should discuss how *Black Rock* deals with the issue of male tribalism that so permeates rape-revenge in horror and thriller. After all, Henry, Alex, and Derek are ex-soldiers, veterans of war; that is, they have been indoctrinated into a fraternity culture built, partially, on masculine bravado and masculine tribalism. Popular culture is rife with images of the male, sex-crazed, young soldier, and certainly our three soldiers from *Black Rock* fit that stereotype well. As for tribalism, observe the position soldiers are in during war: two sides of, largely male, combatants fight against one another and rely on the, largely male, members of their own respective teams to keep them alive. Such reliance on a team for survival necessarily breeds a tribalist mindset whereby one is inculcated into elevating one's team over and above most other considerations.[6]

Masculine tribalism, *Black Rock* suggests, risks toxicity. Said toxicity arises when Alex and Derek turn on the women and assault them following Henry's death. Whereas Sarah and Lou immediately believe Abby's story, the men do not; even worse, Derek insists to Alex that they owe Henry. So their loyalty to their fallen comrade, their fellow soldier, eclipses whatever other considerations they might have, including any anti-rape attitudes they might possess. To be clear, though, the men did not witness Henry's attempt to assault Abby. But, then, neither did the women. Therefore, *Black Rock* suggests male tribalism can deafen men to the voices of rape victims, leading to today's real-world refrain of believing women.

Such deafening is not inevitable, though, as we see in another non-rape, rape film: *Rust Creek* (2018, directed by Jen McGowan). This movie follows Sawyer (Hermione Corfield), a hard-working college student who runs afoul of a meth-cooking ring after getting lost in the Kentucky forest. The film opens with Sawyer running laps at her college's track before getting a call for a job interview in Washington D.C. She packs and begins the drive to D.C. only for her GPS to prove unreliable on the dense backroads. Pulling into a wrong road, Sawyer

---

[6] Here, one might object to my characterizing the military as a largely masculine enterprise. There are, after all, many female soldiers whose experiences my analysis appears to elide. To be clear, my assertion is that formal, professional armies have, traditionally, been majority male because of the sociocultural and sociopolitical systems whence said armies emerge. Furthermore, the continued revelations about sexual violence aimed at female soldiers in the United States military reveal that, unfortunately, the United States military continues to have a masculine, fraternity-esque culture that, at the very least, allows sexual abuse of women under its purview.

nearly stumbles upon Hollister and Buck, two brothers who help run a meth ring and are in the process of burying a body. Fearing Sawyer saw them (she did not), the brothers follow her, finding her pulled over to the side of the road, consulting a map in lieu of her GPS. They approach her and offer directions before inviting the increasingly and visibly uncomfortable Sawyer to eat dinner with them.

Hollister blocks Sawyer from entering her vehicle despite her blunt statement that he is making her uncomfortable. He continues making advances and then grabs Sawyer's rear, whereupon she defends herself, breaking his nose and turning Buck's knife back on Buck himself. She is wounded in the struggle, however, when Buck's knife impales her leg. Thus hurt, her typically strong running abilities weaken, and Sawyer limps into the forest, away from the two hurt, angry brothers.

Feeling they have no choice but to find and kill her, the brothers head home to prepare to hunt Sawyer down. Sawyer, meanwhile, spends the night in the wilderness, awakening cold and weak. The next day, she watches as Hollister and Buck roll her car off a small cliff. Though she scavenges her cell phone, she is unable to get help and ultimately collapses near a dumping ground in the forest. From there, she awakens in a trailer, her leg bandaged. The man who rescued her, she learns, is Lowell, cousin of Hollister and Buck, and the meth cook in their operation. Whereas Sawyer is initially wary of Lowell, he assures her he wants to drive her to safety but must wait until the latest batch of meth is ready so he will have an excuse to borrow Hollister and Buck's truck without arousing their suspicions. Despite her eagerness to leave, Sawyer's injury continues to hamstring her ability to flee on foot, forcing her to follow Lowell's plan.

That plan becomes more complicated, however, when Hollister and Buck grow suspicious of Lowell; they have tracked Sawyer's trail to near Lowell's trailer, and Lowell is uncharacteristically evasive, unwilling to allow them inside. Likewise, the local sheriff, whom we learn is part of the drug ring as well, also grows suspicious of Lowell. The sheriff, O'Doyle, leans on the brothers to find and kill Sawyer, as the state police threaten to take over the case of her disappearance. Thus, Hollister and Buck storm into Lowell's trailer, discovering Sawyer there.

As a last resort, Lowell and Sawyer manage to kill Buck and wound Hollister by blowing up the trailer. Hollister and Lowell struggle, but O'Doyle arrives and guns them down. As O'Doyle drives Sawyer from the scene, Sawyer recognizes his voice from his earlier visit to the trailer. Realizing this, O'Doyle tries to drown Sawyer in the nearby creek, intent on framing the brothers for the events, but Sawyer manages to stab O'Doyle, leaving his body in the creek. The film ends with her walking down the road, state trooper cars beginning to pull up behind her.

As this summary shows, *Rust Creek* lacks a rape scene. The closest the film comes to one is Hollister's sexual battery of Sawyer when he grabs her butt. Still, while this scene does not explicitly show rape or attempted rape, it clearly shows sexual battery and unwanted advances. Moreover, it foregrounds the undercurrents of sexual violence women can face in every day life; what may have merely been the threat of physical assault and murder against a male (presumed) witness becomes a threat of physical and sexual violence against a female (presumed) witness. Hollister's insistence that Sawyer join him and Buck for dinner carries sinister implications about Sawyer's fate, implications the brothers would, presumably, not have made to a male victim. In this way, *Rust Creek* mirrors the rape-revenge film's narrative arc, which I described earlier in this book. Not only does the film focus on a female victim against her male attackers and their threat of physical and sexual violence, but it also follows the familiar beats of the urban/country conflict (as we saw in *I Spit*).

What stands out in its contribution, then, are Sawyer and Lowell. And both of these contributions boil down to the same story element: realism. Like the other heroines in this volume, Sawyer is strong and capable. She is not only a high-achieving student but also resilient and capable of defending herself against two male attackers. Indeed, one might think the scene of her initial assault would have played out differently if she were not so talented in self-defense. And yet, unlike some of the other rape-revenge heroines (say, Zoe from *Avenged*[7] and Jennifer from *I Spit* (2010)), Sawyer is a grounded character. Though capable, she never becomes the sort of superhuman avenging figure some of her fellow heroines do. There is no supernatural spirit animating Sawyer,[8] and she shows no preternatural ability to construct traps to torture her assailants.[9] Instead, *Rust Creek* realistically portrays the effects of injuries, as the initial wound to Sawyer's leg hounds her throughout the film, severely limiting her mobility and forcing her to rely more on others for assistance.

That assistance, of course, comes from Lowell. Whereas some of the films in this volume (e.g., the original *I Spit*) treat the country as unrelentingly hostile toward urban outsiders, *Rust Creek* pushes against such a depiction of rural America. Rather than a purely hostile tribe intent on her death, Sawyer encounters a mixture of characters, one of whom actively puts himself in danger to protect her. And so, *Rust Creek*'s depiction of the urban/country

---

[7] *Avenged* is a 2013 rape-revenge film directed by Michael S. Ojeda and starring Amanda Adrienne.

[8] See *Avenged*.

[9] See *I Spit* (2010).

divide is not as stark as that in other films, offering the country some redemption through the figure of Lowell. Indeed, central here is how Sawyer finds her salvation more so through Lowell than through a return to nature or to her own primal instincts (as in *Black Rock*).

Moreover, through Lowell, *Rust Creek* challenges the notion that male tribalism will always and necessarily blind men to questions about sexual violence. Tribally, we would expect Lowell to align himself with Hollister, Buck, and O'Doyle. All four are from the country (and so their alignment would respect the urban/country divide around which these films often revolve), all four work together, and Lowell is kin to the former two. And yet, Lowell stands firm in his moral convictions, ultimately sacrificing his home, cousins, and life in an effort to protect Sawyer.

Rust Creek, therefore, asks the audience to question their presumptions. Rather than a source of help, the local sheriff becomes a key threat.[10] Rather than a source of danger, the local meth cook becomes Sawyer's most important ally. Ergo, *Rust Creek* maintains its realism by insisting on how inaccurate initial impressions may be. And yet, while Lowell remains an important reminder of humanity's potential for goodness, his character may become the source for possible objections to this film. Whereas Jennifer exacts revenge for herself, Sawyer largely takes a backseat in gaining the upper-hand over her assailants. Lowell instructs her on how to kill Buck, O'Doyle kills Hollister, and Sawyer independently kills only O'Doyle, who did not participate in the initial assault.

To be sure, in this movement, *Rust Creek* departs from the traditional rape-revenge formula. After all, Sawyer does not get direct revenge on Hollister for sexually battering her.[11] At times, therefore, Sawyer appears as a supporting character in her own story. In light of our earlier discussion of *I Spit*, it would therefore appear that Sawyer does not recapture the agency she lost when assaulted. And yet, that is too simplistic a reading, for Sawyer does not completely lose her agency during the initial assault. Note how she thwarts Hollister and Buck's attempts to kidnap and/or murder her and how she

---

[10] The reader may rightly note here that the sheriff in *I Spit* (2010) is also a threat, and, to be sure, it is common for these films to show law enforcement as unhelpful at best, actively malicious at worst. Nevertheless, the cultural perception of police as a source of aid instead of a source of danger remains noteworthy in this context, especially as *Rust Creek* goes out of its way to depict law enforcement as a possible force for good. Whereas the sheriff is corrupt and a murderer, deputy Katz is not. In contrast to the sheriff, Katz and the state police seem actively invested in finding and saving Sawyer.

[11] That is, aside from when she immediately hits him the face right after he gropes her. This hit, however, hardly gets revenge against the stab wound to her leg and the brothers' hunt for her.

manages to wound both the brothers while also eluding them. Sawyer, ergo, never fully loses her agency, and so what she seeks to regain is her safety, not her agency. In regaining the latter, though, she must rely on Lowell, who does, consequently, lessen Sawyer's role as the heroine of the story.

Still, it would be easy to overstate this effect. While forcing a heroine to rely on another, particularly a man, for assistance, may be problematic, we should note, nevertheless, that Sawyer emerges from her ordeal as strong and determined as she was at the movie's beginning. The film's final sequence, as aforementioned, follows Sawyer walking down the road, the creek and Sheriff O'Doyle's body behind her, staring ahead and walking doggedly forward even as the state troopers begin to arrive. Like Eve from *Bound to Vengeance* and Jennifer from *I Spit on Your Grave*, Sawyer finishes her film moving forward, symbolically leaving the past behind her. Unlike with her predecessors, Eve and Jennifer, however, Sawyer seems to have a clearer sense of where she is going: back to her college, to her worried mother, and maybe to salvage a job opportunity after her missed interview.

Rape-revenge films have a habit of ending immediately after the revenge is complete. And while *Rust Creek* demonstrates that non-rape, rape-revenge films can overcome this pitfall, *Black Rock* shows they do not always. At the end of the latter, Abby and Lou try to swim to shore, but it is unclear if they will make it. Wounded and in cold waters, they may drown before reaching shore. And *Black Rock* is not alone here, as other non-rape rape-revenge films likewise have unclear endings.

Of particular interest on this note is Quentin Tarantino's *Death Proof* (2007), which Heller-Nicholas has noted as a rape-revenge film despite its lack of any scenes containing actual sexual assault (attempted or otherwise).[12] Indeed, it is her observation that some rape-revenge films do not show rape that has inspired this chapter on "non-rape, rape-revenge films."[13] *Death Proof* is divided into two largely independent stories, united in the presence of antagonist Stuntman Mike (Kurt Russell), a stunt-driver turned serial killer whose weapon of choice is his customized car.

Outfitted with numerous safety features, Mike's car is "death proof," designed to complete dangerous stunts while allowing the driver to survive. The first story section follows a group of three women, "Jungle" Julia (a local DJ), Shanna, and Arlene. Celebrating Julia's birthday, the three visit a few bars in Austin while Mike stalks them. The night ends with the three women and a fourth, Lanna, driving toward Shanna's family beach house. Mike follows them and

---

[12] Heller-Nicholas. 2nd edition. 80.
[13] Ibid.

intentionally crashes his car into theirs at high speed, killing all four women and hospitalizing himself. The local sheriff declines to pursue charges against Mike, however; though he recognizes Mike's motives and knows Mike murdered the women intentionally (and for sexual gratification), he lacks evidence with which to charge the stuntman.

And so the film enters its second story segment, this time following a new group of three (then four) women. This time, the group is Abernathy (Rosario Dawson), Kim, and Lee, three women working on a local film production. Abernathy is a make-up artist, Kim is a stuntwoman, Lee an actress. Later, they gain a second stuntwoman, Zoe, Kim and Abernathy's friend who has just flown into the States. Zoe convinces the other women to go with her to view (and hopefully test drive) a Dodge Challenger for sale in the area. Upon seeing the car, Zoe convinces Kim to test drive it with her and engage in a game of "Ship's Mast." Refusing to stay behind, Abernathy convinces the other two to bring her with them and convinces the car's owner to stay behind and "get to know" Lee, whom the other girls leave (in perhaps the movie's most troubling moment) as a sort of collateral.[14]

Thus, the game of "Ship's Mast" begins. With Kim in the Challenger's driver seat, Zoe climbs onto the car's hood and takes hold of two belts tied to the front window frames. The women's daredevil game turns deadly, however, when Stuntman Mike, who has been stalking them, interrupts. Entering the fray in his own car, he starts ramming the Challenger, threatening to send Zoe flying off the hood at high speeds, likely to her death. Eventually, he succeeds, and Zoe disappears behind some bushes. Stuntman Mike emerges from his car to gloat for a moment, only for Kim to shoot him in the arm with her concealed carry handgun. Bleeding and in pain, Mike flees, after which Zoe emerges from the bushes, unscathed. From there, the three women give chase, turning the tables on Mike. With Kim still driving, they wreck Mike's car, drag him from the wreckage, and beat him to death. The film ends after Abernathy delivers a fatal axe kick to the head of a prone Mike.

As aforementioned, Heller-Nicholas has already made the case for why *Death Proof*, despite its lack of rape scenes, is, in fact, a rape-revenge film. Central to this classification is the film's equation of car crashes with sexual violence. After the crash that kills the first group of women (i.e., the crash Mike uses to murder the women), the local sheriff muses the crash is "a sex thing," a connection the film's female protagonists also make, as Lee says of Mike when the latter revs

---

[14] *Death Proof.* Directed by Quentin Tarantino, performance by Rosario Dawson, Dimension Films, 2007.

his engine and speeds away, "Little dick."[15] This connection between vehicular violence and sex[16] becomes even more explicit during the final chase scene, during which the repeated ramming evokes images of penetration, as Kim implies when she asks Mike: "Don't like it up the ass, do ya?"[17]

And, of course, just before the final chase, a shot shows Mike watching the women through binoculars while sitting on the hood of his car, his crotch pressed against his hood ornament. This shot visually equates Mike's penis with the hood ornament and, by extension, his car. Thus, even though the film has no scenes of sexual assault (attempted or otherwise), it is clearly about sexual violence. And, indeed, it follows the typical rape-revenge structure, starting with a male villain who sexually assaults the female protagonists only to then fall victim to similarly sexualized violence when his victims return for their revenge.

As I suggested before, though, *Death Proof* ends as soon as the protagonists have taken their revenge. In fact, the film never addresses what happens to Lee, how the Challenger's owner reacts to its condition upon return (it was wrecked during the final chase), or how the women will explain their situation to law enforcement. One must assume law enforcement will have many questions about the deceased Mike and the two wrecked cars (to say nothing of all the broken traffic laws). Of course, many rape-revenge films leave such questions up in the air.

The original *I Spit* has Jennifer boating away with four dead bodies in her proverbial wake (two of them in her literal wake). The film does not address how Jennifer will navigate the authorities, who will surely have questions about the four dead men. Notably, though, the remake cycle of *I Spit* films actually covers this ground since, in *I Spit III*, we learn Jennifer changed her name and is, in fact, wanted for questioning in connection to the killings from *I Spit* (2010).

And, furthermore, other rape-revenge films address this question in other ways. In *I Spit II*, Katie receives assistance from a Bulgarian police officer who saves her at the last minute and makes no effort to detain her when she leaves for the American embassy, instead apologizing for his failure to help her earlier in the film. Yet, these films are something of exceptions within rape-revenge stories. Rape-revenge films are often unconcerned with questions of what happens after the revenge.

---

[15] *Death Proof.*
[16] Heller-Nicholas. 2nd edition. 81.
[17] *Death Proof.*

While we might not fault *Death Proof* for ignoring the question of legal consequences for its heroines,[18] we may still be concerned with its treatment of Lee. In her analysis of the film, Heller-Nicholas astutely observes how the film allows the women to assert control over a traditionally masculine domain: automobiles.[19] Like Mike, Kim is a stunt-driver, and she repeatedly shows her skills are comparable to his. Not only does she manage to keep herself, Abernathy, and the vulnerable Zoe alive during the initial chase, but she also chases Mike down, overcomes his attempts to elude her, and totals his car.

This assertion of feminine strength taking ownership over traditional symbols of masculine power allows *Death Proof* to overcome some of its more troubling elements. For example, when Abernathy, Zoe, and Kim approach a badly injured Mike to finish him, the camera lingers in a medium shot focused on the women's backsides, ostensibly sexualizing them in what should be a moment of female empowerment. And yet, because this shot comes at the tail end of an extended sequence in which the women gain the aforementioned power over a stereotypically masculine domain, this shot, rather than merely reducing the women to sexual objects, asserts their power, their control over their own bodies, and the threat they can pose to self-professed predators.

And so, *Death Proof* ends up being a rather empowering film, pushing a message of female strength. Yet, from this strength, we return to the film's weakness: Lee. Though Lee is a sexually liberated, successful actress, the film leaves her in a vulnerable position charged with sexual implication. When the other three women leave her behind, they do so after Abernathy says Lee is a pornographic actress and after she tells Zoe and Kim she plans to imply to the Challenger's owner that Lee might give him oral sex. And where, one might ask, is Lee in all this?

She is napping in a chair, blissfully unaware her so-called friends are using her as a bargaining chip. They do not awaken her until they are ready to leave in the Challenger, leaving Lee to wake up with the car's owner standing in front of her. He chuckles, and Lee's final line is "gulp."[20] Thus, even when the rest of the surviving female protagonists are showing their empowerment, Lee is

---

[18] To be clear, this is not to suggest I, the author, believe the heroines deserve legal punishment for their actions. Rather, this is to suggest they are likely to face them if only because it will be difficult for them to prove their case that Mike attacked them. It is also unclear whether they can legally claim self-defense given how they pursued Mike and attacked him after he ceased being a threat. In particular, I suspect the final axe kick against a downed and incapacitated Mike could easily become a crime in the eyes of the legal system.

[19] Heller-Nicholas. 2nd edition. 81.

[20] *Death Proof.*

reduced, apparently, to a bargaining chip of sexual favors, and the film leaves her in a vulnerable position that remains unresolved, as we do not see her again.

Also troubling is how Lee is the most traditionally feminine of the four women. Even her clothing suggests her femininity; whereas the other three dress somewhat practically, Lee wears her character's costume, a bright yellow cheerleading uniform, the skirt short enough to reveal her panties in one low-angle shot when she bends over to get a drink from a vending machine. The film itself even lampshades Lee's traditional femininity when the four women eat an early lunch together and discuss the disparity between masculine and feminine interests. Kim acknowledges she likes both cars and typical 'girly' movies like *Pretty in Pink*.

Lee immediately chimes in, saying: "Aww, I love *Pretty in Pink*," almost as if she has not realized the other women are contrasting themselves to such stereotypical or limited views of femininity.[21] To be clear, this is not to say the film denigrates or dismisses traditional views of the feminine. Indeed, even the badass stunt driver Kim admits to liking traditionally feminine media even as she also enjoys traditionally masculine activities (e.g., stunt driving). Thus, *Death Proof* instead advocates for a non-binary view of gender roles wherein women can thrive in, even claim, domains the patriarchy has typically deemed masculine.

And yet, despite this avowed gender progressivism, the film and women's treatment of Lee is troubling. It is easy to read Abernathy, Zoe, and Kim's willingness to leave Lee behind as they're abandoning the traditionally feminine, and not just abandoning it but rather they're sacrificing it to the threat of male sexual violence. Not only does *Death Proof* imply Lee may be sexually assaulted, but it plays this moment as if it were a joke, Lee's audible "gulp" contrasting with the scene's extremely serious implications. Now, on the one hand, such a contrast could be to ease the audience's concerns, to show the scene is not as serious, not as dangerous as the audience takes it to be. On the other hand, it is difficult to view the scene as a joke or anything less than seriously disturbing, as Abernathy and Jasper, the Challenger's owner, have directly sexualized Lee, and, as aforementioned, Lee's final scene is dripping with sexual implications.

It would be easy, therefore, to guess the scene is leading to Lee's being coerced (or feeling coerced) into sexual activity. That we never see what happened to Lee, that the film never confirms she is safe and has not been victimized, is, to my view, the film's most unsettling implication, not only because the man

---

[21] Ibid.

might attack Lee but also because the film's otherwise powerful and progressive protagonists, well-written female characters, allowed this to happen; in fact, and moreover, they made it happen. And their making it happen suggests progressive, non-binary feminism may abandon the traditionally feminine along the way, may toss it to the wolves, so to speak, thus leading to yet another prescriptive view of femininity, one which forces women to adhere to the non-binary progressivism the other three women embody, not allowing the typical femininity Lee visibly embodies.

Here, though, one may object to my classification of Lee as "traditionally feminine," as she repeatedly proves sexually liberated. Indeed, throughout her scenes, Lee makes references to sex and her active sex life, including her ongoing sexual relationship with a member of the film's production team. We should also note how "Lee" is a more unisexual name than "Zoe," "Abernathy," and, arguably, "Kim."[22] Still, these facts do not undermine how Lee is the most traditionally feminine of the group, as evident from Lee's outfit and demeanor. These facts do, however, further demonstrate how *Death Proof* seeks to undermine binary views of gender roles, suggesting one can be feminine while not feeling entirely beholden to patriarchal gender norms. To be sure, however, Lee's lack of complete adherence to traditional gender norms does not mean that her final scene becomes untroubling; it is still deeply problematic.

Still, as we have seen, rape-revenge stories are rife with problematic subject matter. So, it should be unsurprising that *Death Proof*, in my analysis, still runs afoul of this issue, albeit to a lesser extent than many films do. In the wide world of rape-revenge media, *Death Proof* remains a largely successful entry. That rape-revenge media have a wide variety should be evident from our discussion thus far; indeed, it is the primary argument of Heller-Nicholas's book on the matter.[23] And contrasting to *Death Proof* is David Slade's very different 2005 film *Hard Candy*, which, unlike the other films I have discussed so far, addresses pedophilia, a topic that immediately puts the movie into troubling territory.

Hard Candy features a minimal cast, following just two characters for the majority of the film: a photographer, Jeff, and a young girl, Hailey. Most of the film's action occurs in Jeff's house, with only him and Hailey on screen. Hailey

---

[22] "Kim" will vary by the culture, as some countries in Asia do not limit the name to women as often as Western cultures do.

[23] Heller-Nicholas. 2nd edition. 2. Heller-Nicholas notes that, far from a single, unified treatment of rape or revenge, rape-revenge films offer a large variety of often differing, even contradictory, treatments.

(Elliot Page)[24] pitches herself as a young teenage girl, and the film opens with her and the adult Jeff flirting via online chat, agreeing to finally meet in person. Their meeting occurs in a small coffee shop, whence they decide to go to Jeff's house. There, Jeff shows Hailey his collection of photos; images of models adorn his walls. He describes them as his portfolio, evidence of his skills as a photographer. As if these photos have inspired her, Hailey asks Jeff to photograph her after she pours them drinks.

Jeff grows disoriented, however, and passes out. Waking up, he finds himself bound to a chair, with Hailey searching his house. She reveals to him that she drugged his drink and that she knows he was involved in the recent kidnapping of a local teenager, Donna Mauer. Naturally, Jeff denies his involvement. He also accuses Hailey of seducing him when she points out he has lured her, an underage girl, back to his home and given her alcohol. Hailey does not buy it, however, and, after Jeff attempts to escape, she ties him to his kitchen table and threatens to castrate him.

She pantomimes the castration, convincing Jeff she has gone through with it. By this point, she has also found a photo of Donna Mauer tucked away in Jeff's safe. Jeff manages to escape his binds once more, however, only for Hailey to subdue him again. When Jeff wakes up, he has a noose tied around his neck. Hailey has moved into her endgame; she offers Jeff the opportunity to commit suicide, saying if he does, she will destroy the evidence of his crimes. Rather than take the plunge, though, Jeff escapes for a third time and chases Hailey onto his roof. There, however, he learns Hailey has called Jeff's ex-girlfriend Janelle, with whom he remains obsessed. Under the threat that Hailey will reveal Jeff's crimes to Janelle, Jeff hangs himself from his roof, secure with Hailey's promise she will destroy the evidence. Before jumping, though, Jeff reveals he was present at Donna's murder and that his accomplice, Aaron, killed her. He even offers to reveal his accomplice if Hailey lets him live, only for her to confess she already killed Aaron, who claimed Jeff was the murderer. Once Jeff has hanged himself, Hailey reneges on her promise and slips away before Janelle sees her.

As this summary shows, *Hard Candy* is atypical of the films (let alone films and literature) I discuss in this volume. First, it deals with the issues of pedophilia and pederasty, issues I have not yet addressed in this book. Second, it shows no explicit images of sexual assault yet is clearly about sexual violence and revenge against said violence. Third, *Hard Candy* offers a remarkably well-

---

[24] Actor Elliot Page is a transman. At the time of *Hard Candy*'s production, he had not yet transitioned, and, thus, was billed as Ellen Page. This volume will refer to the actor as Elliot Page, though original materials from the film's production may yet bear his deadname.

rounded portrayal of its antagonist, Jeff. To be clear, Jeff is a monster. He knowingly flirts with and tries to seduce teenage girls, and he was involved in the kidnapping, rape, and murder of at least one such girl. Jeff is despicable. And yet, through Hailey's investigation, we learn a lot about him.

Jeff is a talented photographer, but he is very insecure, particularly with women. This insecurity, we learn, stems from when Janelle broke up with him. Jeff has never managed to move on from her; indeed, even his safe combination pertains to her, and the threat of her finding out about his crimes drives him to suicide. The film even hints that this insecurity may be one of the reasons why Jeff pursues underage girls. Again, to be clear, while one might sympathize with Jeff's being devastated at a bad breakup, it would be a rare viewer indeed who finds Jeff a sympathetic character. His backstory in no way justifies his abominable actions. But, still, it is rare for rape-revenge films, even non-rape, rape-revenge films, to give such extended backstories to their antagonists. *I Spit* reveals little about the men. And even most of the films in this chapter do not bother to give such backstories. In *Death Proof*, Mike claims to have worked as a stunt driver on a number of television shows he mentions by name.

We never learn, however, whether his claims are true. And, at one point, he claims to have a brother, Stuntman Bob, suggesting he is willing to lie about his personal history for the sake of a joke. And Mike may be one of the more developed rape-revenge villains. Le Tenia from *Irréversible*, for example, gets no backstory at all.[25] With Jeff, we learn a bit about what makes him tick, and his motivations extend beyond his merely being a sexual deviant or psychopath.

Hard Candy, therefore, humanizes its antagonist even though it does not redeem him. Notably, one of the few on-screen characters other than Jeff and Hailey is Jeff's neighbor, Judy Tokuda. Judy is only in a couple scenes, and she shares one of them with Hailey. Hailey poses as Jeff's niece, and Judy asks Hailey if she babysits. This scene is rather undramatic, contrasting with the rest of the film and especially with the noose-wearing Jeff in the house while Hailey and Judy are talking. And that is the point. To the outside world, Jeff is a regular person with neighbors who make pleasant chit-chat and ask Jeff's niece if she babysits.[26]

While such a pedestrian depiction of evil, such a revelation that the monster lives next door and looks just like us, is not unique to *Hard Candy*, it is something of an outlier in a narrative form that frequently marks its villains as such. Moreover, *Hard Candy* hereby places itself outside the mythic world that

---

[25] I discuss *Irréversible* at length in chapter five.
[26] That is, the girl the neighbor believes to be Jeff's niece.

so many rape-revenge films occupy. Like *Irréversible, Black Rock,* and *Rust Creek, Hard Candy* occurs in the real world, where Hailey has to cover her tracks to avoid going to jail herself.

On a similar note, Jeff's Achilles' heel stems from his place in the real world, a world where image matters. Jeff is obsessed with image and reputation. Notice, for example, how it is Hailey's threat of outing Jeff as a pederast to Janelle that ultimately drives Jeff to suicide. Indeed, Jeff's obsession with image is evident from his occupation. Adorning his walls with his photographs, he is preoccupied with appearances, including his appearance to others. And it is his earnest desire to maintain this image that leads to his downfall. On the surface level, he dies because he fears Janelle learning he is a rapist and murderer. On a deeper level, though, he dies because of his insecurities, his needs to appear impressive and successful drive him to prey upon underage girls.

Given Jeff's preoccupation with appearances, it is ironic that Hailey not only deconstructs his façade but also maintains her own throughout the film. The photographer, ostensibly the one with the most control over images, proves to have the least control out of the two main characters. Hailey hereby emerges as a particularly interesting protagonist for a rape-revenge film. As we have seen, most such protagonists follow a predictable arc whereby assailants assault them, they turn into avenging figures, and they get their revenge. Hailey, however, departs from this traditional model. We never see what drives her to hunt down pedophiles. Was she a victim herself? Did she know Donna Mauer and therefore desire revenge for Donna's death? Or has she done this before as a sort of self-appointed vigilante?

Not only do we not get the answers to these questions, but we learn very little about Hailey herself. When Jeff tries to threaten her with the personal information she gave him during the course of their conversations, Hailey notes how all of that information could be false, that Jeff actually knows nothing about her. Realizing his predicament, that Hailey has seen right through his façade, and that he can be sure of little to nothing about the information she gave him, Jeff angrily sputters, demanding of Hailey: "Who are you!?"[27] And that is a question the audience also has to ask since Hailey remains enigmatic.

And perhaps our first question as viewers regards her actual age. Hailey claims to be and presents as a young teenager. Yet, her ability to identify, find, trap, and kill two pederasts and rapists would hint she is actually older than she appears. Otherwise, her detective abilities are precocious, at the least. Of particular interest here is Elliot Page himself; he was 17-18 when making *Hard Candy*, though his petite frame made him appear noticeably younger. Still, that

---

[27] *Hard Candy.* Directed by David Slade, performance by Elliot Page, Lionsgate, 2005.

Hailey calls someone (possibly the older sister she had earlier told Jeff she had) for a ride at the film's end suggests she may actually be a young teenager, albeit an oddly capable one. Also aligning with this reading of Hailey's age is the number of mistakes she makes.

Remember how Jeff escapes his restraints three different times. And while Hailey seemingly predicts his second escape, claiming she is going to shower but instead hiding in the bathroom and ambushing Jeff when he moves toward the running shower and drawn curtain, she still struggles to keep control of the situation she engineered. Her apparent lack of control contrasts with her otherwise powerful, enigmatic demeanor. The contrast between these two Haileys makes it seem Hailey is merely a precocious young girl.

Of all the heroines in this book, Hailey's mistakes make her most akin to Eve from *Bound to Vengeance*.[28] While both Hailey and Eve present as capable avenging figures, their films show them repeatedly making mistakes, nearly to the point of appearing inept. Though I identify this as a major flaw in *Bound to Vengeance*'s design, *Hard Candy* does not suffer as much from this issue, as Hailey's ostensible age (which the weight of the evidence suggests is accurate even as it belies her precocity) justifies her making errors. One might wonder how capable and lethal Hailey might become if she continues down this path of being a self-appointed avenger. Here, we should also note that Hailey differs from Eve not merely in age but in another key way: Hailey stays in psychological control.

In *Bound to Vengeance*, Eve remains psychologically under her captor Phil's thumb even after she has gained the upper-hand, physically.[29] Hailey, by contrast, flips Jeff's attempts at psychological warfare back on him. When Jeff tries to tear her down, she plays along, feigning upset, and then laughs, dashing Jeff's hopes of gaining the advantage. In this way, Hailey becomes a remarkable heroine; though her physical control is weaker than that of many of the heroines' I have discussed in this volume, her psychological control is another matter. Unlike the many rape-revenge heroines and avengers who (understandably) remain psychologically damaged from their respective films' events, Hailey appears to emerge largely unscathed. I say "largely" because one

---

[28] I discuss *Bound to Vengeance* at length at the end of this chapter.
[29] Daniel Stidham, *Cutprintfilm*, June 23, 2015, https://web.archive.org/web/2015062510 0050/http://www.cutprintfilm.com/reviews/bound-to-vengeance/.

might convincingly argue that Hailey's willingness to push men to suicide is a hallmark of a damaged psyche.[30]

Still, as I have shown, Hailey's psyche remains elusive, as we do not get her backstory, or, at least, cannot be sure how much she says is true and how much false. As such, it is hard to tell to what extent Hailey is psychologically damaged. Indeed, the way she casually calls up her ride seems to suggest she compartmentalizes very well, though, again, this is a case of my having to work with limited information.

This limited information does not preclude us from discussing some other matters about *Hard Candy*, though. For instance, whereas I earlier noted how *Hard Candy* remains more grounded, more realistic, than many other rape-revenge films do, we should also note *Hard Candy*'s mythic elements. Chief among these is the film's connection to the "Red Riding Hood" fairy tale, a connection viewers have made much of, but that was a happy accident for the film's prop department.[31] Throughout the film, Hailey wears a red sweatshirt. When she raises its hood, she, therefore, looks like Little Red Riding Hood. *Hard Candy* also invokes the folkloric rule of three with Jeff's three attempted escapes.

And, ironically, Hailey's Little Red is one who traps the wolves by tricking them into thinking they are hunting her when she is hunting them. Not only does Hailey accordingly invert the positions of hunter and hunted, thereby challenging the view of young girls as prey by presenting one of them, instead, as a hunter, but she also upsets the broader societal structures at play. Because we learn little about Hailey as a person, the film implies any girl could be Hailey, any girl could be that avenger, that fake victim waiting to trap her would-be predator. Furthermore, such girls may be innate avengers rather than transformed avengers.

Notice how, throughout this volume, avengers are almost always created. That is, trauma causes otherwise benign women to become violent, creative killers. With Hailey, though, it is possible someone may be such a killer innately, without the intervention of outside, abusive forces. Of course, as I have established, *Hard Candy* remains unclear on this point, but the argument stands nonetheless. And the pre-existing avenger would be an outlier in the rape-revenge narrative. We see this figure in *Avenged*, where the spirit of Mangas Coloradas, already an experienced warrior, possesses the protagonist

---

[30] That is, one might argue, vigilantism is indicative of a moral flaw. It is, however, beyond the scope of this volume to argue for or against the ethics of vigilantism. Thus, for now, I but acknowledge that arguments against personal revenge exist.

[31] "Making *Hard Candy*." Directed by David Slade. In *Hard Candy*, Lions Gate, 2006.

Zoe only after she is raped and left for dead. So even *Avenged* does not make the avenger innate to the rape victim.[32]

And neither does the last non-rape, rape-revenge film I wish to discuss here: 2020's *Alone*, directed by John Hyams. This movie almost seems to start in media res, as protagonist Jessica (Jules Willcox) packs a small U-Haul trailer. She appears eager to leave the city, as she abandons a potted plant that will not fit in the limited space, and her mother later says over the phone that she had thought Jessica would wait.

Jessica, however, embarks on a long road trip, only to repeatedly encounter the same man in a number of disparate locations: the road, a gas station, a hotel, and a rest stop. Afraid this man is following her, Jessica rushes away from the rest stop and ends up in a ditch when one of her tires gives out. Inspecting the tire, she realizes someone has slashed it. But a few minutes later, the man pulls in behind her and, abandoning all pretense, immediately shatters her window with a tire iron and renders her unconscious.

Jessica awakens in a basement, where her captor physically and psychologically torments her. He orders her to strip and slams her into the wall when she then tries to flee. Rather than force her to undress, however, he instead lays on the floor with the hurt, scared Jessica and spoons her while forcing her to watch a video on her iPad, which he has been inspecting. This video shows Jessica with her now-deceased husband. Here, we learn Jessica left the city because her husband recently died from suicide; she is fleeing to start a new life away from the life she had with him.

After the man leaves her, she realizes he has left the key to the basement in the keyhole on the other side of the door, and, with some ingenuity, she retrieves the key and escapes the room. She waits to flee the house, though, as she almost encounters the man, who sits at a table upstairs, eating a small lunch. While Jessica hides nearby, he takes a call from his wife and daughter, whereupon we learn he has lied to them about being on a business trip. Once she gets the opportunity, Jessica flees the cabin, but the man quickly gives chase, starting a cat-and-mouse struggle extending into the next day. The chase ends in a field where, as a search and rescue helicopter closes in, Jessica calls the man's wife and reveals his crimes to her. Enraged, the man attacks her, and Jessica kills him in the struggle. She collapses as the helicopter closes in to rescue her.

---

[32] I refer to Zoe as a rape victim rather than rape survivor because her rapists also murder her. Her revenge occurs during her undeath when the aforementioned spirit possesses her body.

What is most interesting about *Alone* in the context of rape-revenge is how it replaces physical trauma with psychological trauma, focusing on explicit portrayals of psychological assault rather than upon physical assault. And yet, we would be remiss to thereby dismiss *Alone* as a rape-revenge story. When the man orders Jessica to undress, the implications are clear even though he does not follow up on them. And, of course, we should also note how the film's format fits easily into the rape-revenge plot model: an urban woman embarks into the country, a man more familiar with the area attacks her, she fights back, and she kills him. Given this model and the implication of the man's order, it is but a small leap to classify *Alone* as a non-rape, rape-revenge film.

In *Alone*, therefore, we have an example of a rape-revenge film that centers on psychological violence rather than physical violence. Particularly uncomfortable is how the man pries into Jessica's personal life and then uses it to attack her. When she hides in a small body of water, he invokes her husband's suicide, saying she is to blame, as she must have missed the warning signs. This is a poignant, vile psychological attack intended to prey upon the guilt the man perceives in Jessica. Interestingly, though, Jessica does not fall for this attack, which the man hoped would provoke Jessica into emerging from her hiding spot. Soon thereafter, in fact, she turns the tide on the man by ambushing him in his car and wounding him with his own knife, a symbol of phallic power, which, when turned against him, suggests the man's declining dominance.

Between these knife-based assaults and Jessica's impaling her foot on a small stick, it is clear *Alone* does not forsake all physical violence, even as it emphasizes emotional violence. Of course, we should be careful here to note that many rape-revenge films do show emotional or psychological violence in addition to physical violence. In *I Spit*, Jennifer's assailants read her manuscript aloud to her in mocking voices, thus dismissing her prose and her work in a base personal attack that augments their assault on her physical person. And so, as rape-revenge films often show, rape is sometimes about an attempt to destroy an entire person.

That is, rapists in these films are not always content with physical destruction; they must dominate their victims mentally as well. *Alone*, ergo, is not unique in showing psychological violence, but it is distinct in how it focuses on this violence rather than the physical violence whence we derive rape-revenge's name. Such a focus diminishes, perhaps, the film's evocation of disgust. While viewers may grow uncomfortable when the man torments Jessica with images of her dead husband, said discomfort is still a form of disgust, albeit a less visceral version than that evoked in, say, *I Spit* and *Irréversible*.

Speaking of, professional social worker Hilary Jacobs Hendel observes that disgust arises in an attempt to expel dangerous stimuli.[33] In the case of *Alone*, the viewer's disgust is a longing to move past the emotional torment the man inflicts on Jessica. Disgust, therefore, can still reside in the non-rape, rape-revenge film. Said disgust arises in our other non-rape, rape-revenge films when, for example, Stuntman Mike messily eats nachos (a visual and auditory indicator of how Mike should repulse the audience, how they should be aware his charm is but a mask for his misogyny and murderous intent) in *Death Proof*.

We see it, too, in the attempted rape in *Black Rock* as well as in Jeff's pederasty and willingness to sexualize underage girls in *Hard Candy*. In these two films, disgust toward the antagonists motivates the audience to long for their punishment, which comes from the films' conclusions. And in *Rust Creek* disgust arises when Hollister gropes a visibly and admittedly uncomfortable Sawyer. Thus, disgust lingers in non-rape, rape-revenge films; like a miasma, it clings to rape-revenge, leading us to condemn sexual violence, even when said violence is merely hinted or metaphorical.

Of course, it is unclear to what extent these films convincingly push anti-rape messages. These films can still struggle with the paradox of disgust, albeit a diminished version of it, but their largely indirect approaches to sexual violence can allow audiences to miss the point. That is, these movies often lack an edge. They do not shock or provoke the way *I Spit on Your Grave* does, and as Bressack claims is necessary for such material to work.[34] On this topic, consider how the Marquis de Sade wanted his audiences to react to the sexual and violent imagery in his works.[35]

One can watch *Death Proof* without construing it as a rape-revenge film. And even when non-rape, rape-revenge films are more direct about their generic roots, it is unclear whether they show rape for the horrific act it is. *Hard Candy* is likely one of the more successful on this note, partially because it chooses a pederast and child murderer as its antagonist. Yet, Jeff's crimes are implied, not shown, meaning the film relies on its audience already condemning the sort of crimes Jeff commits. And hiding horror can bring its own issues, as Julian Hanich observes that filmmakers can withhold horror to lure or titillate their audiences.[36] To be clear, I am not accusing any of the directors of the films I

---

[33] Hilary Jacobs Hendel, LCSW, "Disgust: A Natural Emotional Response to Abuse," *Psychology Today*, October 14, 2019, https://www.psychologytoday.com/us/blog/emotion-information/201910/disgust-natural-emotional-response-abuse.

[34] *The Found Footage Phenomenon.*

[35] Cowan. *The Forbidden Body.* 231.

[36] Hanich. *Cinematic Emotion.* 86.

have discussed in this chapter of trying to lure or titillate.[37] Rather, I am pointing out a potential shortfall of this particular approach to telling rape-revenge stories.

Returning to *Hard Candy*, I hope we would all like to think our neighbors condemn these crimes, but, unfortunately, we know some people do not. And, as we will see with *Clarissa*, a person with immoral views about sexual violence is unlikely to find these texts persuasive. On a similar note, we have seen how even non-rape, rape-revenge films offer mixed accountings of female agency. While the non-rape, rape-revenge films suggest fiction can evoke rape-revenge traditions in a large variety of ways and, moreover, can do so without needing to show graphic sexual violence, they have, as my analysis has shown, failed to overwrite the sociocultural value of more traditional (and more visceral) rape-revenge works.

We should further observe how these films' very existence may result, partially, from criticisms of other films for portraying rape at all. As we have seen, the presence of rape on screen is problematic. Projansky, for example, argues that portrayals of rape in popular culture naturalize rape by making it consumable and ubiquitous.[38] In making this assertion, however, Projansky gets the causal chain backward. The ubiquity of rape and sexual violence is responsible for their presence in our fictions.

To observe this fact, one need only look outside fiction at the frequency of sexual assaults and the increasing cultural conversation about them. These issues would exist even if fictions did not put them front and center in their narratives. Furthermore, the depictions of rape in such films as *I Spit* (both 1978 and 2010) are so shocking, so grotesque that they have, I argue, a de-naturalizing effect. That is to say, they defamiliarize the common issue of sexual violence by confronting complacent audiences with the stark, disturbing reality of rape in a way that is difficult for audiences to ignore. And so while the non-rape, rape-revenge narratives offer interesting insights into a variety of issues, we should be careful to note that some of the (possible) rationale for their existence may stem from well-intentioned but misguided beliefs about the ethical pitfalls of depicting rape on screen.

Thus, we have seen how the non-rape, rape-revenge films contain their own shortcomings when we view these movies through the lens of narratological feminist potential. And yet, more explicit rape, hidden through editing and plot, does not necessarily solve this conundrum. To see this, let us (briefly) trace

---

[37] Ibid.
[38] Projanksy 13-14.

rape-revenge's development over time. To that end, I now compare and contrast the original *I Spit* with *Bound to Vengeance*.

As we have seen, since its release, *I Spit* has been the subject of revulsion, even condemnation, holding a mere 40% approval rating on Rotten Tomatoes,[39] a 5.6 rating on IMDB,[40] and a rating of zero from the late, esteemed Roger Ebert. Ebert even said the film was "without a shred of artistic distinction."[41] The question, therefore, becomes why one should consider these films at all. If they are truly "without artistic distinction," then what value do they have?[42]

Well, as I discussed in chapter one, for all *I Spit*'s exploitative tendencies, for all its stark violence, there is a current of social progressivism underlying its portrayal of sexual assault. In fact, the film is pushing a message condemning sexual violence, and it aims to empower its female protagonist. For all its brutality, *I Spit* is a deceptively intelligent film which plays its social message underneath the overt sexuality and deplorable violence which have largely been the focus of discourse on the film.[43]

Fittingly, we notice this message as it plays out across Jennifer's body, namely her clothing (both puns intended). At the beginning of the film, Jennifer wears loose, revealing clothing that emphasizes her free spirit and figure. After the men rape her, she covers herself in dark clothing, which masks her body and, therefore, her personality. And yet, once she embarks on her quest for vengeance, her clothing begins to revert back to its initial state, head-to-toe blackness giving way to shorts and, finally, to a dark green bikini, the revealing nature of which suggests to the audience that Jennifer has regained a sense of herself, that, through revenge, she has recaptured part of her lost identity.[44]

In addition to my close reading of the film, we can also go to the source itself, the film's writer and director, Meir Zarchi. As I discussed in chapter one, Zarchi originally entitled the film *Day of the Woman*, and he has said on record that his inspiration for the movie came from his experience with law enforcement's indifference toward sexual violence.[45] In other words, Zarchi intended to craft

---

[39] "I Spit on Your Grave." Rotten Tomatoes. https://www.rottentomatoes.com/m/i_spit _on_your_grave.

[40] "I Spit on Your Grave (1978)." IMDB. https://www.imdb.com/title/tt0077713/. This score is actually a bit higher than I would have expected.

[41] Roger Ebert, "I Spit on Your Grave," July 16, 1980, https://www.rogerebert.com/ reviews/i-spit-on-your-grave-1980.

[42] Ibid.

[43] Clover 115-116; Creed. *The Monstrous-Feminine*. 128-129; Heller-Nicholas. 2nd edition. 35-36.

[44] Jackula Parts 1-2.

[45] Ibid.

a feminist, anti-rape narrative, one which vindicates its protagonist's quest for revenge and demonizes her rapists.

Of course, the discourse is still split on whether the film actually achieved this goal. Statements lauding the film as a feminist parable meet with eye rolls or even condemnation, much like the film itself. And, while I do not fully agree with these critics, they are on to something. After all, the film is rather harsh in its presentation, depicting sexual violence in vivid detail and, more pressingly, having the protagonist use sexual violence to revenge sexual violence. This last facet, the recursive nature of sexual violence, undermines the film's progressive message. How, after all, can we uphold as a feminist icon a woman who, after being raped, has consensual sexual contact with one of her rapists before killing him? Is Jennifer recapturing her agency by using her sexuality as a weapon, or is she using the only weapon available to her, thereby being forced into becoming the sexual object the men already viewed her as?

Part Two: Partially Showing Rape

And thus, we reach the dilemma at the heart of the rape-revenge sub-genre: the difficulty of at once showing rape for the violent, despicable act it is and avoiding sexualizing its protagonists, not glorifying violence, and finding a way to return agency to its heroines. This is a tricky line to navigate, indeed. If our 1970s rape-revenge films fail on this count, how do our more modern films fare? Here, we reach a film which largely implies rape but is more clearly a rape-revenge film than the other movies I discuss in this chapter: 2015's *Bound to Vengeance*.

In the film, a young woman, Eve (Tina Ivlev), is the captive of an unnamed man. Eve flips the tables on him, beating him with a brick and freeing herself. Upon finding photos of other women in the house where she was held, Eve realizes she is not the man's only captive. So she binds him and forces him to take her to the houses where he is holding the other women, whom she endeavors to free. She has mixed success, as the first two girls end up dead, but she does save several by the film's conclusion. In the end, she drops her captor, whose name we now know is Phil, off at his house, where his wife and daughter find him, badly wounded. Eve walks down the street, a cold look on her face, before returning to Phil's house.

From this summary, we already get *Bound to Vengeance's* first departure from the standard rape-revenge narrative, as *I Spit on Your Grave* typifies it. That is, *Bound to Vengeance* (*Bound*) starts where so many other such films end: with the protagonist taking revenge and escaping her attacker's clutches.[46] Thus,

---

[46] Stidham.

from the beginning, we realize *Bound* is departing from some of rape-revenge's established traditions, setting out on its own path and attacking the question from a new angle.

This new angle is the conspicuous lack of explicit rape scenes. As Daniel Stidham notes, *Bound* skips the rape and goes right to the revenge.[47] The story almost seems to begin in medias res. As a rape-revenge film, *Bound* seems to resemble *Clarissa* more than it resembles *I Spit*. After all, it has no rape scene on-screen. Rather, *Bound* heavily implies rape. When Eve saves Lea, she also kills two men entering the house where Lea was kept bound.

These two men make references to how Phil, Eve's captor, whose van Eve has left outside the house, "likes to take the first ride."[48] Phil insists he never touched Eve[49] but also makes references to getting "top dollar" for her, unlike for other girls. And, when Eve sees the two men, she immediately recognizes one of them, and the audience gets some distorted audio reminiscent of a graphic rape scene between Eve and that man.[50] Eve then shoots the two men to death and rescues Lea, making this her first successful rescue attempt.

So, as we can see, *Bound* is definitely a rape-revenge film, but one that spares us all but hints of the rape and instead goes for the revenge.[51] What occupies the last act of *I Spit* occupies the main narrative of *Bound*. Then again, as Bamford's discussion of *Bonduca* shows in chapter one, the question of rape's placement within the plot is essential for the rape-revenge narrative.

Recall how, because the play begins after the rapes, it only ever shows the women acting violently.[52] Connecting this issue to modern rape-revenge films allows us to understand why directors like Zarchi, who want to push a message against sexual violence, would want to portray that sexual violence. Zarchi wants to show why Jennifer's violent revenge is justified. He wants to show how Jennifer is not the monster; her rapists are. So he has to show the acts motivating her revenge. But, intentionality aside, *I Spit* has long suffered from criticism leveled at its stark portrayal of such disgusting sexual violence. While that portrayal may have had good intentions, its success has been decidedly mixed. Ebert, for instance, notes how the crowd seemed to enjoy the rape

---

[47] Ibid.
[48] *Bound to Vengeance*. Directed by José Manuel Cravioto, performance by Tina Ivlev, IFC Midnight and Scream Factory, 2015.
[49] Of course, Phil is a reprehensible and probably untrustworthy source.
[50] *Bound to Vengeance*.
[51] Stidham.
[52] Bamford 116-117.

scenes, very much the opposite of Zarchi's intended reaction as well as my own actual reaction.[53]

Thus, when *Bound* enters the discourse, it tries a new approach: hinting at the sexual violence and its depravity to establish why its heroine is justified in her actions but downplaying the lurid details and giving critics less to seize upon: less, but surely not nothing. While *Bound* has tried a new approach, attempting to balance the regressive rape apologia of Jacobean drama and the violent, exploitative methods of 1970s-era rape-revenge films, it nevertheless seems to fall short of its presumed mark to liberate the rape-revenge tale from critical and popular scorn, to make it a clear narrative of feminist empowerment. Stidham writes: "Moreover, the name Eve (first woman, mother of all women) clues us in that our heroine is not just a girl but *the* girl, a paragon who must rouse her sisters to fight against the patriarchy."[54] In other words, the intention is evident. But the film does not seem to achieve its apparent goal.

Writing for *Slant*, Ed Gonzalez elaborates on this point: "Think of the film as a grindhouse version of *Unbreakable Kimmy Schmidt*, trivializing victim trauma by treating its main character's best-laid plans as punchline fodder."[55] The film has a bizarre obsession with undercutting itself and its protagonist. Eve fails the save the first two girls, both of whom end up dead. She also gets recaptured at one point, only for Lea to save her.

While the protagonist's struggle is a hallmark of fiction, we understand from the film's beginning that Eve has struggled. Not only do we see her as a captive, but we also realize she is dealing with heavy emotional baggage. Throughout the film, we get cuts to a home video of Eve and another young woman. The two appear close, laughing and hugging one another. Toward the end of the film, we learn this other woman was Eve's younger sister, Dylan, who was also kidnapped and held captive with Eve, and who died when she refused to let Eve share food with her. Eve blames herself for her sister's death, and the film hints she feels compelled to save the other girls because of that guilt.

Thus, when I see Eve continuously fail, I get the sense the film is hardly empowering her. Eve can say badass lines like "Then I kill them" all she wants, but when she appears largely incapable of delivering on that bravado, she ends up falling short of the feminist ideal she ostensibly embodies. Stidham compares her to a new form of final girl in recent horror films, the hyper-competent variety, perhaps the best exemplar of whom is Erin from *You're*

---

[53] Ebert 1980.

[54] Stidham.

[55] Ed Gonzalez, "Review: Bound to Vengeance," *Slant Magazine*, June 20, 2015, https://www.slantmagazine.com/film/bound-to-vengeance/.

Next.[56] But not only does Eve fail to compare to female protagonists from other modern horror films, she even appears less confident than Jennifer from *I Spit*, who lures her victims into ambushes and forces them to play by her rules.

Conversely, as Stidham notes, Eve plays by Phil's rules.[57] Thus, even when badly wounded, Phil holds power over Eve, constantly taunting her by dangling hints about her boyfriend Ronnie's involvement in her kidnapping, and making references to her sister, blaming Dylan's death on Eve. Even when she beats Phil, binds him, strangles him, and shoots him, he can still sink his teeth into her psyche. Conversely, *I Spit* does not drag Jennifer's post-assault torment out. Whereas Phil psychologically torments Eve, Jennifer psychologically torments her assailants. Matthew, for example, is clearly afraid of her.

All of this is to say that, even when seemingly pushing rape-revenge forward in some respects, leaving behind the controversial depictions of sexual violence, *Bound* still struggles with controversy and with delivering what appears to be its intended message. It currently sits at a mere 37% on Rotten Tomatoes,[58] and, as we have seen, its critical reception contains views that it does not wholly achieve its goal of empowering its protagonist. This alone does not mean, however, that *Bound* does not manage to achieve anything within the rape-revenge sub-genre of horror and thriller films.

Writing about the problem of graphic violence in films, John Bailey describes how he tried in one of his own films "to deglamorize violence and to focus on its human consequences."[59] And, to some degree, *Bound* does achieve this, showing violence as horrific rather than glamorized or fun. Nevertheless, it is also still clear that *Bound* has its own array of issues which hold it back from delivering an unadulterated feminist message. Not only does the film's narrative undermine Eve and often make her appear incompetent, but the audio of Eve's rape does not achieve a lot. The clip is brief, an interlude into a more pressing scene, and too distorted for the audience to discern much.

Today, nine years beyond *Bound to Vengeance* and over 40 years beyond *I Spit on Your Grave*, we continue to struggle with the issue of sexual violence. After the #MeToo era, tales of female empowerment have a clear place in the cultural zeitgeist. And yet, the rape-revenge film's place is still controversial and still

---

[56] Stidham; See, also: *You're Next*. Directed by Adam Wingard, performance by Sharni Vinson, Lionsgate, 2011. *You're Next* is a 2011 horror film directed by Adam Wingard and starring Sharni Vinson.

[57] Ibid.

[58] "Bound to Vengeance." Rotten Tomatoes. https://www.rottentomatoes.com/m/bound_to_vengeance.

[59] John Bailey, "Bang Bang Bang Bang, Ad Naseum [sic]." In *Screening Violence*, edited by Stephen Prince. (Rutgers University Press, 2000), 84.

unclear. As rape-revenge moves forward, it must find a way to reconcile its paradoxical need to show violence with the need to simultaneously avoid glorifying or exploiting said violence. As with the issue it addresses, rape-revenge remains difficult. Easy answers or solutions remain elusive. Like Jennifer and Eve, we seem to be moving forward, eyes looking in the distance but unsure of where we are going.

Chapter 3

The Aesthetic of Disgust: Rape-Revenge Fiction's Moral Shortcomings

To now, we have examined how films that explicitly show rape, films which imply rape, and films which briefly show rape all seem to encounter their own issues with portraying this sensitive subject matter. In this chapter, I articulate what I see as the major problem hounding this type of analysis of rape-revenge. The paradox of disgust, I argue, makes creating a compelling anti-rape, rape-revenge narrative a remarkably challenging endeavor rife with ambivalence and the potential for misinterpretation.

Introduction

A young, ambitious writer, horrified after some experience, writes a tome aimed at social change.[1] This writer is certain their words will change the world. When the reviews come back, however, the author finds, to their horror, that the audience has missed their point.

This story should seem familiar. Many an idealistic or socially-minded writer has been its protagonist at some point. Indeed, the frequency with which people fail to communicate their meaning is so great that "*mis*communication is, in fact, an inevitable consequence and, arguably, an essential component of the richness and complexity of human interaction."[2] When this miscommunication occurs in a work of fiction, the audience may misconstrue or overlook the writer's moralistic message, causing the fictional work to fail in its goal.

And such miscommunication is particularly rife in our key sub-genre: rape-revenge. In this chapter, I will explore rape-revenge in fiction by contrasting

---

[1] I am not claiming all authors and directors of rape-revenge works are well-intentioned. While I have established how some are or at least appear to be, I raise the morally conscious writer here as an example of one of the issues these sorts of works can encounter. Morally bankrupts creators would be a separate problem.

[2] Maria Stubbe, *"Was that my misunderstanding?" Managing miscommunication and problematic talk at work.* (Victoria University of Wellington, PhD thesis, 2010), 205. https://core.ac.uk/download/pdf/41336781.pdf.

three works: *I Spit on Your Grave* (2010), *I Spit on Your Grave III: Vengeance is Mine* (2015), and *Clarissa, or the History of a Young Lady* (1748). In this analysis, I will treat the two films as a single work, telling one cohesive story.[3] The nearly three centuries separating my texts will allow me to examine the issue of rape-revenge across much of rape-revenge's history. I have cast a wide net precisely to analyze the largest portion of the narrative that my space will allow, and I am going to discuss how the texts approach the matters of rape, revenge, and agency.

To do so, I will relate each of the three works to the aesthetic of disgust, whence comes their anti-rape messages.[4] My first step will be to refine my theoretical framework of the aesthetic of disgust and the motivation for revenge in fiction, whereby I draw on the works of Margrethe Bruun Vaage and Ellen Spolsky. My second step will build off Bruun Vaage's work and show how the films derive their power from the aesthetic of disgust. Then, I will challenge Bruun Vaage's theory by showing how disgust can become self-defeating and can, in fact, undermine a work's message. Step three will further complicate matters, as I will show how *Clarissa* avoids disgust's self-defeating aspect only to fail precisely because it is not sufficiently disgusting. And thus, we will arrive at step four, wherein I will argue that the aesthetic of disgust is largely responsible for rape-revenge's failure to fully communicate anti-rape messages because the aesthetic is, itself, a paradox.[5]

---

[3] *I Spit on Your Grave II* follows a formula similar to the first film, but its story and characters are otherwise unrelated to those of the other films in this series. As such, I will limit my discussion to the first and third films, which both follow main protagonist Jennifer Hills. In this chapter, I will also focus on the 2010 version of *I Spit* rather than on the 1977 original because the remake is more recent and tells a longer story when put in conversation with its sequel. The new films give us a glimpse into Jennifer's life after her initial revenge against her rapists and, therefore, more material to cover. There has also been a follow-up to the original *I Spit on Your Grave, I Spit on Your Grave: Déjà vu* (2019), though I am not discussing that film in this book.

[4] The phrase "the aesthetic of disgust" is not my invention. Michelle Meagher uses a similar phrase in her essay "Jenny Saville and a Feminist Aesthetics of Disgust."

[5] Again, this is not to presuppose that all rape-revenge texts are supposed to communicate such a message. While I have shown that at least some of these texts do have this authorial intention, I am more concerned with looking at rape-revenge texts and seeing whether they communicate such messages since these messages are socially important.

Disgust and Audience Reactions to Fiction

While the exact number remains contentious, current psychological theory holds there are a few "basic emotions" that are truly innate in humans.[6] Most important among these for our purposes is disgust, that emotion we experience when we, for example, step into poop or see an animal dead in the middle of the road.[7] That disgust is apparently foundational to human psychology enhances Bruun Vaage's take on the role of disgust in rape-revenge narratives.

She argues in "On the Repulsive Rapist and the Difference between Morality in Fiction and Real Life" that people adopt different moral outlooks when viewing fictional events than they do when viewing real-life events.[8] Specifically, she says, people tend to leave their rational selves at the door when engaging with fiction, meaning they rely on emotion to make moral judgments of actions in fictional works.[9] Thus, according to Bruun Vaage, audiences make quick, emotionally driven moral judgments of fictional actions that differ from their judgments of the same actions when they occur in real life.[10] The latter decisions are more apt to be rational and slower.[11]

If our reaction to fiction is emotionally driven, as Bruun Vaage argues, our reaction to fictional depictions of rape is most often disgust.[12] As a carnal act, rape is uniquely suited to eliciting this response from an audience, and, therefore, in fiction, rape becomes particularly potent, particularly immoral. Unlike murder, which Bruun Vaage notes a character can still commit while remaining an anti-hero, rape is unforgivable, the mark of a villain. And our response to fictional rape hereby exceeds our response to rape in real life, where it remains underreported and under-prosecuted.[13] Into this void of judicial failings comes the rape-revenge narrative, often bearing with it a message of social change and justice.[14] With its potent evocation of disgust, one would

---

[6] Alessia Celeghin, et al., "Basic Emotions in Human Neuroscience: Neuroimaging and Beyond." *Frontiers in Psychology*, (August 24, 2017), doi: 10.3389/fpsyg.2017.01432. https://www.ncbi.nlm.nih.gov/pmc/articles/PMC5573709/.

[7] Ibid.

[8] Margrethe Bruun Vaage, "On the Repulsive Rapist and the Difference Between Morality in Fiction and Real Life." In *The Oxford Handbook of Cognitive Literary Studies* 1st edition, edited by Lisa Zunshine. (Oxford University Press, 2015), 421; See also: Spolsky 179.

[9] Bruun Vaage 433.

[10] Ibid. 421.

[11] Ibid. 433.

[12] Ibid. 421.

[13] National Research Council. *Estimating the Incidence of Rape and Sexual Assault.* (Washington, DC: The National Academies Press, 2013); "Criminal Justice System Statistics." RAINN. https://www.rainn.org/statistics/criminal-justice-system

[14] Spolsky notes that revengers seek revenge when the justice system fails them (178-180).

hope the rape-revenge story could alter audience perceptions of this crucial social issue. After all, research shows disgust operates as a call to action, compelling one to cast off the offending stimulus.[15] But, as we shall see, this story type's record is decidedly mixed.

Violence and Disgust

To begin our discussion of the texts properly, let us start with our two films, which take a blunt, visceral approach to the issues of rape and its associated revenge. Both films follow a young woman named Jennifer Hills, who experiences brutal sexual assaults in the first film (*I Spit* 2010). That film then sees her exact equally brutal vengeance on her rapists, leaving multiple bodies in her wake. The third film picks up this story thread and finds Jennifer living under an assumed name and attending a support group for survivors of sexual assault. This Jennifer, however, has notably changed and lacks the former Jennifer's vivacity and passion, both of which she starts to recapture when she begins hunting down men who have assaulted other women. Jennifer's quest for vengeance, so pivotal it is in the film's title, branches out from the men who assaulted her, to the men who assault other women, to practically any man unlucky enough to cross her path, as she transforms from writer to psychopath, completing a descent into violence and all-consuming rage.[16]

These films are, in a word, graphic. Even I, a career horror fan, find them uncomfortable and difficult to watch, as I should.[17] The first film subjects us to multiple explicit rape scenes, in which several men brutalize Jennifer. Then we get scenes in which Jennifer violently murders her assailants, using such techniques as castration via garden shears and anal rape via shotgun.[18] And while the third film largely forgoes the explicit portrayal of rape, it does not hold back on the violent revenge, as we see Jennifer rip a man's penis in half and kill another man via sodomization.[19]

---

[15] Andrea C. Morales, et al., "How Disgust Enhances the Effectiveness of Fear Appeals," *Journal of Marketing Research* 49, No. 3 (June 2012): 389. https://www.jstor.org/stable/41714433.

[16] Dyer observes that one moves toward serial killing once one begins targeting a group instead of individuals (*Lethal Repetition* 28). As such, in *I Spit III*, Jennifer arguably transitions into being a serial killer.

[17] Charles Derry argues that violence should revolt (16).

[18] *I Spit on Your Grave.* Directed by Stephen R. Monroe, performance by Sarah Butler, Anchor Bay Entertainment, 2010.

[19] *I Spit on Your Grave III: Vengeance is Mine.* Directed by R.D. Braunstein, performance by Sarah Butler, Anchor Bay Films, 2015.

It is easy to see where the aesthetic of disgust comes into play. Even writing these sentences has made me lose my appetite. And so, I apologize to the reader. But we should be careful to note that our disgust arises not only from the rapes but also from the revenge. On the first point, Bruun Vaage writes, "We find the rapist disgusting because he seems to enjoy, and perhaps also be sexually aroused by, the victim's pain and humiliation. To the observer, there is something fundamentally sick and suspect about this."[20] She further states, "What about murder then?" before giving the answer:

> I propose that the degree of moral disgust is determined by the degree of pleasure the perpetrator finds in tormenting his victim. We find it disgusting to take pleasure in evicting horror and pain. This could perhaps explain why even antiheroes do not rape, and why rape is used to clearly mark some characters as unsympathetic. When Tony Soprano kills a competing mobster, or an unruly subordinate, we do not find these acts as morally disgusting (unnatural, perverse, and sick) as we would if he had tracked innocent people down in order to enjoy slowly tormenting them. With some narrative stage setting, these murders can appear as legitimate, and they do not seem to trigger moral disgust to the same degree as rape does.[21]

In other words, Bruun Vaage does not rule out the possibility that murder, like rape, might be morally disgusting, but she does observe that rape tends to be particularly morally disgusting in its sadism. Here, we happen on a common equation for rape-revenge fiction.

We have established that our two films are very violent. Jennifer's revenge is difficult to watch precisely because of how violent and visceral it is. The films, therefore, need to justify the inclusion of this violence if they are to avoid alienating their audience, and, hence, we reach the formula: for the films to warrant their over-the-top revenge sequences, they need counterbalancing rape sequences to motivate the revenge.[22]

The need for such a balance is well-established in the critical discourse around rape-revenge texts. Heller-Nicholas quotes Linda Ruth Williams as saying, "The less seen of Jennifer's rape, the better, one might think; but this may have the curious effect of making the revenge less defensible, since less of the rape is evident."[23] Similarly, Heller-Nicholas herself writes, "spectator

---

[20] Bruun Vaage 429.
[21] Bruun Vaage 430.
[22] Ellen Spolsky, *The Contracts of Fiction: Cognition, Culture, Community.* (2015), 178-179.
[23] Heller-Nicholas. *Rape-Revenge Films.* 36.

engagement with the ensuing revenge is a direct result of our emotional investment in [the rape]."[24] And Clover makes a similar claim: "...the force of the experience, in horror, comes from 'knowing' both sides of the story."[25] Finally, Spolsky argues that the audience's resistance to revenge and its consequent violence erodes when the audience shares the shock and pain of the event motivating said revenge: "...the power of the visual in the revenge plays carry us from a lawful world to sympathy with an outlaw."[26] Our critics are clear, then: for the films to show the revenge in all its brutality, they must likewise show the rape in all its brutality. Only by doing this can they properly motivate the audience to cheer on the revenge and applaud vigilante violence.[27] Of course, we have already encountered a major problem with this conception. As we saw in chapter one, explicit portrayals of rape make the original *I Spit on Your Grave* potentially problematic.

That these films can have a vested interest in showing the rapes is therefore clear, but we must also note how this interest connects to the films' message. The original *I Spit* was supposed to be an anti-rape narrative.[28] Its director and writer, Meir Zarchi, wrote the film as a response to law enforcement's indifference to sexual assault victims.[29] Originally entitling his film *Day of the Woman*, he clearly intended for it to return agency to its heroine.[30] While our focus here is not on the original film, knowing the series' origins is useful for elucidating its intended message against sexual violence.

That this message carries over into the new films, at least as an intention, is clear from Steven R. Monroe's statements about the 2010 remake he directed. Monroe has said that part of his motivation in making the film was in fictionally acting out his own desire to kill the man who raped his, Monroe's, ex-girlfriend.[31] Monroe's film also takes additional steps above the original to justify its heroine's revenge. Why, we might ask, did Jennifer not go to the police in the original film?[32] Well, the remake directly addresses this issue by having the local sheriff be one of Jennifer's assailants.

---

[24] Ibid. 3-4.

[25] Clover 12.

[26] Spolsky 178-179.

[27] Bruun Vaage 434.

[28] See Jackula Parts 1 and 2.

[29] Jackula Parts 1 and 2. Heller-Nicholas. *Rape-Revenge Films*. 36.

[30] Ibid. I repeat this point from chapter one because it is important for my examination and because I think the reader should bear it in mind here.

[31] Heller-Nicholas. *Rape-Revenge Films*. 176.

[32] In truth, her choice to not go to the police is a direct, fictionalized response to Zarchi's experience with law enforcement's callous indifference toward sexual assault. And it

Moreover, he assaults her when she goes to him for help, after her initial assault. Similarly, while the third film does not portray law enforcement as malicious and officers as rapists, it still gives us a legal system that repeatedly fails victims of sexual assault. Notably, the local detectives fail to prosecute Marla's ex-boyfriend for her rape and murder, fail to prosecute the step-father sexually abusing a member of Jennifer's support group, and appear to devote far more resources to pursuing Jennifer and other murderers than it does to finding and punishing rapists. In fact, throughout the film, the police only punish murderers and not rapists. Even when they shoot a man who is attempting to rape Jennifer, they do so because he is poised to attack them, not because he is a sexual assailant.

Thus, these films have spent considerable time and energy trying to get us to align ourselves with the heroine enacting violent revenge for the sexual violence her assailants inflicted upon her. For this alignment to work, for the audience to have the intended reaction of cheering the violence on, this same audience must also feel the repulsion of disgust at the scenes of sexual violence.[33] This disgust becomes our motivation to see the revenge enacted; it primes us to condone, even celebrate, the graphic scenes of revenge.

But, as we noted earlier, these same scenes of revenge are also disgusting. Indeed, the films play them for disgust. Whereas glamorized depictions of violence may eschew on-screen portrayals of pain,[34] rape-revenge films do no such thing, showing instead brutal, painful violence. On this topic, Stephen Prince argues that, when it is aesthetically lacking, on-screen violence can be disgusting or alienating,[35] which the violence in these films certainly is. Here, the films' relatively cheap production values enhance their messaging.

And yet, we can also look at how Jennifer sexualizes her murders, not once, but twice in the course of the two films, killing a man via sodomy. And here, the aesthetic of disgust upon which the films rely becomes self-defeating. As I stated earlier, for the films to work, we have to cheer the violence on. But

---

reflects the real life worries of many sexual assault victims; Doolittle observes how law enforcement does not always investigate rape cases (xii).

[33] Heller-Nicholas. *Rape-Revenge Films*. 3-4. Heller-Nicholas asserts here that our support for revenge is predicated on our emotional reaction to the rape. As we have seen, the emotional reaction we have to rape is disgust (Bruun Vaage 421). Thus, our emotional investment comes in the form of our disgust at the rape, the disgust pushing us to want to see the heroine's revenge.

[34] Stephen Prince observes that films are more likely to lead their audience members to violence if they, the films, do not show characters experiencing pain from the on-screen violence (21).

[35] Prince 29.

disgust, the same disgust we experience not just from the rapes but also from the hyper-visceral revenge, is a repulsing agent.[36]

It makes us recoil from the material at the precise moment when the films want us most invested, and this means the films risk alienating the audiences they seek to capture. And that the films do alienate audiences is easy to document. Roger Ebert gave both the original *I Spit* and the 2010 remake zero stars.[37] In his review of the latter, he writes: "First, let's dispatch with the fiction that the film is about 'getting even.' If I rape you, I have committed a crime. If you kill me, you have committed another one. The ideal outcome would be two people unharmed in the first place."[38] So Ebert rejects the lex talionis upon which the films rely.[39]

This is the wrinkle I wish to add to Bruun Vaage's conception of the aesthetic of disgust. While Bruun Vaage argues, as I have, that fictional portrayals of rape elicit disgust, she does not consider how this disgust can undermine the rape-revenge narrative's message. When the *I Spit*s are receiving zero stars from America's most famous film critic, when they are banned in the UK,[40] and when they get widespread condemnation from mainstream audiences and critics,[41] their message has clearly fallen on mostly deaf ears. In fact, Bruun Vaage's argument that we engage with fictional morality on an emotional rather than a rational basis further weakens the rape-revenge narrative's efficacy.

On the emotional level, the *I Spit* films alienate many potential viewers. And the reader may observe that I and the other critics who have come to the films' defense have done so not via emotion but via rationality, breaking down the

---

[36] Meagher writes, "disgust is an attempt to render oneself distant from that which disgusts" (11).

[37] Ebert 1980; Roger Ebert, "I Spit on Your Grave." October 6, 2010, https://www.rogerebert.com/reviews/i-spit-on-your-grave-2010.

[38] Ebert 2010. Conspicuously absent from Ebert's review, however, is acknowledgment of how idealistic his statement is. While, yes, ideally we would (I hope) want no one harmed rather than 2 people harmed, the fact is that we live in a world where people frequently become harmed. Ebert's idealism elides this stark reality, one which the *I Spit* films tackle head on. And because people do get harmed, we and the *I Spit* films must reckon with that reality and decide what we are to do about it, both in real-life and in fiction.

[39] Clover 115-116; Young 46.

[40] Laurence Phelan, "Film Censorship: How moral panic led to a mass ban of 'video nasties,'" *The Independent,* July 13, 2014, https://www.independent.co.uk/arts-entertainment/films/features/film-censorship-how-moral-panic-led-to-a-mass-ban-of-video-nasties-9600998.html.

[41] See the films' scores on Rotten Tomatoes, which show how most viewers do not approve of these movies. Yes, these movies do have an audience, but that audience is demonstrably more niche than that of many other types of texts.

films' logic, narratives, and intentionality to make arguments about their messages and merits. That we have to do so, that we have to undertake this rigorous study to merely mount a defense of the films, shows they have taken the aesthetic of disgust too far. The films do their job too well; they are too disgusting, so disgusting (virtually) no one wants to look at them. Rather than focusing their disgust on the rapes, viewers double back on their disgust and direct it at the filmmakers, the people who created these films and subjected the audience to them. The viewers point fingers, make moral accusations, and say these films never should have been made. For all their strengths, as anti-rape narratives, the *I Spit*s fall short.

They also fail to return full agency to Jennifer. The third film is the story of Jennifer's trauma consuming her. She suffers from intrusive thoughts of her rape, is hostile toward those around her, and is no longer the same Jennifer we see at the beginning of the series. Professional therapist Ghislaine Boulanger notes that trauma often leads to a loss of one's sense of self as well as a lost sense of reality whereby the external world and the inner world of nightmares (in which the trauma victim—Jennifer—experiences flashbacks to their trauma) blur together until the victim cannot distinguish them.[42] This is what happens to Jennifer. Her trauma is so horrific she loses herself. The violent, sadistic Jennifer we see at the end of the third film is a far cry from the sociable writer we meet at the beginning of the first. Jennifer fantasizes about violence and sees threats wherever she looks. In some ways, the end of the third film seems to caution us against the pursuit of revenge by showing us how revenge destroys the revenger, a message, we may observe, antithetical to an anti-rape intention.

Clarissa's Agency: Peaceful Resistance and the Moral High Ground

Let us now turn to this chapter's final primary text, Samuel Richardson's *Clarissa*.[43] Some may object to my inclusion of the novel in this chapter and argue it is not a rape-revenge narrative. While the novel does not center on the rape and revenge as the *I Spit* films do, *Clarissa*'s inclusion of both a rape and a revenge are sufficient grounds to make it relevant to our discussion. Moreover,

---

[42] Ghislaine Boulanger, *Wounded by Reality: Understanding and Treating Adult Onset Trauma*. (Mahwah, NJ: Analytic, 2007), 62 & 114-115.

[43] Summarizing *Clarissa* can be a daunting task, owing to its prodigious length (well over 1,000 pages). As such, this will be a very succinct summary that purposefully omits many details from the text. *Clarissa* is a successful and famous epistolary novel depicting the trials and tribulations of the virtuous Clarissa, who finds herself in the crosshairs of the lascivious and unscrupulous Lovelace. Lovelace eventually rapes Clarissa but finds himself unhappy in the aftermath as, rather than possessing Clarissa, he finds her slipping through his grasp as she allows herself to wither away and die.

its treatment of agency and disgust as relating to these two issues makes it a fruitful point of comparison between the two films: *Clarissa* succeeds in places where the films fail. *Clarissa* is also a useful counterpoint to the more modern *I Spit* films as it illustrates how societal attitudes toward rape and rape-revenge have changed in the intervening centuries.

The first of the places where *Clarissa* succeeds is the issue of returning agency to its protagonist.[44] Throughout the novel, Clarissa has little, if any, control over her circumstances. Surrounded by hostile forces and deceivers, she is like a rat in a maze of Lovelace's construction. While she experiences her choices as if they are her own, Lovelace manipulates the circumstances to steer her decisions, rendering her life deterministic. This is how he tricks her into Sinclair's house: she believes she is choosing the place to reside for herself, but, in reality, Lovelace has arranged matters so as to push her to make that particular choice. And Sinclair's house is nothing like Clarissa expects. At every turn, Clarissa has, at best, an illusion of agency. Her situation is precarious, to put it lightly.

Lois A. Chaber goes even further, arguing Clarissa gets reduced "from an autonomous agent to a passive patient."[45] Chaber connects this loss of agency to Richardson's desire to put "a considerable vein of Christian patriarchal authoritarianism" into the novel.[46] Chaber is not the only scholar to highlight the central role Christian theology plays in the text, as Tom Keymer construes Clarissa's departure from her father's house as analogous to the biblical Fall, where her father's house stands in for Eden and Lovelace for the serpent.[47]

On both accounts, we see there is a strain of scholarship arguing against my point about Clarissa regaining her agency. And I will concede that Clarissa's agency at the end of the novel still seems wanting. Indeed, Chaber observes how the novel's ending has not aged well.[48] These strong Christian overtones,

---

[44] This area is, perhaps, one strength novels have over films. A novel, especially one as long as *Clarissa*, has more space to develop its characters and explore each stage of its narrative than a film typically does. Commercial pressures push modern films to remain largely within a standard run-time that allows audiences to view the films' narratives entirely within a single sitting. By contrast, the same pressure does not apply to novels, which audiences do not expect to finish in a single sitting.

[45] Lois A. Chaber, "Christian Form and Anti-Feminism in Clarissa," *Eighteenth-Century Fiction*, 15, no. 3-4 (2003): 508.

[46] Ibid.

[47] Tom Keymer, *Richardson's Clarissa and the Eighteenth-Century Reader*. (Cambridge University Press, 2009), 111-114.

[48] Chaber 537.

moreover, carry with them the sexist implications of the Fall narrative.[49] As such, our shifting cultural mores leave me and modern critics unsatisfied with Clarissa's "revenge." Nevertheless, I do think there is an aspect of Clarissa's agency we must consider before concluding Clarissa does not regain agency.

This is key: Clarissa never loses herself. At the beginning of the novel, Clarissa is a young woman of virtue who impresses those who meet her with her purity.[50] At the end of the novel, Clarissa is a young woman of virtue who impresses those who meet her with her purity.[51] Unlike Jennifer, who transitions from a lively and sociable writer to a violent, paranoid psychopath,[52] Clarissa never ceases to be a virtuous, too-good-for-this-world type. At the end of the novel, while she has lost her family, her virginity, and her life, she has not lost herself, which, recall, is a frequent component of trauma.[53]

Unlike with *I Spit on Your Grave*, where I took issue with how the story was ambivalent on feminist issues, with *Clarissa*, the problem is not so much the story but instead the author. Because Richardson treats passivity as the ideal form of femininity, he forecloses much of his text's feminist potential. Yes, Clarissa stays true to herself, meaning she regains agency in-universe, but that self is a patriarchal archetype of Richardson's theological imagination, not a realistic person. And because Clarissa operates as an ideal instead of a person, Richardson hamstrings his own narrative's potential from the beginning.

That Clarissa does, however, remain true to herself is also clear from her "revenge." Throughout the novel, we never see Clarissa be vindictive. She wants to see the best in others, and she never loses the desire to see Lovelace reform. Clarissa is a Christian of the "turn the other cheek" variety as opposed to

---

[49] Mary McClintock Fulkerson, "Sexism as Original Sin: Developing a Theacentric Discourse," *Journal of the American Academy of Religion* 59, no. 4 (1991): 662, http://www.jstor.org/stable/1465528.

[50] Lovelace writes the following to Belford about his meeting Clarissa: "That am I not now; nor have I been from the moment I beheld this angel of a woman. Prepared indeed as I was by her character, before I saw her: for what a mind must that be, which thought not virtuous itself admires not virtue in another?" (Richardson 143).

[51] Belford writes to Clarissa, "The happiness of approaching you, which this trust, as I presume, will give me frequent opportunities of doing, must necessarily promote the desirable end; since it will be impossible to be a witness of your piety, equanimity, and other virtues, and not aspire to emulate you" (Richardson 1177).

[52] One of this volume's anonymous peer reviewers made the insightful comment that Jennifer in 2010's *I Spit* finds her person destroyed. Indeed, I would add, Jennifer's use of a pseudonym in *I Spit III* metaphorically represents this destruction of Jennifer's fundamental self.

[53] Boulanger 62 & 114-115.

Jennifer's affinity for "an eye for an eye." In fact, it is because of this distinction that I have felt the need to justify my calling *Clarissa* a revenge narrative at all.

Clarissa does not appear to treat her revenge as such. Staying true to her virtuous self, she maintains the moral high ground throughout the novel's end, living as an ascetic, wishing that Lovelace will reform, and preparing herself for death. In doing so, she also not so coincidentally aligns herself with the ideal of true womanhood as passive.[54] Indeed, Clarissa is by far the most passive protagonist I discuss in this book, making her an invaluable point of comparison. Her passivity reveals the stark differences in how storytellers approach the dual issues of rape and revenge now versus in the 18th century. Endemic to *Clarissa* is an (I hope) antiquated notion of proper femininity as inert. In contrast to this problematic depiction, the modern rape-revenge narratives in this chapter take a very different approach by making their female protagonists stunningly, even grotesquely, active.

That she never damns Lovelace and certainly never, say, sodomizes and kills him, means Clarissa, unlike Jennifer, never succumbs to a base desire for vengeance. And because she does not succumb, the novel's characters treat her death as an ascension. Lovelace, for example, dreams of angles lifting Clarissa into the clouds: "...the most angelic form I had ever beheld, vested all in transparent white, descended from a ceiling...and, encircling my charmer, ascended with her to the region of seraphims..."[55] By contrast, Jennifer descends into rage and paranoia. Thus, the two protagonists move in opposite directions. Whereas Clarissa ascends the symbolic height of her moral superiority to her rapist Lovelace, Jennifer descends and, if we take Ebert's view, becomes morally compromised.

I call Clarissa's revenge a revenge because it torments her rapist and punishes him for his actions. As with Jennifer and Clarissa, Lovelace and Clarissa move in opposite directions, the former descending and the latter ascending. Lovelace transitions from a confident, manipulative rake to a pathetic and desperate man who feels his schemes and victim slipping away from him; he is losing his control and, by the end of the novel, loses it completely, his machinations backfiring and leaving him and Clarissa dead in true tragic form.

Moreover, these deaths do not begin to approach the violence of deaths in the *I Spit* films. Lovelace dies in a duel, which, owing to the novel's epistolary form, occurs off-screen, so to speak. Clarissa wastes away and dies peacefully. Her

---

[54] T. Walter Herbert, *Sexual Violence and American Manhood*. (Harvard University Press, 2002), 113.

[55] Samuel Richardson, *Clarissa, or, The History of a Young Lady*. (St. Ives, United Kingdom, Penguin Group, 1985), 1218.

death, we should note, further reinforces her ability to recapture her agency. Boulanger writes that the self is necessarily embodied, meaning control over one's body is central to forming the experiential self.[56] And Clarissa, a woman who, in being raped, had control of her body wrenched from her, regains this control by discipling her body into a willing death, an act that would require immense self-control and, we should note, that resembles the anorectic's actions.[57]

And so we can see that *Clarissa* succeeds as a rape-revenge narrative on two counts, as it returns (some) agency to its protagonist and avoids alienating its audience through grotesque portrayals of violence. And yet, here we also see where *Clarissa* falls short as a rape-revenge narrative. Where is the anti-rape message? We might argue that perhaps Richardson did not intend for *Clarissa* to be an anti-rape narrative, but we know that he did intend it to be an anti-rake narrative.[58] And on this count, it failed. Contemporary audiences remained enamored of Lovelace and, even after the rape, wanted Clarissa to marry him.[59] It is still clear, then, that *Clarissa* was not fully successful at the time of its release. Today, our cultural sensibilities have changed, and we do not wish for such a terrible union. So today, *Clarissa* remains only partially successful.

Feminist theory is helpful for understanding why *Clarissa* falls short on this topic. Namely, while Clarissa certainly comports with an extreme pacifist Christian ideal, many audiences are liable to find identifying with her difficult. Now, to be sure, those who followed the passivity ideal back when *Clarissa was* released might have identified with Clarissa's passive strength. It is, however, harder to see how female readers frustrated with societal sexism would have identified with Clarissa's "revenge." It is likewise difficult to see how male readers, conditioned to be more prone to exercising an active form of strength, would identify with her.

Considering female readers who might find Clarissa difficult to identify with, we can look to Creed's observation of how female spectators enjoy seeing

---

[56] Boulanger 85.

[57] "Self-Control and its Connection to Disordered Eating," *Eating Disorders Review* 27, no. 5 (2016), https://eatingdisordersreview.com/self-control-and-its-connection-to-disord ered-eating/. This is not to say that anorectics seek death. Rather, a desire for self-control is central to anorexia, and Clarissa's immense self-control over her body resembles the actions of an anorectic.

[58] Shirley Van Marter describes how Richardson, unhappy with audience affection for Lovelace, revised *Clarissa* to make the character less likeable (Van Marter 120).

[59] Shirley Van Marter, "Richardson's Revisions of 'Clarissa' in the Third and Fourth Editions," *Studies in Bibliography* 28 (1975): 122, www.jstor.org/stable/40371613.

powerful female characters.[60] Clarissa's form of power would not allow for the cathartic release of violent retribution in fiction, nor would it allow for the chance to break out of societal misogyny (even if briefly via fiction). Compounding the issue, Doane argues that fiction's pleasures revolve around its ability to corroborate the audience's identities.[61] Clarissa's lack of action, then, her Christian patience, stakes a rather rigid stance on this issue, foregoing resonating with those readers who would prefer action, even if only in the realm of fictional escapism.

On this topic of identification, Greven argues action heroines compensate "for the male spectator's fear of loss of phallic mastery."[62] Clarissa does not do this. And while Greven's argument focuses on film, it applies to literature as well. Whereas Jennifer and even Evadne return power to the audience members who identify with them by picking up weapons and exacting violent retribution, Clarissa forecloses this possibility. Audience members who identify with Clarissa are, therefore, left to imagine her wasting away.

The rape is a turning point in *Clarissa*, but it occupies only a small portion of the narrative, buried amid literally hundreds of letters and countless details and plot events. In a work of such considerable length, the rape loses some of its prominence and, consequently, power.[63] And when it does occur, it is anticlimactic. Lovelace, for instance, is unsatisfied with it.[64] For all their stark brutality, one could never accuse the rapes in *I Spit* of being glossed over and unimportant. For better or worse, they fundamentally shape and define the narrative. They occur right in front of us in all their unrelenting brutality. Conversely, in *Clarissa*, the rape is not central and not seen.

And because the rape occurs off-screen, so to speak, where is the disgust in *Clarissa*? This is essential: *Clarissa* falls short of an anti-rape narrative because

---

[60] Barbara Creed, *Return of the Monstrous-Feminine: Feminist New Wave Cinema.* (Routledge, 2022), 1.

[61] Mary Ann Doane, "Woman's Stake: Filming the Female Body." In *Feminism and Film*, edited by E. Ann Kaplan. (Oxford University Press, 2000), 86. Doane is concerned, specifically, about the identities of film viewers, but we can apply her argument to bring up an interesting point about the identity negotiation of *Clarissa*'s readers as well.

[62] David Greven, *Representations of Femininity in American Genre Cinema: The Woman's Film, Film Noir, and Modern Horror.* (Palgrave Macmillan, 2011), 158.

[63] Damrongpiwat argues that Clarissa's letters after the rape reveal her trauma, that her writing operates almost as an agent in its own right (43). Nonetheless, that we have to read Damrongpiwat's (very astute) article to recognize the trauma shows how Lovelace's rape of Clarissa is not the story's central event, rather just part of Clarissa's gradual downfall.

[64] Lovelace writes to Belford, "nor did thy Lovelace know what it was to be gloomy, till he had completed his wishes upon the charmingest creature in the world" (Richardson 888).

it does not sufficiently evoke the aesthetic of disgust. While the modern audience does not cheer for Lovelace, it is unclear whether they fully condemn him, and, moreover, that the narrative repels them. *Clarissa* lacks *I Spit*'s poignancy. Where the latter falls short because it is too visceral, too disgusting, the former falls short because it is not gross enough. A person with a regressive (and immoral) view of sexual violence will not reconsider their view because of *Clarissa*, nor will the narrative repel them.

So we have seen that *Clarissa* lacks the disgust of *I Spit* and other rape-revenge stories. This matters because, as it turns out, disgust is central to the work's meaning. Carolyn Korsmeyer argues that disgust helps promote insight into artistic works:

> For an emotion such as disgust, a cognitivist solution makes the most sense for the most profound works. By 'cognitivist solution' I mean that pleasure can be traced to the fact that one gains insight from the art work... It is the emotion itself that delivers insight in its own intimate, visceral manner. Without the affective response, one simply would not experience the same degree of insight. That is, disgust is not just the nasty price that must be endured to achieve the point of the work; the emotion itself delivers the point.[65]

Readers do not learn much about rape from *Clarissa*. While the narrative returns some agency to its heroine and does not alienate us, it also fails to teach about sexual violence. Thus far, then, we have seen how all these rape-revenge works ultimately fall short as they relate to the aesthetic of disgust. It is time to pull these threads together and discuss why this is, why these stories keep failing to fully hit the mark I and others have drawn.

Disgust as Paradox

It is my central contention that the aesthetic of disgust is a paradoxical tool insofar as it is self-defeating. For a rape-revenge work to succeed, to convincingly push an anti-rape message, it must evoke disgust sufficient to show rape for the horrible act it is. When a work does this too well is so disgusting no one wishes to see it. But when a work does not do this well enough, it keeps its audience but loses its message. On this point, we turn again to Clover:

---

[65] Carolyn Korsmeyer, "Disgust and Aesthetics," *Philosophy Compass* (2012): 760, doi: 10.1111/j.1747-9991.2012.00522.x.

If something gets gained in this most civilized version of the rape-revenge story, something also gets lost. There is a sense in which the third party, the legal system, becomes the hero of the piece...we lose sight of what the lower forms of the rape drama unfailingly keep at center stage: the raped woman herself.[66]

To evoke the aesthetic of disgust is to walk a tightrope, sheer drops on either side. Evoke too much or too little disgust, and your narrative will fall short and emotionally driven audiences will accuse you of moral bankruptcy. This tightrope act, as I have called it, stems from disgust's repulsive character. It is a powerful emotion, but it is a primarily negative emotion as well. As such, the creators of rape-revenge fiction have the unenviable task of having to evoke this aesthetic to communicate their message and treat their subject matter with its due gravity while also having to be respectful of sexual assault victims and conscious of audience alienation. It is not clear that there is a proper balance here, the right amount of disgust to mix into the fictional blend. Because of the aesthetic's core character, maybe it cannot be done, cannot be properly balanced, for, at the end of the day, there will always be someone rushing out of the theater and to the nearest toilet stall.

Thus, the paradox of disgust is integral to rape-revenge texts and warrants further study. The paradox of disgust already exists in the literature, albeit in a different context. Aural Kolnai identifies the paradox of disgust in the tension between its simultaneous pushing and pulling mechanisms.[67] That is, though disgust's ostensible aim is to cast off the offending stimulus, disgust nevertheless has a strong allure. Whereas Noël Carroll asserts audiences do not seek out feeling disgust,[68] the existence of shock sites as well as games designed to evoke disgust (not to mention the prevalence of rape-revenge fiction) all indicate this is not the case. And Kolnai notes how disgusting objects seem to force themselves upon us.[69] So the paradox of disgust, as Kolnai elucidates it, is how disgust both allures and repulses. Dyer similarly observes disgust's push and pull mechanism as well as disgust's consequent ambivalence.[70]

---

[66] Clover 147-148.

[67] Aurel Kolnai, "On Disgust," edited by Barry Smith and Carolyn Korsmeyer. (Open Court), 43.

[68] Noël Carroll, "Why Horror?" In *Horror, The Film Reader*, edited by Mark Jancovich. (Routledge, 2002), 37.

[69] Kolnai. "On Disgust". 41.

[70] Richard Dyer, *Lethal Repetition: Serial Killing in European Cinema.* (Bloomsbury Publishing, 2019), 73-74; Isabel Pinedo also notes that disgust carries desire (67), and Julia Kristeva similarly observes the desire for and rejection of the abject (11). Thus, this observation is well-established in the literature on disgust and on the horror genre.

This mechanism is crucial to how the paradox of disgust operates in rape-revenge fiction, even though it is not the exact way in which I have explained the issue.[71] Kolnai builds on the paradox of disgust to observe the ultimate ambivalence of disgust as an emotion and experience.[72] Kolnai's observations, therefore, support my interpretation of rape-revenge fiction's ambivalence via the paradox of disgust. His work also helps us better understand why disgust is so well-suited to rape-revenge works. Not only does Kolnai point out the connection between sexuality and disgust,[73] but he also notes how disgust reifies values.[74]

Thus, even consensual sexual activity can arouse disgust, and because audiences so often condemn rape, they are liable to feel especially disgusted when encountering fictional portrayals of rape. This may be why rape-revenge works so often focus on examples of stranger rape since those are the types of rape scenarios most widely condemned.[75] Furthermore, because disgust and hatred resemble one another[76] and because hatred aims to destroy its object, disgust aimed at fictional depictions of rape aims to destroy the fictional rapist(s).[77] I will expound upon the feeling of disgust in the next chapter when I explore the pleasures disgust can offer audiences.

Before getting there, however, there is one other matter I need to consider. Namely, the paradox of disgust is not the only paradox we encounter in horror fictions. Carroll has long since articulated the paradox of fear, that is the paradox of people actively seeking out that which repulses them.[78] As such, the paradox of disgust, as both Kolnai and I have described it, resembles Carroll's more well-known concept, a fact which necessitates my mentioning the paradox of fear here. I also bring up the paradox of fear because, even though I am focusing my analysis of rape-revenge fiction on the issue of disgust, I want to be clear that I am not trying to dismiss the importance of other matters and

---

[71] The differences stem from how Kolnai and I have different missions. Whereas Kolnai sets out to describe disgust as a feeling, I have set out to identify its role in rape-revenge stories.

[72] Kolnai. "On Disgust". 43.

[73] Ibid. 51; Gina Wisker, *Horror Fiction: an Introduction.* (Continuum, 2005), 178.

[74] Kolnai. "On Disgust". 31.

[75] "Perpetrators of Sexual Violence: Statistics." RAINN. https://www.rainn.org/statistics/perpetrators-sexual-violence. Accessed December 2021.

[76] Aurel Kolnai, "The Standard Modes of Aversion: Fear, Disgust, and Hatred," edited by Barry Smith and Carolyn Korsmeyer. (Open Court), 100.

[77] Kolnai. "Modes of Aversion". 104.

[78] Carroll. "Why Horror?" 35; See also Cowan. *Sacred Terror.* 46.

other emotions to these fictional works.[79] And, as we see in the next chapter, there are a number of possible resolutions for this paradox.[80]

---

[79] Focusing his discussion on fear, Julian Hanich nevertheless specifies that horror films do not play to only one emotion (*Cinematic Emotion* 8). There are possibly innumerable ways of approaching these texts, meaning my discussion of rape-revenge fictions with a focus on disgust is not meant to be the exhaustive, universal method of interpreting these works. As I mentioned in the introduction, my method is meant to be one approach.

[80] For far more thorough and enlightening discussions of the paradox of fear, see, first, Noël Carroll's original *The Philosophy of Horror: Or, Paradoxes of the Heart* (1990) and Julian Hanich's more recent *Cinematic Emotion in Horror Films and Thrillers: The Aesthetic Paradox of Pleasurable Fear* (2010).

Chapter 4

Pleasures of Disgust

Part One: Enumerating the Pleasures

Though disgust offers a paradox, risking the alienation of audiences and critics alike, our image of disgust to now is far from complete. After all, disgust is clearly one of these texts' appeals,[1] meaning there must be some pleasure in disgust. Indeed, Richard Dyer observes: "It is widely held that people like nastiness."[2] And Julian Hanich writes that "the main functions of disgust...[are] pleasure and provocation."[3] As such, it is too simple to merely dismiss disgust as paradoxical in the rape-revenge story. As befitting this sub-genre's complexity, its core aesthetic of disgust is very complicated.[4]

And so are disgust's pleasures, varied as they are many. As such, in this chapter, I am not identifying the panacea that will explain disgust away once and for all. I am not, in other words, solving the problem I have identified. Instead, I am identifying some of the pleasures these films offer in and through disgust. Here are those pleasures as I see them. Disgust offers audiences pleasure through catharsis, through embodiment, through masochistic maturity rites, through socialization, through cognition, through teaching valuable lessons, through ritualistic repetition, and through play via the carnivalesque. I do not claim this list is exhaustive.[5] But I will describe each of

---

[1] I would like to credit one of this volume's anonymous peer reviewers, who first suggested I investigate this aspect of rape-revenge fiction.

[2] Dyer. *Lethal Repetition.* 59.

[3] Julian Hanich, "Dis/Liking disgust: the revulsion experience at the movies," *New Review of Film and Television Studies* 7, no. 3, 293. I am not going to devote a paragraph to provocation and will instead address it here. It seems to me that disgust's ability to provoke fits into its roles as a maturity rite and a mechanism for social bonding, both of which I elaborate on in this chapter.

[4] Writing about horror, Hanich notes that we need to consider the pleasure in a particular feeling (he was focusing on fear) and that a film or genre does not necessarily offer one type of pleasure (*Cinematic Emotions* 5-6).

[5] That said, this list does exhaust my current assessment of disgust's possible pleasures. I remain open, however, to the possibility that I have overlooked some, even many, other pleasures disgust may offer.

these in turn.[6] And, at the end of this chapter, I will conclude with an examination of these pleasures in the 2007 horror-comedy, rape-revenge *Teeth*.

Catharsis is the first pleasure on my list, and it gains its primacy because of its age, being the oldest explanation for the pleasure audiences derive from so-called negative emotions in fiction. Aristotle was the first to articulate a theory of catharsis, and though he was writing about tragedy rather than horror and thrillers (let alone rape-revenge), his theory is applicable here. The idea is that negative fictions allow us to purge (note that word) our negative emotions.

So, in this conception, disgusting fictions allow us to cast off these negative feelings. Already, the reader may object to my classification of catharsis as a potential pleasure of disgust. After all, why would someone feel disgusted without having seen something disgusting? Put another way, if I want to avoid feeling disgusted, I could just avoid watching these movies or engaging with any other disgusting stimuli.

In this theory's defense, we should consider how our negative emotions (i.e., the baggage we carry through our daily lives, the accumulation of stress) become, through these films, off-loaded onto disgust. Disgust in fiction, in other words, lets us purge a collection of our negative emotions, not just pre-existing feelings of disgust in the absence of any noxious stimulus. Furthermore, the connection of disgust to purging is all too apparent. As one of my brothers sagely told me: "Sometimes you won't feel better until you've thrown up." Disgust, that run to the toilet stall, therefore, offers us a way to experience the pleasure of relief.

In aesthetics, there are two types of pleasure: sustaining pleasure and relief pleasure.[7] While aesthetics mostly attends to the former, the latter is a clear role of nausea if not disgust properly.[8] But the case is more complex than this, I think. Relief pleasure arises when we cast off an unpleasant stimulus, meaning vomiting is one such example. Hanich, however, has noted that relief alone does not account for the pleasure of horror, and I think we can say the same for the pleasure of disgust.[9]

---

[6] I must stress now that each of these pleasures could well form the basis for an independent study. Indeed, some of them have already received such studies. Therefore, what I offer now will necessarily be truncated views of these different pleasures since my focus is rape-revenge and disgust therethrough rather than any of these individual pleasures disgust may offer.

[7] Bence Nanay, *Aesthetics: A Very Short Introduction.* (Oxford University Press, 2019), 12.

[8] Ibid.

[9] Hanich. *Cinematic Emotion.* 100.

But can disgust offer sustaining pleasure? Nanay writes that sustaining pleasures control the audience's attention.[10] Thus, according to this view, in rape-revenge, we start with attention to the rape, feeling that initial disgust at the immorality and carnality. After the rape scenes have ended and we enter the revenge scenes, we experience the relief of disgust's abatement (and possibly of throwing up). Thereafter, we attend to the disgusting violence, meaning we are now entering into a sort of sustained pleasure. We have, in other words, encountered a sort of aesthetic catharsis, especially by the story's end.

Part of the difficulty in charting the pleasures of disgust, however, arises when we consider Kolai's point that disgust seems to serve a limiting function on pleasure.[11] If disgust limits pleasure, how is disgust, itself, pleasurable? First, we need to be aware that Kolnai is specifically tying this idea to how we begin to feel disgust when we overindulge.[12] Second, per Kolnai's observation, I think we can make the case for disgust's potential for pleasure. If disgust limits pleasure insofar as it stops us from overindulging, then disgust offers temporary displeasure, which counterintuitively clears the path for future pleasure. This is disgust's sustaining pleasure. By setting boundaries on our indulgence, disgust makes us refrain from either habituating ourselves to the pleasurable stimulus such that we can no longer enjoy it or from indulging to the point where we adversely condition ourselves to dislike the stimulus.[13]

This conception of the pleasure disgust offers fits neatly into Kolnai's paradox of disgust, whereby we try to hold the disgusting object at a distance even as we imagine imbibing it, combining it with our very being, as it were.[14] Since the casting off process (purgation) is part and parcel of experiencing disgust, it makes sense that this casting off could also form one of the affect's pleasures. Catharsis, however, does not exhaust the pleasures disgust offers, nor is it without problems of its own. On this point, Prince observes how catharsis lacks

---

[10] Nanay 13.

[11] Kolnai. "On Disgust". 63-64.

[12] Ibid.

[13] In the first case, consider the issue of thresholds in drug use. Each time you use a drug, you grow more habituated to it, meaning you must take increasing amounts of the substance to achieve the same level of effect. In the second case, consider eating too much of a food because you are enjoying its taste. Only, you eat until you overdo it and get sick. Thereafter, you can no longer stomach the taste of that food. Every time you try to eat it, you start feeling nauseous again.

[14] Kolnai. "On Disgust". 43.

empirical support.[15] And Cowan notes in *Sacred Terror* that catharsis does not last.[16]

The latter of these objections is the easiest with which to contend. Compare the cathartic experience with any other sort of relief. When in pain, I may take a Tylenol and feel my pain abate. But the pain often comes back unless I address its root cause. Relief is ephemeral. What about Prince's objection, though? I must admit this one is more damning and much harder to argue against. Finding empirical evidence of catharsis would be an entirely different project than this one is. Nevertheless, I want to note here that the existence of catharsis as Aristotle envisioned it is fairly immaterial for my overall argument about disgust. If catharsis is not an actual phenomenon, that does not negate the paradox of disgust in rape-revenge, as I have articulated it. In that case, though, catharsis may not be one of disgust's pleasures. Disgust may be complicated, even paradoxical, but it cannot offer pleasures that do not exist.

It seems to me, however, that relief clearly exists. And I have experienced this very feeling when watching rape-revenge films. Indeed, two of the films I examine in this book made me nearly vomit: *I Spit* (2010) and *Irréversible*. The former sent me to the bathroom, where I feared I would puke (I did not). And I felt better after that nauseous feeling passed. Meanwhile, the beginning of *Irréversible* gave me motion sickness, a feeling I got relief from through a couple of tablets of Dramamine.

All of this is to say that removing an offending stimulus (even a fictional one) does offer its own sort of pleasurable release. And, of course, there is also the possibility of endorphins here. Endorphins are the human body's natural painkillers, which it releases after such activities as strenuous exercise. And research shows the body can also release them after vomiting.[17] So it is, in fact, possible to experience not just relief but also a bit of a rush after vomiting, after purging, after catharsis-ing.

That rush, moreover, brings us to the second pleasure of disgust I have identified: embodiment. Disgust, and especially vomiting, can be an intense physical experience. In throwing up, you feel your body tense, sometimes to the point of feeling it may break. It is a powerful bodily experience. Such an observation jives with Linda Williams' discussion of body genres, wherein she

---

[15] Prince 19.

[16] Douglas E. Cowan, *Sacred Terror: Religion and Horror on the Silver Screen.* (Waco, Texas: Baylor University Press, 2008), 260.

[17] HD Abraham and AB Joseph, "Bulimia vomiting alters pain tolerance and mood," *International Journal of Psychiatry in Medicine* 16, no. 4 (1986): 311-316, https://pubmed.ncbi.nlm.nih.gov/3030947/.

writes: "Visually, each of these ecstatic excesses could be said to share a quality of uncontrollable convulsion or spasm—of the body..."[18] While vomiting and disgust are not among Williams' list of experiences here, they fit her observation to a surprising degree.

Vomiting is, after all, an experience in which the body uncontrollably spasms. Here, the experience of purgation fits with a far different experience in ways I think most of us would rather not imagine. That is, vomiting bears at least a passing resemblance to the orgasm. If the orgasm is the "little death," it is at least partially so because orgasm sees the mind lose control as the body's machinations take over, much as they do in the moments preceding death. And vomiting does the same. Like arousal, then, disgust can lead to intense bodily sensations (and contortions). And, as we saw above, that experience is not always negative.

Because it is so intense, though, disgust can make us attend to our own bodies while we are experiencing a rape-revenge text. On a similar note, Hanich describes cinematic fear as the pleasurable foregrounding of the body.[19] Hanich elaborates by pointing out that fearful emotions let audience members experience themselves.[20] Given its powerful bodily aspects, disgust has the potential to do the same. Sitting in my desk chair, watching *I Spit* (2010), I felt myself withdrawing from the narrative, my immersion breaking, as I became aware of something: a knot in my throat, an unpleasant sense of being a little light-headed. I was disgusted and nauseated. Disgust, ergo, made me attend to myself, become aware of my own limitations, those cinematic factors I could not stomach, so to speak. This was a powerful sensory experience that sticks with me even years later.

Powerful bodily moments are part and parcel of the next possible pleasure of disgust: masochistic maturity rites. Above, I noted how *I Spit* (2010) confronted me with my own limitations regarding the sort of cinema I could view.[21] This experience meshes well with the idea of disgust as a maturity rite. On a related topic, Darryl Jones argues that the purpose of horror is "to force its audiences to confront the limits of their tolerance."[22] Similarly, noted folklorist Jan Harold

---

18 Williams 269.

19 Hanich. *Cinematic Emotion*. 234.

20 Ibid.

21 It is possible my tolerance for extreme cinema has risen since then and/or that my particularly strong reaction to *I Spit* (2010) was contextual, possibly based on my own dread of the film, given the graphic nature of the subject and the movie's predecessor, the original *I Spit*.

22 Darryl Jones, *Horror: a Very Short Introduction*. (Oxford University Press, 2021), 13.

Brunvand observes that gross-out urban legends function as maturity rites.[23] And Kolnai argues that disgust issues a challenge.[24]

Thus, the idea of disgust (and even horror) as a form of maturity rite is well-established in the literature. Allow me to illustrate with an example. Years ago, I encountered a game called BeanBoozled. The game involves two components. First, there is a wheel of jellybean favors the players take turns spinning to determine which flavor jellybeans they must eat. Second, there is an assortment of jellybeans corresponding to those flavors.

At first, this hardly seems like a game since there is no challenge. In fact, the challenge lies in the jellybeans themselves, which are of half regular flavors (e.g., berry) and half disgusting flavors (e.g., rotten cheese). The game, then, is a challenge, whereby players risk the chance of eating truly repugnant candies. Between the two players lies the game: each player dares the others to take the same risks to prove their bravery equal to the other player's bravery. Accordingly, being able to tolerate disgusting flavors becomes a way for players to demonstrate their prowess to the other player(s).[25] This is, of course, almost identical to the nature of horror as a maturity rite wherein adolescents try to prove their fortitude to their friends.[26]

By proving one can engage with the disgusting object, one can prove one is, in some sense, mature or strong. This is not far off from the idea of a sporting contest to prove athletic prowess. It is, perhaps, unsurprising, therefore, that Clover found the audience for rape-revenge films to be primarily adolescent males.[27] There is, of course and unfortunately, the possibility of prurient interest in these films, of viewers seeking them out because they, the viewers, get sexual gratification from graphic depictions of sexual violence. But the above discussion suggests another possibility, that of viewers seeking these films out to test their mettle, whether individually or in a peer group.

It makes sense that adolescents might be the primary audience for such material, moreover, because of what adolescence means. Adolescence is a liminal state between childhood and adulthood, a period in which people must

---

[23] Jan Harold Brunvand, *The Vanishing Hitchhiker: American Urban Legends & Their Meanings.* (New York: W.W. Norton and Company, 1981), 75.

[24] Kolnai. "On Disgust". 76-77.

[25] I am only a little ashamed to admit I bowed out of the game almost immediately after getting a rotten cheese flavored jellybean. My nephew was, however, a good sport about my early departure.

[26] See Evans' work on horror films and initiation rites.

[27] Clover 6. Brigid Cherry has, however, challenged this assessment of horror film audiences, noting they have a larger number of female viewers than discussions such as Clover's tend to allow (170).

try to define themselves while navigating myriad personal, emotional, and social hurdles. Said hurdles fit into Williams' argument that disgusting movies show feelings "on the edge of the respectable."[28] In trying to define themselves, adolescents will, almost invariably, test the boundaries of acceptable conduct. Accordingly, it is natural that gross movies like the rape-revenge film might appeal to this sort of audience.

Even more interesting to me, though, is the masochism these sorts of maturity rites evince. In a sporting contest, one proves one's athleticism and, depending on the sport, strategy. Of course, one also proves one's toughness, but the audience's focus tends to glom onto athleticism and strategy instead of onto toughness.[29] The same is not the case for the sorts of maturity rites disgust allows, where the rites revolve around not athleticism or strategy but, rather, solely toughness, the ability to withstand the noxious and repulsive. The pleasure here comes from proving one's worth.

Said pleasure immediately overlaps with disgust's next appeal: socialization. I derive this pleasure from Hanich's argument that cinematic fear and disgust make audience members feel powerless and, consequently, push audience members to bond.[30] That is, captive in their theater seats, audience members feel helpless against the graphic material on screen. Thus pushed to attend to their bodies,[31] audience members seek relief through bonding (if implicitly) with their fellow audience members, imagining their fellow viewers are feeling the same negative emotions.[32] Hanich's argument centers on the movie theater experience, but my discussion of disgust as a form of maturity rite suggests disgust can offer socialization well outside the movie theater. While maturity

---

[28] Williams 267.

[29] As a former competitive swimmer, I am aware of toughness's role in sports. But I am also aware of its often limited potential. I am reminded, that is, of the swimming races where, yes, I endured the pain of exertion and pushed myself to swim as fast as I could despite my tiredness but then lost because my competitors were faster than me. In other words, athleticism can trump toughness in a swimming race, meaning endurance is but part of the puzzle. Indeed, thinking back now to the swimming races I have watched, it seems to me that my foremost concern as a spectator is on the swimmers' differing speeds. It is only if one of the swimmers starts to slow down and another to catch up that I begin attending to their differing levels of conditioning. Thus, endurance is a secondary consideration for me in this sort of viewing experience. But such is not the case for a game like BeanBoozled, where the focus is on each player's ability to withstand each awful taste.

[30] Hanich. *Cinematic Emotion.* 55 & 76.

[31] Ibid. 234.

[32] Zillman and Gibson observe that horror plays to social precepts (e.g., morality) and empathy (28).

rites can be individual, they are often social experiences, occurring in largely public spaces. This assessment fits both the movie theater and BeanBoozled.

Socialization offers, however, another dimension, whereby disgust in the rape-revenge film can operate as a moral yardstick. Part of the socialization process is learning proper behavior for social settings. And this entails learning morality. A central part of adolescence, then, is attaining the ability to discern right from wrong, especially regarding how to treat other people. And so, when viewers in a film audience find themselves repulsed by the graphic violence of the rape-revenge film playing on screen, and when they subsequently bond with their fellow viewers by assuming that (and/or by looking around to gauge whether) their fellow audience members are feeling the same, they are, in effect, gauging their and their fellow viewers' moral values.

Such an assessment not only measures the fellow audience members but also provides the assessor an opportunity to reflect on their own moral values. In such a situation, an inappropriate reaction from one viewer can bring social stigma from the rest of the audience and/or feelings of shame from the outlying viewer. This dynamic means that disgusting films like rape-revenge movies offer the opportunity for reflection on morals and values. If I react inappropriately, such as by laughing at the wrong time, I can look around to see the disapproval from my fellow viewers and can thereby learn to behave differently. Peer pressure can teach me the socially appropriate way to behave. Likewise, if I see that my fellow viewers are reacting as I have, I can feel validated in my response and know I am reacting as my peers dictate.

It is perhaps strange to say, but I think disgust offers the possibility for a rather moral experience. On the one hand, society often looks down on those who engage with disgusting material, those who willingly watch such films, for example. And yet, on the other, these disgusting stimuli offer the chance for their audiences to reify their moral values by confirming that they do, in fact, all feel disgusted by the offending stimuli, whether it is fictional or real. Rape-revenge films, therefore, offer an opportunity for moral viewing, as do other hyper-graphic or disturbing works of fiction.

By now, we have moved from more physical pleasures of disgust to more mental pleasures, meaning we have reached the potential cognitive pleasure(s) of disgust. Such pleasures are not, however, limited to moral considerations. Kolnai, for instance, argues disgust is more mentally-oriented than either fear or anxiety is.[33] As such, disgust has a strong cognitive component, even if we divorce it from morality. Disgust pushes us to think, meaning the rape-revenge work consequently does as well.

---

[33] Kolnai. "On Disgust". 43.

The sort of thinking we do because of disgusting stimuli (even if they are fictional) may run in a multitude of directions, of course. One of these directions corresponds well with feminist film theory, namely issues of identification. Writing on this topic, Teresa de Lauretis points out that, to work, films must offer pleasure through, e.g., desire and identification.[34] Christine Gledhill takes this astute observation even further when she argues that identification through cinema relies on negotiation, whereby meaning arises through the struggle between production and reception.[35] In these conceptions, the film offers viewers the chance to redefine their identifications as the movie plays.

Given its central role in rape-revenge films, disgust necessarily forms a key part of the viewer's identity negotiation when the viewer is watching a rape-revenge movie. When a viewer watches *I Spit* (2010) and finds themselves disgusted at the men's rape of Jennifer, they renegotiate their self to align with her. By thinking through the narrative, the viewer plays with the concept of who they are, thus unlocking possible pleasure, not only through experiencing the vindication of Jennifer's revenge but also through experiencing the pleasure of hermeneutics, of interpreting the film's narrative. Disgust pushes us, the audience, to think, which can be its own pleasure.

Of course, thinking can also be pleasurable because of its results rather than merely its process. Many scholars have posited that part of the appeal graphic cinema and horror films offer is the ability for the audience to glean valuable lessons from their narratives. This is the next pleasure of disgust I wish to explore. Vivian Sobchack writes "to know violence is to be temporarily safe from the fear of it."[36] But why would fictional violence make us feel safe from real violence? One of the possible explanations is that these works, including rape-revenge works, teach us how to avoid real-life violence.

We can, after all, recognize when characters are making poor decisions, and we can resolve not to do the same. Bruno Bettelheim has argued this is one of the appeals of fairy tales; they teach children important lessons, including

---

[34] Teresa de Lauretis, "Oedipus Interruptus." In *Feminist Film Theory: A Reader*, edited by Sue Thornham. (Edinburgh University Press, 1999), 85.

[35] Christine Gledhill, "Pleasurable Negotiations." In *Feminist Film Theory: A Reader*, edited by Sue Thornham. (Edinburgh University Press, 1999), 169.

The issue of identification has received much attention in existing feminist scholarship, so much so I believe the question of identification in rape-revenge requires its own extensive discussion elsewhere.

[36] Sobchack 116-117.

those related to survival.[37] For his part, Hanich offers the related observation that scary movies can satisfy our desire for knowledge.[38] This knowledge can relate not just to survival but also to the desire to unfurl a narrative[39] or the desire to experience that which the viewer cannot experience in real life (or, at least, cannot experience safely).[40] Hanich offers another essential point here when he argues that we experience the disgusting in fiction as real rather than as fictional.[41] Terry Heller has made a similar observation about how terror fiction lets us experience what we cannot or do not do in real life.[42]

Hanich's arrangement privileges disgust as a remarkably powerful and intrusive affect, one which, therefore, gives the viewer an especially strong learning opportunity (at least insofar as fiction can teach us). Put another way, disgust's ability to reach through the screen, as it were, makes fictional works evoking disgust applicable in a way many other fictional works simply are not. We can watch disgusting videos to learn what disgusting material is like. And, if we agree with Hanich's assessment, most other affects will not achieve this sort of reality.

These lessons are, however, transitory.[43] Indeed, they are often pretty weak to begin with.[44] Combined, these two facts mean that disgusting fiction's lessons fade quickly, meaning audiences feel compelled to return repeatedly to these fictions. This is the pleasure of ritualistic repetition. Like disgust, the idea of pleasure via repetition can seem oxymoronic at first glance. And there are certainly cases where repetition is more torturous than pleasurable.[45] The fact remains, though, that we do often repeat activities for pleasure. We listen to the same songs over and over again, eat the same foods, and so forth. We not only attempt to recreate pleasurable experiences, but we experience pleasure via repetition itself.

Dyer considers repetition one of the major pleasures of stories about serial killers. In *Only Entertainment*, he writes of the "pleasure principle of seriality,"

---

[37] Bruno Bettelheim, *The Uses of Enchantment: The Meaning and Importance of Fairy Tales.* (New York: Vintage Books, 1989), 4.

[38] Hanich. *Cinematic Emotion.* 6.

[39] Carroll. "Why Horror?" 36.

[40] Martin Tropp observes that fiction is safe (4).

[41] Hanich. "Dis/Liking". 304.

[42] Terry Heller, *The Delights of Terror: an Aesthetics of the Tale of Terror.* (University of Illinois Press, 1987), 29.

[43] Sobchack 117.

[44] Ibid. On a similar note, Fred Botting describes how repetition does not quite manage to satisfy (192).

[45] For a fictional example of this, see Stephen King's "That Feeling You Can Only Say What It Is In French."

a topic he also discusses in *Lethal Repetition*, where he writes of "repetition as pleasure."[46] In this volume's introduction, I noted how the rape-revenge sub-genre often overlaps with the slasher film sub-genre. That overlap indicates how rape-revenge stories frequently invoke tropes of serial killer fiction, making Dyer's assessment relevant to rape-revenge fiction, too.[47] Rape-Revenge fits Dyer's narratological assessment of pleasure because these narratives so frequently follow the same general plot structure.

I know what to expect when going into a rape-revenge film, and I can, in Dyer's account, experience pleasure because of my familiarity with this sub-genre and its formulas. Genres of fiction offer recognizable blueprints, providing a sense of play for the knowledgeable viewer who can attempt to spot the familiar cues and predict the familiar story.[48] Moreover, this is pleasurable precisely because of how it contrasts with our experience of reality. Whereas a work of genre fiction may be wholly predictable,[49] real life is rarely so formulaic, containing as it does a variety of unpredictable events. In fictional works that elicit disgust, we can predict when the disgust will come since it is part of the work's formula.

What is more, the rape-revenge film offers not only a justification for the extreme violence of the heroine's revenge but also offers the viewer a contained portrayal of graphic violence. Violence in the real world is rarely so contained, but in the rape-revenge film we, the audience, know exactly who the heroine's victims are going to be. Because the film presents us with a finite list of victims, we can rest assured of some sense of narrative closure and, moreover, some sense of repetition as we get the thrill of disgusting revenge on multiple, successive, and escalating occasions.

Thus, repetition is pleasurable partially because of its predictability. If we take disgust to its extreme of vomiting, we can see this predictable structure play out. One starts feeling nauseous, one feels a knot in one's throat, a pressure at the back of the tongue, then the feeling of inevitable eruption before the

---

[46] Richard Dyer, *Only Entertainment.* (Routledge, 2002), 71; Dyer. *Lethal Repetition.* 10.

[47] To be clear, slasher films and films about serial killers are not identical. Rather, they sometimes draw of similar ideas and tropes, which is why I bring up the slasher film in this chapter.

[48] Steve Neale has pointed out, however, that genre films do not offer pleasure merely through repetition and that, instead, the pleasure of genre films is based on both repetition and variation (7).

[49] Plenty of fictional works set out to disrupt audience expectations, which is why I specify that works of genre fiction *may* be wholly predictable. They are not always, and that lack of predictability can bring about its own pleasures. Indeed, Wisker lists pleasure at subversion as one of the pleasures of horror (29).

constriction of the purge itself followed by a feeling of exhaustion, relief, and, for some, even mild euphoria.[50] This predictability also connects to a deeper concern with genre fiction, the ritual.

Rick Altman has argued film genres have either ideological or ritualistic functions.[51] Jones further connects this idea to the rape-revenge film when he argues that the pleasures horror fiction offers resemble those of a ritual.[52] As ordered activities that help people make sense of their worlds, rituals connect readily to the idea of control, an idea also central to repetition. The idea that narratives offer pleasure through their predictability and repetition suggests that audiences get a sense of pleasure through a feeling of control over the narrative, an ability to predict the future (of the story). Disgusting fiction (e.g., rape-revenge) thus allows us to experience disgust in a relatively inert setting where we can gain a feeling of control, possibly mastery, over material that, in reality, is typically outside our control.

And control brings us to the final pleasure of disgust I explore in this volume: play via the carnivalesque. Dyer identifies the connection of disgust to the carnivalesque in *Lethal Repetition*, so I am not breaking new ground by merely pointing to a link.[53] Alison Peirse makes a similar observation when she invokes Robin Wood's notion of horror films showing a nightmare in which we disrupt our society's norms.[54] Mikhail Bakhtin was the first to articulate the critical concept of the carnivalesque, a genre that shows participants joining a game in which they gleefully and temporarily subvert traditional authority structures and social norms.[55]

Because horror, its related genres, and its sub-genres (including rape-revenge) allow audiences the chance to temporarily view material society frowns upon and, furthermore, that itself shows disruption of typical societal norms and power structures, this volume's core texts connect readily to the idea of the carnivalesque. Thus, part of the pleasure of disgust and the fictions eliciting it lies in the opportunity to perform, witness, and/or enjoy acts that

---

[50] I am not claiming to experience a euphoric feeling from throwing up, but the research showing how vomiting can trigger endorphin release demonstrates that such a feeling is possible and may help explain such concerns as bulimia. See: "Bulimic vomiting alters pain tolerance and mood" by HD Abraham and AB Joseph.

[51] Rick Altman, *Film/Genre*. (British Film Institute, 1999), 26.

[52] Jones 13.

[53] Dyer. *Lethal Repetition*. 73.

[54] Alison Peirse, "Women Make (Write, Produce, Direct, Shoot, Edit, and Analyze) Horror." In *Women Make Horror: Filmmaking, Feminism, Genre*, edited by Alison Peirse. (Rutgers University Press, 2020), 4.

[55] See: Bakhtin *Problems of Dostoevsky's Poetics* (1929).

are anathema to ordered everyday life. And so disgust is not just a challenge but also a game, one rooted deep in human psychophysiology.

What interests me here, though, is the reactions we have to this game. Extant analyses of the horror genre tend to focus on two visceral reactions audiences may have to horror films: screaming or laughing. Master horror director Wes Craven describes the process of watching a horror movie as one of experiencing mounting tension, tension the horror director then allows us to release in the form of a scream or a laugh (hence the balancing of horror and humor in Craven's *Scream* (1996)).[56] Scholar William Paul also identified this apparent relation between horror and humor in the title of his book *Laughing Screaming*.[57] To this connection, however, I think we need to add a distant third possibility: vomiting.[58]

Craven has already traced the connection between the laugh and the scream for us. And Hanich does the same for screaming and vomiting. Hanich makes the astute (if gross) observation that fear and disgust are both constrictive experiences.[59] Hanich goes further, however, tracing the pleasurable experience of the scream, which creates distance between the self and the offending stimulus.[60] Creating distance is, of course, vomiting's raison d'être. All three actions (laughing, screaming, retching) have, therefore, similar mechanisms and consequences: relieving tension we experience (in this case) because of negatively coded works of fiction. In each of these cases, we cast aside the offending material while signaling we found the material offensive, and, thus, we reify our values and their alignment with those of the others engaging in the game.

Part Two: A (Disgusting) Case Study

Section One: Teeth: Summary and Analysis

Since I have now described each of disgust's pleasures I have identified, let us see them ourselves in the rape-revenge film *Teeth*. In this first section of part two, I summarize the movie and take this opportunity to analyze its plot and

---

[56] Hidden Clips, "Wes Craven Interview (screamography)," YouTube, May 26, 2015, https://www.youtube.com/watch?v=_zmo9fGtcVE&t=1203s.

[57] See: Paul *Laughing Screaming: Modern Hollywood Horror and Comedy* (1994).

[58] Then again, "Laughing Screaming Retching" is a less catchy title.

[59] Hanich. *Cinematic Emotion.* 102.

[60] Ibid. 149.

characters.[61] In the second section, I move on to the pleasures the film offers via disgust. Directed by Mithcell Lichtenstein, *Teeth* (2007) is about high schooler Dawn's experience with her own vagina dentata. The film's first scene occurs years before the main narrative, showing Dawn (Jess Weixler) and her stepbrother Brad as young children. The older, aggressive Brad offers to show Dawn his if she shows him hers. Reaching for her vagina, he draws his hand back, revealing a long cut on his finger.

Flashing forward to the present, teenage Dawn is a life under siege. At home, she still deals with the aggressive and lecherous Brad, as well as her own ailing mother's declining health. At school, she faces frequent mocking from her peers. Dawn, we learn, is a prominent member of the school's abstinence club. Believing firmly in abstinence until marriage, Dawn suppresses her libido and tries to ignore the sexual harassment she faces. Her ability to do either ebbs, however, when she meets Tobey, another member of the abstinence club with whom she shares a mutual attraction.

She and Tobey attempt to avoid one another at first, but eventually, they agree to meet at the local lake. There, they begin kissing. Dawn, realizing the situation is escalating, tells Tobey to stop and attempts to push him away. But Tobey grows more forceful and rapes Dawn, complaining about how difficult abstinence has been for him. As he penetrates her, though, her vagina severs his penis from his body. Dawn flees the scene, leaving Tobey behind. Thereafter, much of the film follows Dawn's attempts to figure out what is going on with her body, why her vagina was able to bite off Tobey's penis. This quest brings her to stories of vagina dentata. Fearing she has these mythical structures, Dawn visits a gynecologist, only for her vagina dentata to bite four of the doctor's fingers off after he molests her.

Dawn flees this gruesome scene and soon discovers (as if from a cosmic attempt to compound her terror) that Tobey died as a result of injuries from her teeth. Meanwhile, Dawn's stepbrother Brad ignores Dawn's mother's cries for help when she collapses at home. Consequently, Dawn's mother becomes hospitalized. Distraught, Dawn seeks comfort from her classmate, Ryan, with whom she has sex.[62] The two spend the night and part of the next day together, and Dawn is happy to find her teeth have not bitten Ryan. The situation

---

[61] This discussion allows me to contextualize each of the pleasures I discuss in Section Two. It also allows me to intervene in scholarship of this movie, which I believe misconstrues the film's feminist potential.

[62] Ryan gives Dawn a sedative when she comes to him, so one could make the case that he rapes her that night given her lack of a clear head, owing to the drug. The two do have consensual sex together the next day, though, indicating Dawn does not think of their first sexual encounter as non-consensual.

changes, however, when Ryan reveals he bedded Dawn because he bet a friend that he could. Ryan even brags about getting Dawn to break her abstinence pledge, mocking her indignity over his exploitation of her. His mocks turn to screams, though, when the teeth activate and chomp his penis clean from his body.

Disgusted, Dawn leaves Ryan behind, and, learning her mom has passed away, seduces Brad, who reveals he has always had a crush on her. Once he penetrates her, Dawn uses her teeth to slice off his penis. With her life torn apart, Dawn runs away, hitching a ride with an old man as she journeys into an uncertain future. When she awakens, the old man driver refuses to let her out of the car. Instead, he gestures with his tongue to indicate his repulsive demand that Dawn sexually perform for him. Dawn, visibly frustrated, slowly turns from the passenger side door to face the driver, tossing him a seductive look.

In writing about *Teeth*, Heller-Nicholas finds the film "far from unproblematic," since, in her view, the film shows Dawn's vagina dentata as less a deterrent to or weapon against rape but instead an impediment to Dawn's ability to enjoy sexual activity.[63] Kyle Buchanan similarly takes issue with how Dawn's consensual sex scene with Ryan culminates in her castrating him, ostensibly indicating she cannot enjoy sex.[64] While I appreciate Heller-Nicholas's work in cataloging and reading rape-revenge fiction, I disagree with her reading of this relatively obscure film.

Heller-Nicholas and Buchanan believe Dawn is incapable of enjoying sex, and her yonic dentine is a problem for her as much as a problem for her rapists.[65] Such a reading, however, elides the true arc of Dawn's character as I see it. Far from being hampered by her unique adaptation, Dawn receives power from it. Without realizing it, Heller-Nicholas and Buchanan have adopted a view similar to Dawn's, a view in which a "hero" is necessary for conquering the vagina dentata.[66]

In the film, Dawn peruses material about the vagina dentata myth, discovering versions of the myth wherein a heroic male character quells the untamed fires within the troubled woman's loins. Such a view, as I have dramatically phrased it, is clearly problematic in that it lays the onus of a woman's sexuality at the feet of a male character, a charge similar to the one these critics level toward *Teeth* itself. They are not entirely unjustified in doing

---

[63] Heller-Nicholas. 2nd edition. 57-58.

[64] Quotd. In Heller-Nicholas 2nd edition 58.

[65] Ibid.

[66] *Teeth*. Directed by Mitchell Lichtenstein, performance by Jess Weixler, Roadside Attractions, 2007.

so, of course, for Dawn herself believes Ryan is the "hero" up until her teeth turn on him, after which she sarcastically quips "Some hero" while leaving Ryan to find help or die of exsanguination.[67] Heller-Nicholas further asserts Dawn's teeth sever her gynecologist's fingers because Dawn perceives he is taking perverse pleasure in examining her.[68]

This reading, however, overlooks important sub-text within the scene. The doctor is a predator, and Dawn's teeth bite him because he is molesting and hurting her (all without Dawn's conscious input). In the scene, the doctor questions Dawn about her gynecological history. After he learns she has never been to the gynecologist before, his demeanor shifts. Because this is Dawn's first visit to such a doctor, she does not know what to expect, meaning she does not know what behavior from her doctor is inappropriate. And so, thus confident in his ability to molest Dawn with impunity, the doctor removes his glove before testing Dawn's "flexibility."[69]

That is, he inserts his bunched fingers into her vagina under the pretense of seeing how far he can stretch her sex. When he does not relent despite Dawn's protestations, her teeth react. Notably, then, her vagina dentata are reacting not so much to the doctor's enjoyment of tormenting Dawn (though this is part of it), but more so to Dawn's pain and fear. Her pain and fear, moreover, stem from the doctor's assault upon her person (i.e., his sexual assault of her).

That Dawn's teeth respond to her pain is clear from how the teeth attack unwanted intruders into Dawn's genital cavity. Her teeth do not masticate the objects they bite. Instead, they cleanly sever those objects from the offending person. Thus, their evolutionary purpose (regardless of their origin) is to punish sexual assault to prevent their body (of which they are an extension) from this manner of attack. Reading this scene and Dawn's vagina dentata in light of how the teeth respond to Dawn's pain is essential because it shows why Dawn's consensual sex with Ryan ends with yet another castration.

While having sex with Dawn, Ryan receives a call from a friend. While actively penetrating Dawn, Ryan brags to his friend about having bedded her, thus showing he does not value her as a person or consider their sex a form of pair bonding. Instead, his bragging indicates he sees Dawn as a sexual object, a wager for him to win. He callously incites Dawn to reveal she is there with him, and when Dawn objects that Ryan has disrespected her agency, he trots out the

---

[67] Ibid.
[68] Heller-Nicholas. 2nd edition. 57.
[69] *Teeth.*

cliché and immoral observation that Dawn's mouth is saying one thing, but her "sweet pussy" is saying another.[70]

In other words, Ryan is dismissing Dawn's agency, outright saying he does not care what she says, only how her body physiologically responds to him. Certainly, such a statement aligns (rather too comfortably) with the real-life phenomenon of rape victims experiencing orgasm during the horrific event.[71] Physiological response, therefore, neither equals nor implies actual interest or consent. Dawn, by contrast, has a unique physiology, one which does respond to interest and consent. When Dawn consents to have sex with Ryan, the teeth remain innocuous. Once Dawn is no longer interested in having sex with Ryan (i.e., after he treats her like an object and rejects her personhood), then the teeth bite.

We would be remiss, it follows, to read this scene as an indication that Dawn cannot enjoy sex. The scene shows her enjoying sex. Instead of a lack of enjoyment, the scene reveals another facet of Dawn's unusual biology, that is, her ability to physiologically revoke consent. Whereas human beings typically lack this function (despite numerous politicians' bigoted assertions to the contrary), Dawn has it in spades. If someone disrespects her personhood or attempts to override her consent mid-coitus, then her teeth respond as they would if had she been unwilling from the start. Her teeth, it seems, have a better understanding of consent and its revocation than many people do.

And on this point, *Teeth* is somewhat unusual as a work of rape-revenge, as most such works depict stranger rape, rape which begins as non-consensual and then increases in violence and violation. Conversely, in the scenes with Ryan, *Teeth* shows an example of sex beginning as consensual and then becoming rape after one partner revokes consent. This is, however, but a muted example since the revocation comes swiftly and with little chance for Ryan to pull out. Ryan is also useful for illustrating how *Teeth* returns power to its heroine more fully than scholars like Heller-Nicholas and Buchanan allow.

Let us return to the paradigm of the hero in the vagina dentata mythos, a corpus into which this film boldly enters. After discovering the concept of the hero in this context, Dawn hopes she can find such a person. Unbeknownst to

---

[70] Ibid.

[71] Roy J. Levin and Willy von Berlo, "Sexual arousal and orgasm in subjects who experience forced or non-consensual sexual stimulation—a review," *Journal of Clinical Forensic Medicine* 11, no. 2 (April 2004): 82-88, https://pubmed.ncbi.nlm.nih.gov/15261004/; Research, such as that cited above, demonstrates that survivors of sexual assault can experience arousal and even orgasm during the assault. In the above study, Levin and Berlo conclude that orgasm does not, therefore, indicate consent or enjoyment.

her, however, she already has. That person, she decides, is Ryan; unlike every other man who has penetrated her, Ryan remains unharmed throughout their initial copulation. And so, Dawn concludes, Ryan is the hero, and her teeth are tamed.

Only, as I have already mentioned, Dawn misreads the situation, as Ryan is despicable and taking advantage of her. Ryan, as Dawn declares after castrating him, is no hero. Moreover, any person with whom Dawn shares consensual sex is not the hero either since, as we have seen, her teeth respond whenever the sex is non-consensual. The hero, therefore, the only one who can control the teeth, is Dawn. The arc of the film is that of Dawn deciding to be her own hero, taming the beast that is actually her (i.e., coming to terms with the power of her own sexuality).

Thus, even though, as Heller-Nicholas observes, Dawn is more terrified of her own body than she is of sexual assault, it is clear the film vilifies sexual assault and upholds Dawn's bodily autonomy, the importance of her giving and maintaining consent to sexual contact.[72] As I have asseverated, Dawn is able to enjoy sex. Furthermore, her control over the teeth increases as the film progresses. On this note, Heller-Nicholas indicates Dawn embraces her teeth at the film's conclusion.[73] And indeed, she does.

But because the teeth are part of Dawn's self, Dawn's embrace at the end is an acceptance of her own sexuality. *Teeth*, I assert, is an extended metaphor for the process of puberty and sexual awakening. From her beginnings in the early parts of the film, as a young woman committed to abstinence to her ability to enjoy (guiltlessly) her sexuality with Ryan (until he reveals his true nature), Dawn gradually comes to terms with her teeth and sexual identity as the film progresses. These two facets of Dawn's self, teeth and sexuality, are inseparable.

And Dawn's acceptance of one correlates with her acceptance of the other because of their inextricable link. As Dawn gains the confidence to embrace rather than suppress her libido, so too does she gain the confidence to wield her teeth as a weapon instead of treating them as an unwanted side effect of her biology. On this topic, the reader may recall their own experience with puberty and sexual awakening, the initial rejection of the uncomfortable bodily changes entailed therein, as well as their eventual acceptance or even enthusiastic embrace of them. Dawn, as I have written, follows the same trajectory, the same story beats.

That is, she comes to terms with her identity as a sexual being as well as with her sexual desire. Instead of rejecting such desire as she does with Tobey, she

---

[72] Heller-Nicholas. 2nd edition. 58.
[73] Ibid.

accepts this desire with Ryan, and even after chomping his penis off, she seems no longer afraid of her sexuality. We see this transformation in her when she subsequently begins to use her atypical anatomy as a weapon with which to punish others. Whereas Dawn's initial revenge against her various assailants is unconscious, the teeth reacting without Dawn's intentional input, Dawn's revenge against Brad is premeditated.

Before seducing Brad, Dawn dons makeup; and during the act, she insists on having Brad penetrate her vaginally instead of anally, as is his wont with his girlfriend.[74] Her intentions are clear: she coaxes Brad into penetrating her so she can use her vagina dentata against him, sending his penis to join the likewise severed appendages of the other men who abused her. On a similar note, she appears to consciously choose to use her teeth against the old man at the end of the film. While we do not witness her using the teeth, the implication is unmistakable. And, pivotally, this scene shows Dawn choosing to use her teeth before commencing a sexual act; the teeth, ergo, are now an appendage she can choose to flex. Just as the process of growing up entails gradually learning how to consciously control the various parts of one's body, Dawn's sexual awakening includes her learning how to use her vagina dentata.

In thus choosing to use her vagina dentata as a weapon against male sexual aggression and abuse, Dawn is, as Heller-Nicholas argues, accepting her role abilities.[75] What is more, like the many rape-revenge heroines before her, Dawn is embracing a role as a punisher of sexual violence. This acceptance, however, is not quite as Heller-Nicholas describes it. She writes: "...*Teeth* finishes with a look toward the audience. Here, however, the intent is comical..."[76] Only this, the film's final scene, has Dawn looking toward the audience twice, first when she attempts to open the passenger side door the old man has locked, and second when she turns toward the man, accepting that she must hurt him to gain her freedom.

And, circling back now to Heller-Nicholas's reading of this scene, I can see the comic elements. Dawn tries the door several times, not out of desperation or fear so much as exasperation. But this scene moves from comedic to serious, a tonal shift emblematic of the film's thematic mixing of these two generic elements: comedy and horror; comedy then horror. Nevertheless, the scene ends on a serious note. As Dawn casts her eyes back over her shoulder, her turn is slow, her look seductive, and the implications grim. Still, one can hardly feel any pang of sympathy for the lecherous driver, who kidnaps a young woman

---

[74] An earlier scene in the film shows Brad's girlfriend arguing with him about how he always wants to penetrate her anus rather than her vagina.

[75] Heller-Nicholas. 2nd edition. 58.

[76] Ibid.

and pressures her into sex. The man is a rapist, and by the law of rape-revenge texts, he has sealed his fate. We might note, however, that most of the male characters in *Teeth* fit this mold. Like *Ms.45* before it, *Teeth* is a critique of rape culture. That is, Thana (the eponymous *Ms.45*)[77] and Dawn find themselves in a world rife with sexual violence, whereby they find themselves assailed from every side, from every man in their respective stories.

In fact, the only man in Dawn's life who does not abuse her is her step-father, who, to his credit, seems genuinely caring and trustworthy.[78] Nevertheless, nearly every other man Dawn encounters is over-sexed, crude, or sexually abusive. Rather than find a safe haven, then, as she tries to do with Ryan, Dawn has to create her own haven—carve it, with gritted teeth—right out of the rape culture around her. That rape culture, moreover, is a source of comedy in *Teeth*, where it becomes a target for mockery. Perhaps the funniest scene of the film is one of the most gruesome: the gynecologist scene.

When Dawn's vagina dentata snap down on the doctor's fingers, he begins thrashing. As he tries to pull his hand free, he jerks from side to side, pulling Dawn along with him. Here, Dawn's genitals resemble a pit bull clamping down on the doctor's arm, moving with it as he struggles. Furthermore, the doctor invokes vagina dentata by name, dramatically shouting about them. Between the struggles, his flinging Dawn around on the table, and his shouts, the scene becomes comedic even as it treats rather gruesome material, that of a doctor sexually abusing his underage patient.

That the film does evoke comedy is indubitable; Dawn's reaction to accidentally castrating Ryan is humorous, as is Brad's crying request for his dog, the Oedipally named Mother, to attack Dawn instead of eating his severed penis. The dog chooses the latter. Thus, the target of *Teeth*'s satirical bent is rape culture and men who abuse women; the jokes do not come at the rape victim's expense.[79] Perhaps the film's most grotesque joke comes at Brad's expense.

In naming his dog "Mother," Brad not only signals his Oedipal desires (possibly resulting from losing his mother while young) but also his fear of women. As aforementioned, Brad seems loathe to engage in vaginal intercourse, and because the movie begins with Dawn's vagina dentata cutting his finger, we can infer his fear comes from his experience with Dawn. His

---

[77] *Ms.45* is a 1981 rape-revenge film directed by Abel Ferrara and starring Zoë Lund as protagonist Thana.

[78] Her friend's boyfriend also comes out of the film unscathed, but his role in the narrative is minor, and he spends little to no time alone with Dawn.

[79] Heller-Nicholas observes that rape jokes become more socially acceptable when they target abusers rather than the abused (2nd edition 55).

resulting trepidation leads to his sexual difficulties. He can only perform anal sex, and he treats sex as a one-way transaction, focusing on his own pleasure. Essentially, though, Brad's sexual difficulties also stem from his quasi-incestuous love of Dawn. I write "quasi" before "incestuous" because he and Dawn share no blood relation.

Yet, because they have grown up together, one would expect the Westermarck effect to take root, and one would expect society to frown upon any romantic or sexual relations between Dawn and Brad.[80] Brad himself has internalized this view, as he blames his father for making Dawn his "sister," thus precluding Brad from pursuing her.[81] The self-loathing and internal conflict growing out of his feeling may, therefore, explain some of Brad's behavior, including his choice to name his dog "Mother."

In bestowing this name, Brad attempts to gain control of his sexual anxieties. As a dog, Mother spends most of her time locked in a cage. When she leaves the cage, Brad gives her commands. In other words, he exercises power and control over his "Mother," thereby easing his fears since he is the one in charge of this relationship. Moreover, this mother is the castrating mother Creed describes in *The Monstrous-Feminine*. Creed astutely observes that infants fear their mothers swallowing their identities.[82] That is, ego formation occurs early in the infant's maturation process, wherein they first recognize a being, their mother, as separate from themselves. The mother, as the source of life, becomes an object of fear because of the threat that she might also be capable of taking life. The Other, therefore, embodied first in the infant's mother, represents the threat of disintegrating one's self. In film, folklore, and psychoanalysis, according to Creed, these fears manifest in the figure of the castrating mother.[83]

Connectedly, the myth of the vagina dentata concerns the threats of women as castrating and of women as duplicitous (giving life and death, or giving pleasure and pain).[84] Given the presence of teeth, Creed notes, the dentata-laden vagina evokes comparisons with the mouth.[85] And in *Teeth*, a Mother's mouth features prominently in one scene, when Brad's dog fulfills his fears by turning the mother figure into a castrator. One should note, too, that this

---

[80] The Westermarck effect is the phenomenon whereby people who grow up together tend to lack sexual attraction to one another. Jonathan H. Turner and Alexandra Maryanski, *Incest: Origins of the Taboo*. (Boulder, Colo.: Paradigm, 2005), 163 & 168.

[81] *Teeth*.

[82] Creed. *The Monstrous-Feminine*. 109.

[83] See Creed *The Monstrous-Feminine* Chapter 8, including page 109. See also pages 9, 14, and 23.

[84] Creed. *The Monstrous-Feminine*. 106-107.

[85] Ibid.

turning of Brad's Mother against him comes on the heels of Brad's other greatest fear coming true, his experience of vaginal penetration resulting in his castration. Brad's fears of women, the same fears he tried so desperately to control, prove well-founded, his pretenses of power baseless. So, the film suggests Brad is all bravado.

He fears the vagina, the threat of castration, the idea of women having power over him. And he fears the last of these because Dawn already has power over him when the film begins. Even as a child, she demonstrated her power, albeit unconsciously, when her teeth bit Brad's finger. As a young adult, she has unwitting power in her hold on his mind. This is a power she does not want, mind you, but understanding how Brad's psyche becomes so warped helps us understand the mindset of the abuser. To be clear, none of this discussion is to blame Dawn for anything or to exculpate Brad for any of his actions. Dawn emerges with her morality intact; by contrast, Brad's morality starts the film in tatters and only degrades as it continues. His misogyny and abuse come from a place of fear, revealing his insecurities.

On another note, *Teeth* differs from stories like *I Spit*, which, as I have noted, phallicize their heroines during their revenge. In contrast to the texts from chapter one, though, *Teeth* never phallicizes Dawn, whose weapons, her vagina dentata, remain decidedly feminine, decidedly yonic. Rather than stabbing (i.e., penetrating), Dawn's vagina dentata appear to slice. Their cutting action is of two halves coming together into a whole. Thus, as Dawn's teeth close, they bring her vagina lips together, reminding her of her wholeness, her unity of self.[86]

And so *Teeth* is one of the least problematic films I have discussed in this volume. By finding humor in criticizing rape culture, and by placing the source of power in the decidedly feminine, *Teeth* avoids pitfalls common to rape-revenge stories. None of this is to assert, however, that *Teeth* is unproblematic. Dawn's future is, after all, uncertain. While she has embraced her vagina dentata, she lacks prospects, stability, or a support structure. Even though Dawn is powerful herself, she is still human, still a social animal. Only now, far from her home (or what remains of it), Dawn is alone. And cutting a swath of severed phalluses through the rape culture around her will lead to little long-term happiness, one might surmise. And here, it is tempting for one to blame her vagina dentata for her desolation. Except, it is not really her dentata that leave her there; it is her puberty and the rape culture around her.

Dawn ends the film alone, but upon close examination, we see she basically starts the film alone too. At the beginning of the movie, after the flashback,

---

[86] Luce Irigaray, *This Sex Which Is Not One.* (Ithaca, NY: Cornell UP, 1985), 24.

Dawn has an ailing mother, a supportive stepfather, an abusive and obnoxious step-brother, and only three friends at school. As the film progresses, her mother dies because of her brother's neglect, her brother reveals he has incestuous feelings for her, and one of her three friends rapes her. So, Dawn's support structure is rickety at the film's beginning and collapses as the plot continues. That she ends up alone may be unfortunate, but it is also unsurprising. Moreover, her dentata are not really at fault. They did not make her a social outcast, did not make her mother sick or deceased, did not make Brad a monster, and did not make Tobey rape her.

All of these events could occur independently of Dawn's teeth, which, instead of causing these problems, give Dawn a defense against some of them. The teeth, ergo, are a net benefit for Dawn, even though their positive impact can be hard to discern. Still, since it is so difficult to identify that Dawn's teeth are not really the problem, so difficult that insightful critics have mistaken them for the film's monster, *Teeth*'s problematic nature stems, in part, from its indirectness. It would, perhaps, be better suited if it were to make its point clearer or find greater happiness for Dawn. If the teeth could rescue her rather than merely shield her, it might be more obvious that Dawn's teeth benefit her overall.

Whereas some films eschew explicit depictions, *Teeth* contains numerous shots of severed penises, including one where a crab eats Tobey's severed sex, one where a close shot shows Ryan's crotch squirting blood, and one where a dog eats Brad's penis. Certainly, such gruesome details are bound to alienate some audience members. And yet, *Teeth*'s mixture of comedy with its graphic horror may redeem it in some viewer's eyes. Given *Teeth*'s relatively unproblematic nature (emphasis on "relatively"), it may, therefore, be a good introduction to this often graphic type of fiction.

Section Two: Pleasures of Disgust in Teeth

Now that we have discussed *Teeth* at length, let us consider the (pleasurable) roles of disgust in the film. To do this, I am going to consider each of the 8 pleasures of disgust I have enumerated, in the order I identified them in this chapter. I begin, however, with a disclaimer: *Teeth* does not evoke all 8 pleasures to equal degrees.

The case for catharsis in *Teeth* is relatively straightforward. If catharsis theory holds, the movie's narrative allows audiences to cast off the film's disgusting stimuli and thereafter feel cathartic release. Similarly, after the disgusting scenes are finished, the audience should feel relief pleasure, being glad the disgusting visuals are no longer on screen. Likewise, *Teeth*'s ability to offer masochistic maturity rites is clear-cut. Not only does the film follow a character through emergent adulthood, but it also offers a challenge to audiences, asking whether viewers can stomach images of, e.g., severed penises. Of course, this type of imagery is particularly applicable to young male audience members, who may well imagine their own castration when viewing the fictional castrations on screen.

And so the role of embodiment in *Teeth* also becomes clear. When the film repeatedly offers disgusting imagery of severed penises, it pushes audiences to become aware of their own bodies as they experience feelings of revulsion. While the phallic images may have a particularly strong effect on male audience members, *Teeth* still has a strong appeal for female audience members, given how the narrative follows a young woman coming to terms with her own body and sexuality. Ergo, one would expect *Teeth*'s narrative to offer intense bodily experiences for many (or even most) audience members.

Meanwhile, the film's cognitive pleasures of disgust lie partially in the identity negotiation of following Dawn along her journey, moving as she does from weakness to strength. This journey arms Dawn against rape culture and sees the film's despicable characters suffer at her, err, teeth. That this journey disgusts is obvious from the nature it takes: Dawn moves from rape survivor and unwitting castrator to willing castrator. At each step of her journey, then, lies extreme violence aimed at physically and culturally sensitive parts of the body (the genitals). For me, the cognitive pleasures of this film go further in the movie's analytical possibilities. Discussing the movie this way has been, for me, far more enjoyable than the initial viewing experience. Thus, in mentally grappling with the revolting object, I have been able to derive increased and sustained pleasure from it.

That cognitive pleasure has grown because I have been able to repeatedly engage with this sort of material, meaning the pleasure of ritualistic repetition is reinforcing the cognitive pleasure. Within *Teeth* itself, however, the pleasure of ritualistic repetition lies in the familiar story beats of escalating violence. For the viewer, the punishments Dawn's vagina dentata visit on the reprehensible people in Dawn's life become rewarding.

Unless we have advanced knowledge of the film's story, the first bite against Tobey comes as a surprise. But we can anticipate the bite coming for Brad. We can, therefore, anticipate the violence[87] as the narrative's ritual has established itself in our minds through the story's repetition. We know ahead of time that Brad is about to receive his comeuppance, experience some bit of karma for all his abusive and immoral behavior. Focusing on this element of retribution, we can also discern where disgust connects to survival theory in this film.

---

[87] It is important to note here that anticipation is often key to pleasure.

There is a clear anti-rape message running throughout *Teeth*, as we see one sexual abuser after another suffer gross (though well-deserved) punishment.[88] Then again, what lessons do Dawn and female viewers learn? That rape culture is pervasive? This does, in fact, seem an important lesson, one which gives pleasure to viewers who thereby feel at least somewhat better armed to navigate societal dangers around them. Given its focus on societal dangers, it is clear *Teeth* appeals to the social pleasures of disgust, allowing audiences to bond not only over the shared experience of disgust but also over the film's feminist messaging.[89]

Perhaps, however, *Teeth*'s strongest evocation of disgust's pleasures lies in the carnivalesque. After all, *Teeth* is a horror-comedy, and it is clear from the film's staging and story that it is supposed to be funny. For me, the funniest scene is the one at the gynecologist's office, where Dawn's vagina dentata latch onto the lecherous doctor's fingers. Again, the arrangement here makes it obvious the movie is supposed to be humorous. As evidence of this assertion, I point to a few factors. First, the doctor screams about vagina dentata being real when Dawn's unusual teeth bite him. Something tells me the odds of even a gynecologist being familiar with the legend of vagina dentata are unlikely. Here, humor derives from coincidence.

Second, when the doctor attempts to extract his hand from Dawn's vagina, he begins thrashing from pain and desperation. In doing so, he pulls Dawn along with him. Even understanding this scene's context, including the doctor's decision to sexually abuse a naïve Dawn, I still found myself laughing at the sheer absurdity of it. Thus, this scene from *Teeth* combines coincidence and absurdity to create humor in a work addressing extremely serious subjects, including familial sexual abuse, sexual harassment, rape culture, and rape itself.

Earlier in this volume, I discussed *Bound to Vengeance* at length and argued it falls short as an anti-rape narrative because it treats its heroine, Eve, as if her efforts to save fellow rape victims and punish her rapists are comical. And yet, in this chapter, I have argued one of *Teeth*'s strengths lies in its humor. So, what

---

[88] I consider this one the weaker pleasures of disgust *Teeth* offers.

[89] Unfortunately for my purposes here, I watched *Teeth* alone and so cannot comment on the social experience of watching this film. Indeed, this has been a hurdle for my work on rape-revenge films. Not only do many of my friends and loved ones dislike horror movies, but anyone with a distaste for horror is almost certain to avoid movies like *I Spit on Your Grave* since they tend to be especially graphic. Accordingly, I have found myself watching most these movies alone, which makes it somewhat harder for me to discuss the social pleasures these films offer. Future research could, therefore, build on this shortcoming of my analysis by specifically arranging or attending group viewings of these movies.

differentiates these two films? Crucially, *Teeth*'s humor does not typically come at the protagonist's expense. In the gynecologist scene, for example, the humor comes at the doctor's expense.

At this point, one might object to my argument by pointing out how the teeth inconvenience Dawn, thus meaning humor does actually come at her expense. This is a fair objection to raise, but I do not agree with its conclusion. In the gynecologist scene, the doctor pulls Dawn along as he tries to get his hand away to safety. Does this not make Dawn something like the punchline? I do not think it does, as Dawn is the powerful figure in this scene. Her teeth (albeit her vaginal teeth she is only beginning to learn about) are strong enough to sever multiple fingers and to hold onto a grown man's hand as he tries to retract it. As I mentioned earlier, Dawn's teeth resemble the tenacious grasp of a pit bull, a symbol of power.

Let us consider another scene, then. When Dawn's teeth trigger against Ryan, her exasperated reaction has the potential to elicit a chuckle from the audience. Once again, it can be tempting to read this scene as one in which Dawn becomes the punchline. Her teeth have frustrated her, of course. But such a reading of this scene overlooks how, while Dawn may be annoyed, Ryan is bleeding profusely from castration. Again, the film's comedy casts Dawn as the powerful one. Her annoyance comes in response to her own abilities, abilities that make her dangerous to men like Ryan, who treats her as an object and disrespect her personhood.

We can see, therefore, how *Teeth* treats rape culture as a punchline, its protagonist as powerful. Now, the film does, as I have noted, leave Dawn bereft of friends and a social support network at the movie's conclusion. But the fact remains that the movie's humor does not come at Dawn's expense, making *Teeth* a remarkably carnivalesque film among the rape-revenge sub-genre of horror. *Teeth* invites the audience to laugh at Dawn's assailants as they find themselves castrated and emasculated. It invites, therefore, play within the realm of disgusting rape-revenge imagery.

Chapter 5

Showing Without Becoming

Throughout this volume, we have repeatedly engaged with the question of how a work of fiction can adequately convey what a horrifying and grotesque crime rape is without simultaneously alienating audiences via graphic violence and without running the risk of titillating the sexually sadistic. This is, perhaps, one of the key issues dogging the rape-revenge sub-genre, and it has provided this volume with much of its organization and exigence. Having now established the issue as I conceive it, I want to consider a possible path forward for the rape-revenge narrative.

To that end, in this chapter, I first engage with the question of whether it is possible to portray an action in film without (at least tacitly) endorsing said action. To explore this question and argue, yes, it is possible (but very difficult) to do so, I briefly turn away from rape-revenge fiction to examine the anti-war film *Come and See* (1985, directed by Elem Klimov). Once I have established *Come and See*'s ability to portray war without ever glamorizing it, I turn to the 2017 Belgian rape-revenge film *Revenge* (directed by Coralie Fargeat), which I see as the most successful anti-rape film I examine in this volume. And, to further highlight *Revenge*'s capacity as an anti-rape film, I contrast it with another European rape-revenge film, the French *Irréversible* (2002), which, I argue, is far more problematic.

Scholars have long recognized the issue of how to represent violence while glorifying it. Prince suggests that the very medium of film subverts anti-violence goals.[1] Projansky notes there is a paradox of how to have an anti-message in a fictional work without eliciting pleasure from the thing the text is supposed to be against.[2] And, of course, scholars have specifically aimed this sort of criticism at rape-revenge films. On the related topic of fictional femicide in literature, Meyers observes the problem such texts face when they try to discuss femicide without "essentializing women as victims."[3] Projansky casts the paradox as a tension between the desire to end rape and the need to

---

[1] Prince 29.

[2] Projansky 96.

[3] Helene Meyers, *Femicidal Fears: Narratives of the Female Gothic Experience.* (SUNY Press, 2001), 1.

represent it.[4] Fredriksson picks up on this same issue as she points out that rape revenge has received criticism for perpetuating what it wants to change.[5] Finally, Dyer observes: "Serial killer fictions condemn the slaughter of women, of course, but they also provide opportunities for misogyny."[6] And yet, Derrida argues it is possible to participate in a genre without belonging to it.[7]

So the question becomes: how does one show horrible violence without endorsing said violence? The key, I think, lies in a prescient remark from Prince, who suggests it may be best to critique violence in its absence.[8] I understand this comment may seem counterintuitive, given how I have argued it is necessary to show rape in order to critique it. To be sure, I think absence may be necessary but that it is also insufficient. To see this equation operate outside of rape-revenge, I turn now to *Come and See*.

Come and See is a Belarusian/Soviet anti-war film that follows the tribulations of young Flyora as he joins a band of Soviet partisans to fight against the invading Nazis during World War II. After unearthing a rifle from a mass grave of fallen Soviet fighters, Flyora joins a group of local partisans, only to find himself relegated to non-combat tasks. When the bulk of the partisans move out to fight the Nazis, they leave Flyora behind, much to his chagrin. He does, however, befriend another partisan, a young girl about his age named Glasha. But the Nazis soon attack and destroy the camp, forcing Flyora and Glasha to flee into the wilderness.

Eventually, they find their way back to Flyora's village only to discover the Nazis have murdered most of its inhabitants, including Flyora's family. Flyora and Glasha meet up with the survivors, though, and Flyora agrees to search for supplies to sustain the refugees. That foray sees the Nazis kill Flyora's companions (Glasha remained with the survivors from his village). And Flyora himself almost dies when he encounters an SS group exterminating another village. Flyora narrowly escapes burning to death when the Nazis corral many of the villagers into a barn and set it ablaze. Shortly thereafter, he reencounters his partisan group, who have ambushed and slaughtered the SS. Here, Flyora fires his rifle, for the first time in the film, at a photograph of Hitler lying in a puddle. Envisioning Hitler as an infant on his mother's lap, Flyora stops shooting and rejoins the partisans on their renewed march.

---

[4] Projansky 19.

[5] Fredriksson 61.

[6] Dyer. *Only Entertainment*. 74.

[7] Jacques Derrida and Avital Ronell, "The Law of Genre," *Critical Inquiry* 7, no. 1 (1980): 65.

[8] Prince 32.

I have chosen to include *Come and See* in this volume because it is one of the very, very few war movies recognized as being distinctly anti-war.[9] When first watching *Come and See*, I was impressed with how it never glamorizes World War II. Not once was the action in *Come and See* exciting. Indeed, *Come and See* portrays World War II as horrific from opening to conclusion. Such is the movie's ignominious depiction of war that some have classified *Come and See* as a horror movie, noting its remarkably disturbing perspective on warfare, which sets it apart from most mainstream war films.[10]

Here, Prince's idea of critiquing violence via its absence comes back into play.[11] As I made sure to note in my summary, Flyora does not fire his rifle until the end of the film. Even then, he fires at a photo, an inert target. Flyora, then, offers the viewer a subjugated, vulnerable position of identification. Flyora is a far cry from the typical war film protagonist; he is no action movie hero. Thus, in *Come and See*, war is inglorious, war is suffering, war is hell (as the movie's title, a crib from *Revelation*, attests).

Not only does Flyora never get to become a hero of the Soviet Union by gunning down waves of invading Nazis (or, for that matter, even one invading Nazi), but most of the film's violence occurs off-screen. We see the aftermath of the partisans' attack on the SS, but not its occurrence. When violence does appear on screen (such as when the partisans gun down the final SS survivors), it is quick and brutal. *Come and See*, therefore, meshes with Annette Hill's observation: "Real violence is raw and brutal and not entertaining."[12]

Thus, by keeping the bulk of its violence off-screen and by making the on-screen violence quick and de-glamorized, *Come and See* avoids the common pitfall whereby violent films make violence appealing to the viewer.[13] *Come and See* was the first movie to convince me it was, in fact, possible to portray war on film without making it look fun or exciting. The question remains, however, as to whether any rape-revenge film has managed to achieve for rape-revenge

---

[9] Matthew Mosley, "How 'Come and See' Avoids the Inherent Problem With Anti-War Films," Collider, 2022, https://collider.com/come-and-see-avoids-problems-with-anti-war-films/.

[10] Pat Fox, "The Most Terrifying Film of All Time...*Come and See*," Film Hounds, 2022, https://filmhounds.co.uk/2022/06/the-most-terrifying-film-of-all-time-come-and-see/.

[11] Prince 32.

[12] Annette Hill, *Shocking Entertainment: Viewer Response to Violent Movies*. (Luton, Bedfordshire, U.K.: U of Luton, 1997), 107.

[13] Modern action movies are particularly prone to making violence appealing. The action, revenge film *John Wick*, for example, features intricately choreographed fight scenes as its main appeal. Unlike in *John Wick*, the violence in *Come and See* is never played for spectacle but, rather, for horror. Thus, framing is essential here.

what *Come and See* has for war movies. To this question, I suggest one movie has at least come close. We turn, then, to *Revenge*.

Promotional materials for *Revenge* laud its feminist credentials.[14] And I do think it is critical that *Revenge* has a female director. Of course, Fargeat's mere presence does not a feminist film make.[15] For that, we need to turn to the text of the film itself.

Revenge (2017) relates the story of Jennifer/Jen (Matilda Lutz), who enjoys a brief vacation at her wealthy boyfriend's holiday estate. The English-language Belgian film takes a turn, however, when the boyfriend Richard's friends, Stan and Dimitri, arrive early for the trio's planned hunting trip. When Richard leaves the estate the next morning to run some errands, Stan takes advantage of the opportunity and rapes Jen after she becomes uncomfortable with his advances. Richard arrives back at the estate, where Stan admits his actions. Because Jen is the married Richard's mistress, Richard tries to buy her off, offering her a job in Canada as well as a money transfer to her bank account. Jen declines, however, as she is only interested in going back home. Richard refuses to call the helicopter for her, however, fearing she will disclose his infidelity to his wife. In a rage, he strikes Jen, who promptly flees. So a chase ensues, with the three men cornering her against a tall cliff in the desert mountains surrounding Richard's vacation home.

Richard feigns calling a helicopter for Jen and then shoves her off the cliff, where she lands, impaled, upon a tree. The men leave her for dead, but Jen revives and manages to crawl away in the nick of time. Experienced hunters, the three men set out to track down and finish the badly injured Jennifer. When she encounters Dimitri, however, she wrests his knife from him and stabs him to death, thus turning the tables against the men. From there, she arms herself with Dimitri's hunting gear, including his shotgun, mends her wound, and begins hunting the other two men. She kills Stan during a showdown in the mountains, and the film climaxes with Jen killing Richard in the vacation home after an extended game of cat-and-mouse. The film ends with a victorious Jen, covered in blood, waiting outside as the helicopter approaches.

On the surface, then, *Revenge* resembles the typical rape-revenge film. And yet, its plot synopsis does it little justice here, for *Revenge*, I argue, is one of the most successful rape-revenge films to date. Throughout this volume, I have focused on two primary problems facing the rape-revenge narrative: the

---

[14] "Revenge." Shudder. https://www.shudder.com/movies/watch/revenge/2cef63838 af05b94. Accessed December 13, 2021.

[15] *Revenge* does, however, fit Citron, et al's observation that feminist filmmakers have been trying to change how women are filmed (117).

disgust sexual violence evokes and films taking sadistic pleasure in their heroine's struggles. *Revenge*, however, largely sidesteps both of these issues. While the film is very sexual and features an early scene of Jen performing fellatio on Richard, that scene is filmed from the back such that we see Richard's buttocks but not his penis. His penis, however, receives prolonged screentime later in the film during his and Jen's final showdown, the entire duration of which he spends naked. Jen, by contrast, has less on-screen nudity than Richard does.

Her actress, Matilda Lutz, does show her breasts once, but only in a very quick, voyeuristic scene in which Stan peeps at her from the cracked bedroom door. The duration of her nudity emblemizes the situation under which it occurs. Because Stan has already creeped out Jen and because he is now spying on her dressing (and because the audience probably knows it is watching a rape-revenge film and that the rape is impending), the scene is more suspenseful than titillating. And the rape scene itself consists almost entirely of the lead-up, glossing over depicting the act. Stan gets increasingly aggressive toward Jen until he shoves her against the window and puts his hand down her underwear. From there, he spins her around. And then, the camera cuts to Dimitri in the other room. We hear Jen screaming, but Dimitri turns up the television's volume, drowning those sounds out.

Thus, as an audience, we do not see the actual rape occur even as we witness the sexual battery leading up to the actual assault. And we do not hear much of the rape either. Fargeat, therefore, spares the audience from the more grotesque aspects of sexual assault. And yet, unlike with *Bound*, there is enough material in *Revenge* for the audience to grow repulsed but, perhaps, not enough to alienate audiences. Certainly, I found the experience of watching *Revenge* noticeably easier than the experience of watching *I Spit on Your Grave*, 1978 or 2010, or *Irréversible*. As far as rape-revenge films go, *Revenge*'s portrayal of sexual violence is at once graphic but digestible. That is to say, *Revenge* has the confidence to put sexual violence on screen but the restraint to strategically cut away. And, thus, it finds a sort of middle ground between the extremes of *I Spit* and *Bound*.

Revenge, therefore, balances its evocation of disgust. Whereas *I Spit on Your Grave* and its ilk provide prolonged rape scenes that foreground the horror of sexual violence, and whereas other films leave sexual violence as sub-text (*Alone*) or move it off-screen (*Bound to Vengeance*), *Revenge* does a bit of both. It shows the lead-up to the assault but then moves the camera such that the actual assault plays out off-screen. Jen's screams, however, leave the audience with no doubt. Here, *Revenge* actually offers an interesting intervention into the existing scholarship of disgust, as Kolnai questions whether sound can even be disgusting.[16] Kolnai, I guess, had never heard of misophonia, the strong adverse reaction some people have to the sounds of other people eating. Sound can, therefore, be disgusting, and Fargeat takes full advantage of sound's capacity for disgust in *Revenge*.

Kolnai further holds that sound lacks the immediacy of either senses, even though sound actually possesses a powerful immediacy whereby it seems to force itself upon us.[17] In this volume's early chapters, we saw how the *I Spit* films attempt to de-eroticize sexual violence by foregrounding it. Does *Revenge's* decision to leave Stan's rape of Jen off-screen not, therefore, run the risk of titillating the audience? I would argue it does not for two reasons. First, because we hear Jen's screams. And, second, because we hear her screams in sequence right after seeing the violence of Stan's impending assault on her. On this topic, Hanich argues it is particularly immersive when a horror film plays to both imagination and perception.[18]

Thus, one of Fargeat's major successes with *Revenge* comes from her ingenious decision to show just enough of the assault to spark the audience's imagination and to then move the assault to the domain of sound to avoid the risk of titillation. Hanich argues here that suggested horror pushes back on the notion of the film viewer as a voyeur.[19] The rape scene in *Revenge* is particularly effective because it does not let the audience fetishize it by showing the sexual violence on screen, because it uses visuals to spark the imagination and then sound to sustain it,[20] and because its use of sound to maintain the audience's sense of disgust makes the disgust difficult to escape.[21] *Revenge's* ability to spark the audience's imagination differentiates it from *Bound to Vengeance*, whose brief glimpses of a rape scene do not convey the same sense of visceral horror and pain that Stan's rape of Jen does.

This middle ground, moreover, allows *Revenge* to bestow its heroine with a remarkable degree of unproblematic power. Earlier, I wrote *Revenge* shows Richard nude more often than it shows Jen nude. This is true, but it does not account for how the film frequently sexualizes Jen. Indeed, the film's first shot has her suggestively sucking on a lollipop, foreshadowing the fellatio she will perform on Richard mere minutes of screentime later. Furthermore, after that shot, the camera spends inordinate amounts of time following Jen's butt, particularly whenever she walks. In these (numerous) tracking shots, she is

---

[16] Kolnai. "Modes of Aversions". 102.
[17] Kolnai. "On Disgust". 48.
[18] Hanich. *Cinematic Emotion*. 115.
[19] Ibid. 110.
[20] Ibid. 111.
[21] Ibid. 115.

almost always wearing bikini bottoms or panties, showing skin. And the camera lingers on her rear end as she walks, her hips swaying as she does so. These shots are inarguably erotic and meant to titillate.

They are also obvious examples of the male gaze in cinema. In case there was any confusion on this point, *Revenge* is sure to cut from the camera's focus on Jen's body, particularly her rear, to Stan, thus equating the camera's gaze with that of a male sexual predator. The implication is transparent, and it meshes well with scholarly assertions that the camera embodies the male gaze.[22] And were the film to stop here, the implications would be a bit troubling, and the camera would remain equated with the male gaze. Whenever on screen, then, Jen would be sexualized and objectified, if only implicitly. But *Revenge* does not stop here, and, in fact, it challenges the male gaze by, paradoxically, frequently using said gaze.

After Jen emerges from the cave where she cauterized her wound, she stands at the top of a mountain, surveying the land below her. Her elevation denotes her strength relative to Stan and Richard, who have become her prey. More interestingly, though, despite Jen's power, the camera continues to hold the male gaze. When it films Jen, it still lingers on her butt. The camera, then, still sexualizes her. And yet, the scenes after Richard pushes Jen off a cliff are decidedly unerotic. Drenched in blood and rife with violence, these scenes are frequently graphic, making *Revenge* seem almost a part of the French New Extremity movement.[23] Among these scenes, for example, is one where Jen performs improvised surgery on herself, slicing her flesh apart with Dimitri's hunting knife while the camera lingers in extended close-ups, sparing the audience none of the gory details.

That scene, specifically, is shockingly graphic and, moreover, representative of how *Revenge* cuts away from graphic shots of the sexual violence only to bring the graphic details back tenfold when it comes to physical violence and blood. On the topic of blood, we should note that Richard's extended nude scene at the film's ending, during which the actor is completely naked, making his genitals and butt visible, is also entirely unerotic, as Richard spends the scene in immense pain from his wounds (Jen having just shot him with a

---

[22] Laura Mulvey, "Visual Pleasure and Narrative Cinema." In *Film Theory & Criticism* 8th ed, edited by Leo Braudy and Marshall Cohen. (Oxford University Press, 2016), 624; Indeed, Barbara Creed writes in *Return of the Monstrous-Feminine* that *Revenge* critiques male voyeurism (57). And Fargeat notes how Jennifer moves from defining herself via the male gaze to needing to redefine herself (17).

[23] French New Extremity was a wave of hyper-graphic horror films released in France throughout the 2000s and 2010s. The films were notorious for their explicit violence and subject matter.

shotgun), and inadvertently painting his vacation home with his own blood. All this gore and all this violence desexualize the movie. More importantly, though, they de-eroticize the camera's male gaze.[24]

When Jen stands atop the mountain, and the camera lovingly moves over her body, the shot is noticeably less erotic than previous shots of her body were. Covered in dirt and now armed, Jen becomes less of a sexual object. Pivotally, Jen spends the rest of the film post-cave in her bra and panties. Her attire is sexualized, suggestive. Her demeanor, however, is not. Filmed in a high-angle shot, Jen hunts a wounded Stan on one of the mountains, her shotgun held before her as she scans for her wounded quarry.

This Jen is powerful and dangerous. And her dirt-covered skin is decidedly not sexualized and not appealing, nor is it designed to be. By continuing to film Jen via the male gaze, Fargeat ingeniously de-eroticizes the male gaze by increasingly distancing it from its sexual connotations. As she gets increasingly wounded, scarred, dirty, and bloody, Jen ceases to be a sexual object, becoming instead a symbol of womanly power foregrounded against the diminishing potency of her male counterparts.

That is, she becomes more threatening as they become less threatening. Nowhere, perhaps, is the group leader Richard's declining power more blatant than during the aforementioned showdown where he stands naked, ergo vulnerable and open to assault. The camera may continue to linger on Jen's body, but, as it does so, it gradually begins to thereby grant her agency, emphasizing her power and stature, her status as a hunter, rather than reducing her to an object. And because Fargeat never allows the film to stop leveling the male gaze at Jen, she, Fargeat, subtly undermines attempts to equate the camera's gaze with male power more broadly. Yes, the camera can be a tool to downplay Jen's personhood, but so too can it be a tool for reveling in her personhood. What is more, it can be a tool for exalting her body. Notably, unlike Jennifer Hills (Jen's likely namesake), Jen never feels the need to cover up or hide her body.

Of course, diegetically, Jen has no other clothes to do save, perhaps, for the men. Nevertheless, we can read the production team's decision to leave actress Matilda Lutz in a bra and panties for much of the film as a way of pushing back against any perceived need to hide the female body. Even after her assault, then, Jen remains in control of her body, so much so she manages to perform

---

[24] That the classical cinematic camera tends to have a masculine point of view is well-established in extant scholarship. Christine Gledhill observes that this perspective stems largely from psychoanalytic film theory (166).

surgery on herself. Her sexuality, then, is still hers, just as it was at the film's beginning, and no amount of sexualizing gaze can change that.

At this point, the reader may object that the decision to have the attractive Lutz wear such revealing clothing was merely a marketing decision, an attempt to exploit the actress's body for the movie's commercial benefit and the audience's enjoyment. Such an objection, however, will have to reckon with the bevy of non-sexual elements revolving around Jen's body in the film. As I have mentioned, the dirt, scars, and blood are far from erotic to most people, so it would be difficult to read this decision as an attempt to cash in on the actress's beauty, especially as earlier scenes in the film already did that when the film was first making the point of how the male gaze can view women.

In reading those scenes, though, we still need to be aware that Jen sexualizes herself just as much as the men do. Now, to be clear, this is in no way to victim blame Jen, who is undoubtedly the victim, the men the monsters. What I am asserting, conversely, is that Jen starts the film comfortable with her body and her sexuality. She has no compunctions about dancing suggestively or wearing revealing clothing. Such clothing and such behavior, moreover, in no way suggest her sexual openness, as we see when the film puts any reading to the contrary in the mouth of the wholly unsympathetic Stan, who becomes the film's punchline after becoming its rapist. In this way, then, the film pushes back against any attempt to victim blame. Jen is having fun and enjoying herself, as is her right. Any attempt to read her behavior as coquetry is a projection and representative of rape culture and male feelings of entitlement to the female body, entitlement, *Revenge* reminds us, no one actually has.

Stan, however, disrespects Jen's bodily autonomy and personhood. Not only does he rape Jen, but he rejects her right to have a "type," visibly chaffing at the implication he does not fit her standards and desires.[25] He also (perhaps willfully) misreads Jen's motivations in having him dance with her. Whereas Stan reads the dance as sexual teasing, the scene itself establishes Jen's desire to dance with Richard. Indeed, she seems to choose Stan partially to tease Richard after he declines her invitation to dance with her. Stan may notice this particular bit of context, however, chaffing, also, at his inferiority to the more dominant Richard. As in *I Spit*, then, rape in *Revenge* may hinge partially on male social dynamics, Stan's assault on Jen a manifestation of his annoyance with his subordinate status to Richard.

Revenge, however, depicts the rape in ways *I Spit* does not. In *I Spit*, the rapes, as I established in the previous chapters, are an exercise in male social structure formation. Conversely, in *Revenge*, the rape is an act of interpersonal violence.

---

[25] *Revenge*. Directed by Coralie Fargeat, performance by Matilda Lutz, Rézo Films, 2017.

And so *Revenge* offers a different view of sexual violence than *I Spit* does. Like *I Spit* and *Bound*, however, *Revenge* gives sexual violence an economic undertone. In the first, the wealthier Jennifer suffers sexual violence from comparatively impoverished men. In the second, Eve finds herself sexually trafficked (i.e., forcibly turned into an economic commodity for men to trade amongst themselves). *Revenge* offers a more complicated take on this subject, though, as it never reveals how wealthy Stan and Dimitri are. Given these two men visit Richard's vacation home for their hunting trip, and given Richard is the only one with a helicopter pilot on call, it seems Richard is the wealthiest character in *Revenge*. Regardless of the other hunters' financial standing, though, Jen seems the poorest character.

We see her relative impecunity first in her desire to move to Los Angeles to "get noticed" (i.e., find work).[26] And we see it again when Richard attempts to use Jen's financial position against her. After Stan rapes Jen, Richard offers her money and a job in Canada in exchange for her silence. In other words, Richard thinks his privileged position atop a generous sum of money can insulate him and his all-male in-group. He thinks he can throw money at his problems to make them disappear. When his suppositions prove faulty (i.e., when a distraught and angry Jen rejects his offer), he can only respond with brute force, striking Jen across the face and, minutes later, shoving her over a cliff. In refusing Richard's money, Jen (probably unknowingly) unsettles Richard's privileged worldview, a view reliant on the collective agreement that money has value.

As soon as Jen rejects this notion (even in the highly situational and extreme context of refusing to be paid off for not reporting her rapist), Richard must confront, if but for a moment, the truth: his power is not absolute but, rather, culturally conditional. If Jen can reject his money, can refuse to accept its value, then Richard is left bereft of his primary mode of power. All that is left to him is physical force, and so the façade of civility crumbles at the slightest hint of his impotency. Richard's bravado, then, relies on seeing his own self-view reflected in others.[27] At the heart of capitalistic wealth, *Revenge* hereby suggests, is the drive toward violence. The system itself is violent, a statement which resonates with *Bound*'s depiction of rape culture, in which women are reduced to a commodity.

Revenge reinforces this connection between capitalism and violence during the final fight between Richard and Jen, during which an advertisement plays

---

[26] Ibid.

[27] Molly Haskell, *From Reverence to Rape: The Treatment of Women in the Movies* 1st edition. (Holt, Rinehart and Winston, 1974), 1.

on Richard's television.[28] The connection between an advertisement (extant purely to sell goods in exchange for money) and Richard's materialism is self-evident, and the advertisement's position within the movie makes it a critique of said materialism. Likewise, the film uses the commercial to criticize Richard's treatment of women. During the commercial, two women appear on screen trying to sell the marketed product. The capitalist powers trying to sell the goods, then, use women as commodities to market those same goods. That connection of women to goods and money is a reflection of Richard's treatment of Jen, whereby he thought he could buy her. Of course, this assumption is mistaken, and Jen's erstwhile affection for Richard appears rooted not in Richard's material wealth but in himself. Were this not the case, the audience might expect Jen to accept the bribe Richard offers her.

Revenge, however, offers a more well-rounded and subtle take on these common issues than *Bound to Vengeance* does. Certainly, economic factors recur throughout rape-revenge texts, and the films I discuss in this chapter are not unique in featuring them. For example, *Even Lambs Have Teeth* (2015) sees its two female protagonists kidnapped and turned into sex slaves, much as Eve is in *Bound*. In both these films, the initial motivation behind sexual assault is economic rather than sexual, at least for the slavers. The rapists in both films appear to have more sexual motives. And so, sexual violence in these films can become overdetermined. Such a depiction of sexual violence is helpful because it helps us cultivate a robust understanding of the various causes leading to the crime of rape.

Moving on from this brief vignette on rape-revenge more generally, let us take a look at another aspect whereby *Revenge* distinguishes itself from its counterparts. Part of my criticism of *Bound* stemmed from its treatment of Eve, its use of her as a punchline. Interestingly, whereas *Revenge* avoids denigrating its heroine in this way, it is, nevertheless, funnier than *Bound*, in my estimation. Earlier, I asserted Stan becomes *Revenge*'s punchline and its rapist. His status as the film's source of comedy is easy to discern.

After Richard and Dimitri leave Stan alone in the car so they can track Jen down either side of the lake, the film enters a long-duration medium shot of Stan sitting in the car. The seatbelt light dings routinely, reminding Stan to don his seatbelt. As the ringing continues, Stan grows frustrated and clips his seatbelt in to stop the chime. While describing this anti-joke in prose likely robs it of its comedy, situationally, the humor works, and it injects a miniscule

---

[28] In making (and attacking) this connection, *Revenge* meshes well with Claire Johnston's assertion that films must create new meanings "by disrupting the fabric of the male bourgeoisie cinema within the text of the film" (37).

amount of levity into an otherwise tense, brutal film. The comic relief, however, is small indeed. But, notably, it follows Stan, who experiences an array of embarrassments after he rapes Jen. The morning after the seatbelt episode, Stan urinates on the lake shore before finding Dimitri's body, whereupon he falls into the water. Struggling onto the shore, soaked to the bone, he vomits in the sand.

Shortly thereafter, Richard breaks Stan's nose, and the shot lingers on Stan's pain and torment. Furthermore, after Stan and Richard split up to hunt Jen, Stan's car runs out of gas on the mountain, at which point Jen shoots him. Stan flees, wounded and squealing. And he dies shortly after this scene, in the climax of his confrontation with Jen. As this description should show, Stan suffers an unusual (though well-deserved) amount throughout the film, suffering one embarrassing setback or insult after another. Contrast him with Richard, who likewise loses his power and yet remains unreduced to the squealing, variously humiliated state in which Stan finds himself. The film, therefore, makes a joke of Stan's continued suffering, occasionally cultivating comedy in the process.

And unlike the comedy in *Bound*, based on Eve's dramatic struggles and failures, the comedy in *Revenge* always comes at the expense of the rapist rather than the rape survivor.[29] Thus, *Revenge* avoids another of *Bound*'s pitfalls. And in so incorporating humor, in such a way as to denigrate rapists, *Revenge* makes itself a more palatable film than *I Spit*. So far in my argument, then, *Revenge* comes across as a largely successful rape-revenge film, succeeding in cases where, I have argued, other films fail. But how does *Revenge* fare on the topics of agency and disgust, the topics of chapters one and three?

Revenge makes an interesting contribution to rape-revenge's record on female agency. Here, I observe how these films depict rape survivors transforming into avenging figures following their experience of sexual assault and/or (attempted) murder. Jennifer from *I Spit* follows this character arc, as does Eve, as does Jen. And we have followed each of these three arcs throughout my discussions of their respective movies. Jen's arc, however, adds an element the others' stories lack. As Heller-Nicholas observes, Jen seems vapid at the beginning of *Revenge*.[30] Early shots of her caricature her as shallow, materialistic, and ostentatiously sexualized. The film's first shot shows her riding in a helicopter, sucking a lollipop and wearing sunglasses. The lollipop and her manner of eating it sexualize her; her sunglasses code her as "cool."

---

[29] Heller-Nicholas. 2nd edition. 55.
[30] Ibid. 165.

The next night, she remarks to the men that she wants to move to Los Angeles and "get noticed."[31] When Stan asks her what she wants to get noticed for (e.g., modeling or acting), she responds simply: "...to get noticed."[32] Jen's circular response suggests attention is an end by itself. Consequently, her answer to Stan's fair question colors her insipid. The rest of the film's narrative, however, directly challenges this coloring, gradually revealing Jen's remarkable resilience and resourcefulness. Jen, therefore, problematizes binary interpretations of character.

Whereas some rape-revenge protagonists reveal their initial behaviors as ruses designed to trick their assailants or would-be assailants (see, for instance, *Deeper: The Retribution of Beth* for two different examples of this dynamic),[33] Jen never says anything to suggest her initial, more materialistic, behavior is dishonest, not part of true self and true personality. Because Jen never, by word or explicit action, disavows her earlier personality, the film suggests Jen is at once materialistic and capable. Though the viewer may, at the film's encouragement, dismiss Jen's abilities in the film's earliest moments, deciding instead she is an empty vessel, the film gradually reveals Jen's layers, throwing such judgments in a negative light.

That reading of Jen, moreover, appears to align with that of the male characters. As aforementioned, Stan dismisses Jen's personhood. Similarly, Richard looks down on her. Indeed, he literally looks down upon Jen after he knocks her to the floor and asks: "Who do you think you are?"[34] That he asks her this after Jen threatens to reveal Richard's affair to his wife unmasks his belief that he is superior to her. And that belief implies he lied when he told Jen he would leave his wife for her were it not for his children. Richard, it seems, sees Jen as a sexual object, a sort of plaything that is fun now but that he may discard later, whenever the luster wanes or she becomes inconvenient. Such a dehumanizing view easily explains his decision to shove her off the cliff, as well as the ease with which he offers to buy her silence.

That view, moreover, results from rape culture, whereby Richard, Stan, and Dimitri normalize sexual violence against women. Richard, for instance, tells Jen during their final fight that: "Women always have to put up a fucking fight."[35] Richard's admonishment equates to nothing less than victim blaming. His words suggest he believes the film's events are somehow Jen's fault, that if

---

[31] *Revenge.*

[32] Ibid.

[33] *Deeper: The Retribution of Beth* is a 2014 rape-revenge film directed by Jeffrey Andersen and starring Elise Gatien.

[34] *Revenge.*

[35] Ibid.

she had not teased Stan, if she had submitted to Richard's attempt to bribe her, if she had the decency to die after when he pushed her off the cliff, if she had given up fighting against him, then all would have been okay (for him, that is). Such is Richard's misogyny and immorality that he refuses to accept culpability for his own actions, which include attempted murder, aiding and abetting sexual assault, conspiracy to commit first-degree homicide, and knowingly being friends with a rapist.

We should observe as well that Richard blames Jen's beauty for causing Stan to rape her, as Richard tells Jen: "...but you're so damn beautiful it's hard to resist you."[36] Thus, Richard not only rejects all culpability for his own crimes; he tries to exonerate Stan for Stan's crimes. Richard's allegiance, then, as his generalization about "women" resisting suggests, is to other men.[37] Regardless, therefore, of what wrongs a man commits against a woman, rape culture pushes men to circle the wagons and protect each other from women, even when the men they are protecting are scumbag rapists. In *I Spit* (2010), rape culture manifests in the microcosm of rural Louisiana, where the sheriff, despite his own protestations about being exasperated with the other men, leaps to defend and even help the other men after they rape Jennifer. And in *Bound to Vengeance*, rape culture appears first and most obviously in the sheer number of men participating in sexual trafficking and raping women in Eve's city. It manifests secondly, and more implicitly, when Eve goes to rescue Lea.

When the two men enter the house to rape Lea, they carry fast food with them. Their approach to rape is so casual they brought a snack. That is to say, they approach rape with the casualness of rape culture. Dimitri from *Revenge* shows a similar casualness about rape. Though he sees Stan preparing to rape a crying Jen, Dimitri wordlessly continues eating a chocolate bar and closes the door, abandoning Jen.[38] Then he turns up the television to drown out Jen's screams and goes for a dip in the pool. For Dimitri and for the two men planning to rape Lea in *Bound*, rape is pedestrian, even quotidian. Their blasé attitudes about sexual violence contrast starkly with the women's abject terror, demonstrating they, the men, are inured to both. Rape culture, therefore, destroys these characters' capacity to empathize.

And on this count, *Revenge* offers a more nuanced take than either *Bound* or *I Spit* does. Earlier, I noted how Richard victim blames Jen. Richard's lack of empathy, however, encompasses the other men as well. Not only does Richard

---

[36] Ibid.

[37] Ibid.

[38] During this scene, Stan tells Dimitri to either join him in raping Jen or leave the room. Dimitri, who receives the least characterization of *Revenge*'s three antagonists, evidences little sexual desire in contrast to the lecherous Stan and libidinous Richard.

break Stan's nose, but, after Stan discovers Dimitri's waterlogged corpse, Richard dismisses Stan's despair and Dimitri's death alike. Regarding the latter, Richard merely says: "The desert is sublime but merciless with the careless."[39] But a few minutes have sufficed to let Richard conceive an alibi for Dimitri's demise: Dimitri went off hunting alone and never came back. Such is Richard's callousness even toward his (ostensible) friends.

For his part, however, Stan is no better. Indeed, in this same scene where they discover Dimitri's dead body, Stan blames Richard for Dimitri's death. Stan renders the situation thus: if Richard had not shoved Jen, they would not be out hunting her, and Dimitri would still be alive. Of course, in crafting this narrative of the film's events, Stan elides his own immutable role. In truth, if Stan had not raped Jen, then none of the events would have occurred. Stan, therefore, is eager to heap blame on Richard, who, in turn, refuses to shoulder it and off-loads said blame onto Jen herself. And so the group of men play a game of hot potato with their shared guilt. *Revenge*, ergo, offers a view that rape culture poisons both male-female and male-male relations. Or, perhaps, the causal chain runs the other direction: toxic individuals, trustworthy for neither sex, cultivate rape culture. Whichever is the case, by offering this well-rounded view of rape culture, *Revenge* offers a more insightful view of rape as a cultural force than either *Bound* or *I Spit* does.

Throughout this discussion of *Revenge*, I have upheld it as a largely successful rape-revenge film, one which avoids some of the issues plaguing other notable rape-revenge works. If, as I have done for illustrative purposes, we conceive of these newer rape-revenge movies as an evolution in the narrative form, then we can think of *Revenge* as a more successful successor than *Bound to Vengeance*. Such a perspective, however, while useful from the standpoint of storytelling and illustrating possible narrative shifts, is too simplistic to capture rape-revenge's spirit. For, even as interesting deviations like *Bound* and *Revenge* have emerged, the tried and true formula of the original *I Spit on Your Grave* retains its presence in the narrative form. Indeed, the three films of the *I Spit* franchise's remake cycle, from 2010, 2013, and 2015, demonstrate as much.

These last three films share the original film's explicit portrayal of sexual violence and sexualized violence. They also share the original film cover, depicting a woman, the protagonist, walking away from the camera. The covers for the original film and its 2010 remake have Jennifer's clothes torn, part of her butt cheeks revealed. While her ripped clothes de-eroticize the otherwise revealing images, the partial nudity foreshadows the film's explicit depictions of rape. *I Spit II* offers a variation, having Katie (Jemma Dallender) stand in

---

[39] *Revenge*.

profile and look out at the audience. Katie's stance is more confrontational than Jennifer's, as befitting Katie's robust personality.

Like Jennifer's clothes, however, Katie's are in disarray, the strap of her shirt having slid down off her right shoulder. Meanwhile, *I Spit III*'s cover largely returns to the formula of the other *I Spit* posters. This version, however, zooms in further, putting emphasis on Jennifer's rear, clad in the tight minidress she wears late in the film. And while her clothes are untorn (suitably since Jennifer experiences no rape in this film), the effect's eroticism is not as powerful as it could be, as Jennifer holds a knife in her right hand, and the *III* in the title is stylized to resemble knife slashes.

Cowan observes in *The Forbidden Body* that horror book covers frequently feature partially nude women in danger.[40] On the one hand, then, these movie posters fall into a common generic trap of sexualizing their heroines, an issue Fredriksson also sees in the posters advertising *The Girl With the Dragon Tattoo*.[41] On the other hand, each of the covers I have discussed suits its film in some fashion. For instance, the covers for the *I Spit* movies represent the films' blending of sexual content with violence, the same blend this volume's previous chapters have deemed problematic, their affect paradoxical. *Revenge*'s poster, however, paints a different picture. One version shows the film's final shot (a blood-soaked Jen looking over her shoulder back toward the camera), another Jen pointing her shotgun at the onlooker. These posters, therefore, are uneroticized, their focus on Jen's face as opposed to her backside.

This distinction in focus reveals how, regardless of their anti-rape and pro-heroine messages, the *I Spit* movies remain plagued with accusations regarding their unforgiving depictions of sexual violence. Simultaneously, the focus on the *Revenge* posters centers not on a sexualized body part (the backside) but rather on the face. Whereas the backside is sexualized, the face is associated with agency, folk wisdom deeming the eyes the windows to the soul. And when Jen faces the camera on the poster, she reveals not only her eyes rather than her rear-end but also her mouth, from which she can voice her agency through language.[42] *Revenge*'s posters, therefore, endow their heroine with a sense of agency that the *I Spit* posters leave only implied.

It would be folly, however, to claim posters for the latter merely reduce their heroines to sexual objects, for said heroines also brandish weapons. Thus, even

---

[40] Cowan. *The Forbidden Body*. 102-103.

[41] Fredriksson 66.

[42] The poster for *Bound to Vengeance*, meanwhile, shows Eve's face in close-up, staring out toward the audience. This poster, like *Revenge*'s, emphasizes the protagonist's agency and avoids sexualizing her.

when they are vulnerable (their backs to their audience, their clothing in disarray), they are also powerful and dangerous. Would-be attackers would do well, these posters suggest, to fear what these women can do to them. So my analysis of the posters should not be construed as suggesting the case is binary, the *I Spit* posters eroticized, the *Revenge* posters non-eroticized. Rather, I argue, the latter group does a superior job of foregrounding their heroine's agency, whereas the former problematically and confrontationally blend their heroines' agency with their vulnerability, sexuality, and status as rape survivors.

On the subject of confrontation, we would be remiss, perhaps, to ignore Gaspar Noé's *Irréversible*. This notably grotesque French rape-revenge film tells, in reverse chronological order, the story of a night in Paris, in which a pimp, Le Tenia, brutally rapes and beats Alex (Monica Bellucci). Enraged, Alex's partner Marcus attempts to track down Le Tenia, only to fail when he mistakenly attacks the wrong man. In the ensuing struggle, the other man breaks Marcus's arm, forcing Marcus's friend Pierre to intervene and kill the other man with a fire extinguisher. The police soon arrive and arrest Pierre while paramedics wheel Marcus toward an ambulance.

This brief plot summary does little justice to *Irréversible*'s complexity. While the plot itself may be austere, its reverse chronology and disorienting cinematography complicate readings of the film while making viewing it a uniquely uncomfortable, nausea-inducing experience. At times, the camera spins in circles as if to induce motion sickness in the viewer. According to scholar Laura Wilson, the movie also plays infrasound for the same effect.[43] Arousing disgust, therefore, is a central mission of *Irréversible*, a film that seems to tackle the critique of rape-revenge eroticizing sexual violence by aiming to be the most sickening rape-revenge film possible. Interestingly, *Irréversible* locates the onus of disgust not so much in the act of rape itself but instead throughout the entire film. From the sound design to the cinematography, *Irréversible* tries to make the viewer queasy, perhaps so that no viewer will be in any mood for titillation once the story reaches its climactic rape scene.

That dedication to arousing disgust also appears on the film's cover, which depicts Alex in the underground walkway where Le Tenia rapes her. This Alex, unlike the Jennifer on the *I Spit* films' posters, has not been raped yet, but the poster still communicates the film's commitment to arousing disgust with its Dutch camera angle, presenting a distorted view of the world. That angle, moreover, foreshadows the events to come, just as the red lighting foreshadows the ensuing violence, particularly Le Tenia's beating Alex unconscious. From

---

[43] Laura Wilson, *Spectatorship, Embodiment and Physicality in the Contemporary Mutilation Film* Illustrated edition. (Springer, 2015), 84–85.

the poster, one can, therefore, glean esoteric hints about the film's story. Moreover, this poster avoids eroticizing the movie's sexual violence.

Though Alex on the poster wears the same party dress she wears when Le Tenia assaults her, a sheer and revealing garment that flatters actress Monica Bellucci's beauty, the shot remains unerotic because Alex is obscured. She stands in the mid-ground of a long shot, the details of her body hazy. Thus, even though her rear faces the camera, its shape and details are difficult to discern, meaning the poster does not lavish attention on the actress's body. Moreover, *Irréversible*'s poster achieves this effect while nevertheless mirroring the infamous poster for the original *I Spit on Your Grave* and does so much that it avoids dangers of reducing its female protagonist to a sexual object.

There is, however, an alternative poster (or DVD cover) for *Irréversible* portraying Alex in profile against a dark backdrop. This poster does not feature the complexities I observed above, and a lascivious onlooker could well sexualize this version, as Alex's chest appears prominently in the shot's foreground. One of the issues when discussing posters is that different versions of posters often exist, meaning it can be difficult to draw firm conclusions about them. Nonetheless, my points stand for the posters I have examined, even as they may miss some nuance that would become evident were I to analyze other posters.

Now, the reader may wonder why I have upheld *Revenge* as a largely successful rape-revenge film but have not done the same for *Irréversible*. My reasons for treating these films differently are as follows. First, *Irréversible* questions the ethics of revenge when it depicts Marcus's rampage as self-destructively idiotic. Unlike the resolved and resourceful Jen, Marcus seeks revenge haphazardly, rushing headlong into dangerous circumstances and attacking the wrong man, a man who ironically stands beside Marcus's target, the rapist Le Tenia. Le Tenia, moreover, appears to get away with raping and brutalizing Alex. And so *Irréversible*, while depicting rape as a disgusting and immoral act, does not show the film's foremost rapist receiving his comeuppance.

Second, Le Tenia's rape of Alex forms part of the film's homophobia. David Edelstein, for example, outright accuses the film of being homophobic.[44] And while Noé has disagreed with this reading of his film, one can hardly fault

[44] David Edelstein, "Irreversible Errors: Gaspar Noé's cinematic rape," *Slate*, March 3, 2007, https://slate.com/culture/2003/03/irreversible-a-cinematic-rape.html.

Edelstein and others for arriving at it.[45] For starters, the film establishes Le Tenia as a homosexual man. In fact, even as he rapes Alex, he talks to her about his preference for men and for anal instead of vaginal penetration. So *Irréversible* has a homosexual man violently rape and batter a woman for seemingly no reason at all. While rape is always immoral, my discussion thus far has repeatedly shown how rape-revenge films do provide some rationale for their antagonists' heinous acts. Stan rapes Jen because he lusts after her and is incensed when she does not reciprocate his interest.

Of course, this is not to say *Revenge* in any way justifies Stan's behavior; it clearly does not. Likewise, this is not to say Stan's behavior could ever be justified in any way; it clearly could not. It is, however, to say that Le Tenia's rape of Alex is aberrant insofar as it appears unmotivated, an act of random violence by a rapist not even attracted to the sex of his victim.[46] There is a senselessness to Le Tenia's behavior that codes him as particularly loathsome even among the ignoble company of other cinematic rapists, a dubious distinction, to be sure.

Furthermore, the film's other homosexual characters do not come across much better. After raping Alex and maliciously slamming her face into the concrete floor, Le Tenia, unsatiated, goes to a gay S&M club, The Rectum. It is at The Rectum that Marcus gets his arm broken. The man he fights, moreover, prepares to rape the battered Marcus after snapping his arm. A crowd forms to watch this act, the most noteworthy of whom is a man (played by Noé himself) furiously masturbating at the impending sexual assault. Thus, the film's homosexual characters seem invariably immoral and sexually depraved.

One of them rapes and beats a woman before going to a sex club, one repeatedly asks Marcus to fist him despite the latter's obvious anger and lack of interest, one tries to rape Marcus after beating him in a fight, and another masturbates at the sight of sexual violence. I suppose it is possible that Noé did not intend to make his film homophobic,[47] but the effect is demonstrably homophobic and harmful to a community that continues to face an uphill battle for civil rights and recognition worldwide. It is, at best, troubling,

---

[45] Steve Erickson, " 'Enter the Void' Director Gaspar Noé Talks Sex, Drugs and Narrative Cinema," *Wall Street Journal*, September 21, 2010, https://www.wsj.com/articles/BL-SEB-46231.

[46] Of course, Le Tenia's rape of Alex does align with Brownmiller's observation that rape is about control rather than sex (49). This also means, however, that the film embraces a dangerous and negative stereotype of depicting homosexual men as hyper-libidinous and sexually predatory.

[47] I am offering no assessment of his motives here. Rather, I am arguing that, even if it turns out he did not intend for the film to be homophobic, the film is very homophobic. I am not, however, presuming this was his intention; nor am I assuming the opposite.

therefore, for Noé to portray the gay community in this light. And it is not only the gay community, but also the gay BDSM community receiving this negative depiction. After all, the men in The Rectum clearly do not respect consent and appear willing to engage in and/or vicariously enjoy actual sexual violence, acts of which the real-life BDSM community roundly condemns.[48] *Irréversible* thus has the regrettable distinction of maligning (in effect if not in intention) two marginalized communities, and said maligning comes with real-world consequences, the likes of which it would be irresponsible for me to ignore.

For these reasons, it is difficult to uphold *Irréversible* as an effective anti-rape film. While its rape scene is confronting and unusually brutal even for the graphic narrative mode that is the rape-revenge story, *Irréversible* casts revenge as a fool's errand (at least in the way Marcus pursues it) and leaves its singularly sadistic and inscrutable rapist unpunished. And in doing so the film also casts two stigmatized groups in a remarkably negative light, with no redeeming qualities. Both these characteristics undermine any anti-rape message *Irréversible* might try to communicate. The value of the film instead lies in its depiction of rape as "irreversible" and pervaded with disgust.[49]

A key agent of that disgust, the film's disorienting cinematography, occurs throughout the movie's narrative arc, as the film begins with the camera swaying back and forth (leaving the audience ungrounded and, ergo, prone to nausea) and ends with the camera spinning in a zooming out bird's eye shot of Alex. Both these shots are liable to induce the aforementioned nausea in viewer's like this author, who are prone to motion sickness. And by thus infusing its entire narrative with disgust, *Irréversible* offers a portrayal of rape aligning, unfortunately, with the experience of so many real-world survivors of sexual violence, survivors who may never receive justice and whose attackers may go on to assault others with impunity.[50] This is a bleak fact, but a fact nonetheless. And earlier, I asserted that horror films (including rape-revenge horror films) confront audiences with disconcerting subject matter.[51] It is

---

[48] Cara R. Dunkley and Lori A. Brotto, "The Role of Consent in the Context of BDSM," *Sex Abuse* 32, no. 6, 657-678, https://pubmed.ncbi.nlm.nih.gov/31010393/.

[49] *Irréversible*. Directed by Gaspar Noé, performance by Monica Bellucci, StudioCanal, 2002.

[50] Andrew Van Dam, "Less than 1% of rapes lead to felony convictions. At least 89% of victims face emotional and physical consequences," *The Washington Post*, October 6, 2018, https://www.washingtonpost.com/business/2018/10/06/less-than-percent-rapes -lead-felony-convictions-least-percent-victims-face-emotional-physical-consequences/.

[51] Brandon West, *At the Edge of Existence: Liminality in Horror Cinema Since the 1970s*. (Jefferson, NC. McFarland & Company, Inc., 2022), 104; Jackula Parts 1-2; Clover 20.

hardly surprising, then, that *Irréversible* underscores this real-life, perturbing phenomenon.

Still, I would be remiss to equivocate a somewhat realistic rendering of how frequently rape goes unpunished with the ability to advance an anti-rape message. Certainly, these two qualities differ. And while I readily acknowledge *Irréversible* has the first, I argue it lacks the second. Here, of course, one might object that I have not considered the film's second rapist, the man who fights Marcus. After all, this would-be rapist does receive punishment as befitting a rapist in a rape-revenge narrative, as Pierre caves in the man's face with a fire extinguisher in one of the film's most savage scenes. While one could construe this scene as ameliorating the criticism that *Irréversible* leaves its sexual assailants unpunished, this scene does nothing to counter the criticisms of homophobia I and others have (justifiably) leveled against the film.[52] So even if I accepted this criticism, *Irréversible* would remain, as I see it, a more morally problematic film than *Revenge*. Regardless, though, this criticism is not as convincing as it may appear initially.

When Pierre kills Marcus's would-be rapist, he unwittingly does so at the expense of not punishing Alex's actual rapist. Killing Marcus's assailant lands Pierre in police custody. Starting the fight with said assailant lands Marcus in the hospital. And through all this commotion, Le Tenia remains unscathed. In other words, because one rapist suffers, another gets away with his horrific crimes. Overall, then, the film does not decry rapists, and its most sadistic rapist may be emboldened by his good luck. If anything, Noé's narrative choice to punish one rapist and not the other makes clear the film's dedication to depicting moral questions in shades of grey. While Pierre's killing Marcus's assailant in The Rectum may provide the audience with a moment of catharsis, that catharsis lacks its full impact because this scene comes well before the rape scene due to the film's reverse chronology and comes after the scene of Pierre getting arrested.

Thus, the audience does not understand the full import of the act motivating Marcus's rampage, but it does know Pierre's "victory," if one can even deem it such, is partial at best, hollow and futile at worst. Sometimes, *Irréversible* seems to suggest justice is fickle. Ethical questions linger throughout this troubling film, but they lack definitive answers. Unlike *I Spit on Your Grave*, which makes clear where its ethical allegiances lie, *Irréversible* appears more interested in

---

[52] To be clear, my discussion of *Irréversible* should, in no way, be construed as an attack on Gaspar Noé. While I object to some of the content in *Irréversible*, my discussion of his work focuses on but one of his films and, moreover, does not advance any criticism of Noé as a person. While I find this one film problematic (in the manner I have described), I still consider Noé a talented artist who makes uniquely confrontational films.

raising tough moral questions than in trying to resolve them. Revenging a sexual assault proves possible with Pierre, but doing so leads to an arrest and, presumably, jail time. And with Alex, revenging a sexual assault ostensibly appears impossible.

I have to qualify my point with "ostensibly" because it is possible Marcus could have achieved vengeance had he approached the situation more cautiously. For example, he could have confirmed the man was Le Tenia before attacking him, he could have waited for the two ruffians to meet him at The Rectum so he had reinforcements for the fight, or he could have given the rapist's name to the police rather than trying to become a vigilante.[53] So perhaps the issue is not so much with the futility of seeking revenge but rather with the need not to do so recklessly.

Yet, that it is possible to read *Irréversible* this way reinforces my earlier assertion that the film dwells in moral grey areas. It gives us room to ponder these hypotheticals even as it avoids answering any of them itself. The film does not come out and paint revenge as an inherently pointless, self-destructive endeavor, but it does show how revenge *can* be pointless and self-destructive. This lack of clear answers certainly makes *Irréversible* a troubling film open for analysis, but it also means the film lacks the clear anti-rape rhetoric I have been seeking in rape-revenge narratives.

This lack, moreover, means *Irréversible* does not emerge as a particularly effective anti-rape film even as it does richly evoke disgust in ways many other rape-revenge works do not. The film's creative cinematography certainly serves this role. And, in this way, *Irréversible* connects with McGillvray's observation that some rape-revenge films use "experimental forms and styles" to buck traditional visual pleasures.[54]

The film's rich evocations may be responsible for *Irréversible*'s comparatively successful performance with audiences. As of November 2021, the film sits at a respectable 80% with audiences and a disappointing 57% with critics.[55] Conversely, *Revenge* has an impressive 93% with critics and a mediocre 58%

---

[53] The film itself explains why Marcus does not do this last action; one of the ruffians, Mourad, tells Marcus the police will not do anything but that he, Mourad, and his friend will (provided, of course, Marcus pays them). And, naturally, as I have mentioned elsewhere, rape-revenge narratives often (unfortunately realistically) portray law enforcement as unreliable for investigating and punishing sexual assault.

[54] Maddi McGillvray, "The Feminist Art-Horror of New French Extremity." In *Women Make Horror: Filmmaking, Feminism, Genre*, edited by Alison Peirse. (Rutgers University Press, 2020), 124.

[55] "Irreversible." Rotten Tomatoes. https://www.rottentomatoes.com/m/irreversible.

with audiences.[56] Neither film, then, has managed to gain widespread acceptance with both film critics and audiences, at least not according to these numbers. And the films' IMDB scores are not much different. *Irréversible* rates a 7.4, *Revenge* a 6.4.[57] Both films have their supporters and their detractors, though *Irréversible* is the older, better-known of the two. It is possible, therefore, that my upholding *Revenge* as the more effective anti-rape film may meet with significant pushback, but I believe I have supported my case for rating the films as I have. And I maintain that *Irréversible's* relative popularity does not absolve it of the ethical problems I have identified.

It may also be possible, of course, that *Revenge's* significantly superior performance with critics, as we see from the films' disparate critical scores on Rotten Tomatoes, suggests *Revenge* appeals more to academics than to the lay audience, whereas *Irréversible's* appeal runs the opposite direction. Nevertheless, the data is insufficient to make any definitive judgments at this time. But, I have argued, both *Revenge* and *Irréversible* have achieved the sort of success eluding *I Spit* and *Bound to Vengeance*, and so these two films offer some ways for us to conceive of effective, less alienating rape-revenge films.

Notably, *Revenge* and *Irréversible* couch their rape-revenge narratives in relatively complex cinematography and filmic structures. The former offers a more well-rounded view of feminism and rape culture than either *I Spit on Your Grave* or *Bound to Vengeance* does. The latter offers an art-house approach with unique camera movements and reverse chronology, both of which earn the film appeal it would likely lack were it to favor the stark simplicity of *I Spit* or, to a lesser extent, *Bound*. And both *Revenge* and *Irréversible* sit comfortably in the broader movement of European cinema toward extreme depictions of violence. Their alignment with this movement, I suspect, endows them with some measure of critical respectability they might lack if they had the minimal budgets and fanfare of *I Spit on Your Grave* and *Bound to Vengeance*.

I choose to connect *Revenge* and *Irréversible* for a couple of reasons. First, there is the stark contrast between their approaches to their shared subject matter of rape and subsequent revenge. Second, there is their status as this volume's only European films. *Irréversible* is a French film, whereas *Revenge* is Belgian (but from a French director and filmed in English). As such, these films are more closely connected, geopolitically speaking, to each other than to any of the other films in this volume. While my focus in this book is on the issues of

---

[56] "Revenge." Rotten Tomatoes. https://www.rottentomatoes.com/m/revenge_2018.
[57] "Irreversible." IMDB. https://www.imdb.com/title/tt0290673/.; "Revenge." IMDB. https://www.imdb.com/title/tt6738136/.

disgust and anti-rape messaging in rape-revenge, it nevertheless behooves me to flag these films' disparate origins (compared to my other films,' that is).

Irréversible not only connects to the trend toward extreme violence in French cinema, but also to the issue of femicide in France.[58] *Irréversible*'s particularly bleak story, therefore, reflects the recalcitrant and perennial problem of femicide in France while also reflecting French cinema's tendency toward nihilistic violence.[59] *Revenge*, however, seems to offer a more redemptive view of the rape-revenge sub-genre. While *Revenge*'s origin in Belgian cinema (which has less of a reputation for abject violence than French cinema does) may be partially responsible for this difference, it is, to my mind, more noteworthy that *Revenge* is 15 years newer, entering, therefore, into what Henry has deemed a revisionist stage of rape-revenge cinema.[60]

Either way, *Revenge* demonstrates there is cause for hope for the rape-revenge narrative. The paradox of disgust may, in fact, be avoidable. *Revenge* avoids this pitfall by displacing the onus of disgust onto the rapists and revenge, and not onto the sexual assault itself. And despite not showing the rape of Jen, *Revenge* still evokes disgust toward the rape by relying on sound instead of sight.[61] This auditory approach to the grotesque material proves an effective strategy, at least for this viewer, who finds *Revenge* a less problematic rape-revenge film than any of the other texts in this volume.

Revenge is also noteworthy because it connects Jen to multiple different elements. These multiple elements indicate the film's preoccupation with empowering its protagonist. Whereas the traditional rape-revenge heroine shares an affinity with water (as we saw with Jennifer in *I Spit on Your Grave*), Jen shares affinities with fire and with water. Her connection with fire first arises after she awakens. Impaled on the top of a tree, she fishes for her lighter and

---

[58] "Femicides in France are up – despite attempts to quell the problem," *Euronews*, 2023. https://www.euronews.com/2023/09/02/femicides-in-france-are-up-despite-attempts-to-quell-the-problem#:~:text=Femicides%20in%20France%20are%20up%20%2D%20despite%20attempts%20to%20quell%20the%20problem,-A%20protest%20at&text=A%20new%20study%20has%20found,La%20croix%20de%20la%20Rochette.

[59] Charles Derry, *Dark Dreams 2.0: a Psychological History of the Modern Horror Film from the 1950s to the 21st Century.* (McFarland & Co., 2009), 150.

[60] Claire Henry, "Challenging the boundaries of cinema's rape-revenge genre in *Katalin Varga* and *Twilight Portrait*," *Studies in European Cinema* 10, no. 2+3 (2013): 143. There is definitely much room for exploration here, room I am deliberately leaving under-investigated because I do not wish to stray too far afield from this project's focus.

[61] That is, by moving the rape off-screen and only providing audio of the assault to the audience, *Revenge* diminishes the aesthetic of disgust's alienating effect.

sets the tree ablaze to weaken it so she can break off the part of the tree piercing her abdomen.

Right before this scene, we see Richard burning Jen's clothes back at his home. Thus, Richard hopes to find his salvation in fire, as he uses the flames to destroy evidence that Jen was at his home. Fire, however, is not Richard's source of salvation; it is Jen's. Fire frees her from the tree, allowing her to escape from the men when they come back to retrieve her body. Likewise, fire lets her cauterize the serious wound in her abdomen, likely saving her life.

To accomplish this task, she heats Dimitri's can of beer over the fire. And so, after she presses the heated metal to her body, she comes away with the beer's mascot, an eagle, emblazoned over the closed injury. Fire, therefore, brands Jen with a bird, and the equation of fire and avian evokes imagery of a phoenix.[62] The implication, therefore, is that Jen is rising from the ashes, both literally via those of her dying campfire and metaphorically via her renewed vigor and transition to hunter rather than hunted. Like so many rape-revenge heroines, then, Jen transforms after experiencing sexual assault. Unlike others, though, her transformation occurs foremost through fire rather than through water.

The film visibly connects Jen to a raptor through her new brand, and then it carries this connection into her actions. In the morning, she hikes to the top of the mountain and uses Dimitri's binoculars to locate Stan. Like a bird of prey, therefore, she enjoys excellent long-range vision, enabling her to pick out her target amid the vast expanses below her. In this scene, Jen's vantage point from the high ground, coupled with her connection to an eagle, suggests her power over the men, who occupy the comparatively disadvantaged low ground. Jen can see them; they cannot see her. They think they are hunting her, but, in truth, she is hunting them. From out of the scorching desert, then, Jen returns with a vengeance.

Augmenting the fire and desert, though, Jen also receives aid from the water around her. When the men discover Jen has survived the fall, they follow her extensive blood trail across the desert sands right up until it reaches the shores of a lake. There, Jen's footprints across the mud indicate she has sought refuge in the water. The film then enters a long shot, the camera shooting the men from across the water. Here, the men stand on the shore, the water stretching out before them. And they resolve to hunt Jen on either side of the lake but not

---

[62] Creed. *Return of the Monstrous-Feminine*. 59. While I was revising this manuscript from its first draft, Barbara Creed released her *Return of the Monstrous- Feminine,* in which she makes some of the same observations about *Revenge* that I had in my original draft of this manuscript. As such, I will cite her here when she likewise points out facts about the movie that I included in my initial draft.

across it. Richard goes one direction (toward the right side of the screen), Dimitri the other, while Stan remains at that spot to, he says, wait in case she returns.

It is significant that the men do not enter the water. Of course, on the one hand, they do not have a boat, so entering the lake seems a poor, inefficient choice. On the other, however, the shot's framing, with the men all standing at the edge of the water which stretches to either side of the shot in a remarkably straight line, suggests the lake forms a barrier the men dare not cross. Merely one scene later, the camera finds Jen once more. She wades through the lake and, hearing Dimitri's quadbike approaching, submerges to hide. The water offers her refuge. She then leaves the water to sneak up on Dimitri and gets the drop on him. She fails to kill him, though, as his shotgun, which she has snatched, is unloaded. The movie then cuts to Dimitri standing waist-deep in the water, trying to drown Jen.

As he repeatedly dunks her head, he boasts that he likes to let his prey think it is hunting him so he can surprise it. The audience, however, sees this boasting for what it is: an attempt to save face. Dimitri's shocked expression when Jen confronted him with his own shotgun spoke volumes. Also, his attempts to drown her fail because Jen manages to grab his hunting knife from his belt and stab his eyes out with it. Dimitri, his knife sticking out of his right eye socket, screams, dies, and sinks beneath the water. Dimitri, therefore, dies after he enters the water, Jen's domain. Readers may recognize this scene as remarkably similar to that of Sawyer stabbing the sheriff while standing in the titular *Rust Creek*. Just as water serves as a source of strength for Sawyer, so too does it empower Jen.

And, as in *I Spit* (2010), of the characters in *Revenge*, the heroine is uniquely connected to the elements. Despite their experience hunting, the men in *Revenge*, like the men in *I Spit* (2010), have a hostile relationship with the natural world. Stan, for example, goes out of his way to urinate on a spider he sees scuttling across the desert ground. And Richard goes out of his way to kill a small animal while hunting for Jen. The men, therefore, victimize animals unnecessarily. Their willingness to do so, moreover, highlights their propensity for violence. Their violence also differs from Jen's in that hers is self-defensive, theirs offensive.

Unlike the case with many other rape-revenge heroines, it is unclear whether Jen ever had the chance to end her situation peacefully. How, we might ask, is she to escape or contact the authorities when three armed men are hunting her in a remote desert where help does not appear forthcoming? The film's spate of long shots routinely remind the audience that Jen is isolated from the outside world. No matter how far out the camera shows, no habitations besides

Richard's come into view. Jen, ergo, is on her own and has no resort save violence, as running or hiding seem to offer no hope of rescue.

In her influential essay "Visual Pleasure and Narrative Cinema," Laura Mulvey argues the movie spectator is coded as a masculine voyeur.[63] Clover makes a similar observation when she writes that final girls in slasher films are observant and that they have the power of the gaze as well.[64] This observation, moreover, jives with the work of Isabel Pinedo, who observes how traditional film scholarship that construes the camera's gaze as masculine and objectifying elides the possibilities of female spectatorship.[65]

Pinedo's more extensive reckoning with this area of film studies suggests scholars like Mulvey and Creed are mistaken in essentializing the camera as an instrument of phallic power, the act of film viewing that of male voyeurism. Whereas Creed argues rape-revenge films like *I Spit* (1978) rely on the male viewer's enjoyment of violence, Pinedo points out that such an argument overlooks or denies the possibility that female viewers can likewise enjoy depictions of violence, particularly when said violence punishes a rapist.[66]

So we return to the topic of the gaze and, especially, *Revenge*'s capacity to redeem the gaze. Thus far, I have established how Fargeat de-eroticizes the male gaze. Her achievement in doing so is at odds with Hoeveler's argument that the female gaze objectifies women.[67] Jennifer's power in *Revenge* also challenges the existing trend in horror where female characters are punished for appropriating the gaze.[68] Not only does Jen gain control of the gaze when she looks through a pair of binoculars,[69] but she receives no punishment for doing so.

---

[63] Mulvey 624.

[64] Clover 39;

[65] Isabel Cristina Pinedo, *Recreational Terror: Women and the Pleasures of Horror Film Viewing.* (State University of New York Press, 1997), 76.

[66] Ibid. 68.; Creed. *The Monstrous-Feminine.* 130; For female enjoyment of violence, see Heller-Nicholas 2nd edition 5-6.

[67] Diane Long Hoeveler, *Gothic Feminism: the Professionalization of Gender from Charlotte Smith to the Brontës.* (Pennsylvania State University Press, 1998), 244.

[68] Cynthia Freeland, "Feminist Frameworks for Horror Films." In *Film Theory & Discussion* 8th edition, edited by Leo Braudy and Mashall Cohen. (Oxford University Press, 2016), 565.

[69] Creed also observes in *Return of the Monstrous-Feminine* that Jennifer gains the power of the gaze when she uses the binoculars (60).

Furthermore, Jen subverts the typical cinematic mode in which the male characters' gazes move the story forward.[70] Instead, in *Revenge*, Jen's gaze propels the narrative as she shifts from hunted to hunter. And contra Silverman, who writes that the female gaze in the film is self-entrapping,[71] in *Revenge*, Jen's gaze frees her, gives her some semblance of power over the desert's expansive landscape. And because the movie connects Jen to the landscape, her strength to the elements of fire and water, Jen's relationship with the desert becomes symbiotic rather than adversarial, meaning Jen's female gaze lacks the dominating and possessive characteristics Kaplan attributes to the male gaze.[72]

Here, Jen notably departs from much of the existing scholarship of the gaze and the female character in cinema, distinguishing *Revenge* as an important intervention into existing feminist film theory. Mary Ann Doane, for instance, writes that females with the gaze look for a woman or to submit to a woman.[73] Jen, however, clearly does neither of these as she scans the arid landscape for her male assailants. *Revenge* hereby fits with Doane's other observation that women's films deflect scopophilic energy.[74] It furthermore fits with Kaplan's note that women's films de-eroticize the gaze.[75] Kaplan, however, says that, in doing so, these films disembody the spectator.[76] That criticism does not hold for *Revenge*, as its evocation of fear and disgust makes it an intensely embodying film.

As we can see, "the first horror heroine of the Time's Up Era" complicates (and, in some ways, even redeems) existing feminist film theory concepts.[77] Dyer also

---

[70] Jackie Stacey, "Desperately Seeking Difference." In *Feminism and Film*, edited by E. Ann Kaplan. (Oxford University Press, 2000), 451.

[71] Kaja Silverman, "Lost Objects and Mistaken Subjects," In *Feminist Film Theory: A Reader*, edited by Sue Thornham. (NYU Press, 1999), 104.

[72] E. Ann Kaplan, "Is the Gaze Male?" In *Feminism and Film*, edited by E. Ann Kaplan. (Oxford University Press, 2000), 121; Other scholars have demonstrated how this conception of the gaze is but one culturally-conditioned view, not a true universal (Decker 171).

[73] Mary Ann Doane, "Caught and Rebecca: The Inscription of Femininity as Absence." In *Feminist Film Theory: A Reader*, edited by Sue Thornham. (Edinburgh University Press, 1999), 73.

[74] Doane. "Femininity as Absence". 71.

[75] Kaplan 126.

[76] Ibid.

[77] Quoted in Peirse 2. This comment fits with Henry's observation that the rape-revenge film is currently in a revisionist cycle ("Challenging" 143). I am relegating this observation to a footnote, however, because this volume is focusing on the feminism and disgust in these texts rather than on their historical contexts, which is a project unto itself.

flags one of the shortcomings of conventional feminist film theory, writing: "Thus to look at is thought of as active; whereas to be looked at is passive. In reality, this is not true."[78] Perhaps part of the trouble here is that humans often construe being looked at as natural and automatic. It appears to me, however, that attracting and capturing the gaze are both talents one may have to exercise actively. To be sure, Matilda Lutz's beauty does make her appearance the sort of image traditional feminist film theory holds audiences are wont to look at. Yet, it is also obvious that Fargeat devotes substantial resources toward keeping the audience's attention on Lutz's body. For example, as we have already discussed, *Revenge* features tracking shots focusing on Jennifer's rear end as she walks.

And when we consider Jennifer's own behavior, it is clear she makes an effort to attract the male gaze.[79] Consider, for instance, how she teases Richard when dancing with Stan, actively inviting Richard's gaze and attention. Being looked at (or to-be-looked-at-ness)[80] can, therefore, be an active behavior rather than a passive quality. In fact, most people try to attract such looks at some points in their lives; after all, looking is often the first step toward courtship.

Revenge and Jen herself invite us to see her through the male gaze, probably because this is how she sees herself and construes her own value.[81] This dynamic shifts as Fargeat de-eroticizes the gaze. Through it all, however, we stick with Jen. Even though the movie invites us to see Jen through an objectifying gaze, it nevertheless throws our, the audience's, lot in with her from the beginning. We follow her on her journey, meaning that the tracking shots, even as they objectify the actress's body, force the audience to remain at Jen's side, identifying with her.

Now, traditional scholarship construes female spectatorship as ambivalent,[82] instable,[83] and oscillatory.[84] That oscillation comes from the female viewer's vacillation between masculine and feminine points of view.[85] Yet, *Revenge* complicates this dynamic as it undermines the oscillation in favor of the

---

[78] Dyer. *Only Entertainment.* 128.

[79] To be clear, this is not to say that Jennifer is in any way to blame for being assaulted. There is an obvious, stark difference between trying to get someone's attention and consenting to sexual contact.

[80] Mulvey 630.

[81] Creed. *Return of the Monstrous-Feminine.* 17.

[82] Miriam Hansen, "Pleasure, Ambivalence, and Identification: Valentino and Male Spectatorship." In *Feminism and Film,* edited by E. Ann Kaplan. (Oxford University Press, 2000), 234.

[83] Hansen 230.

[84] Stacey 454.

[85] Ibid.

ambivalence. Because we stick with Jen throughout the film, we remain identified with her even as the camera invites us to objectify and sexualize her. What we lose as the movie progresses is the overt objectification/sexualization, gaining in its stead a greater respect for Jen's personhood as she defines herself apart from the male gaze.[86]

In the same vein, the gaze's gender fluidity supports Judith Halberstam's argument that Clover's view of gender is too essentializing, too polemic, and too prescriptive.[87] Perhaps, then, the gaze does not so much waver between masculine and feminine but rather occupies a liminal space between the two identities; perhaps the gaze is non-binary, unconforming to our limited, constraining notions.[88] Such a conception does make room for intersectional views of the gaze. bell hooks, for example, notes the possibility of the oppositional gaze among black people in the United States.[89] And Decker argues that the assaultive style of gazing may be an Americanized phenomenon.[90]

All of this discussion about the camera's gendered gaze and the woman's thereby subjugated image in cinema leads to one final intervention I think *Revenge* offers in extant feminist film theory. Prolific feminist scholar Mary Ann Doane argues that in cinema, women are associated with the surface of the image, not its depths.[91] Not only has Doane highlighted the unfortunate tendency for cinema to rob female characters (and actresses) of their agency, but she has also brought us back to the earlier discussion of rape-revenge paratexts. After all, Doane's point is trenchant as to the sexualization of actresses and heroines on the posters for these films, which, as we have seen, often focus on their actresses' sexualized bodies, particularly their rears.

---

[86] Creed. *Return of the Monstrous-Feminine.* 17.

[87] Judith Halberstam, *Skin Shows: Gothic Horror and the Technology of Monsters.* (Durham, NC: Duke University Press, 1995), 139, 141, & 143.

[88] Ibid. The gaze is a long-standing, oft-discussed concept in feminist film theory. As such, my discussion of it here is abridged.

[89] bell hooks, "The Oppositional Gaze: Black Female Spectators." In *Feminist Film Theory: A Reader,* edited by Sue Thornham. (Edinburgh University Press, 1999), 308.

[90] Lindsey Decker, "The Transnational Gaze in A Girl Walks Home Alone at Night." In *Women Make Horror: Filmmaking, Feminism, Genre,* edited by Alison Peirse. (Rutgers University Press, 2020), 171. Decker specifically considers *A Girl Walks Home Alone at Night,* an Iranian-American, Persian language vampire film, which she argues construes the gaze very differently from how American cinema has, according to feminist film theorists. Since this volume focuses on American and Western rape-revenge works, it does not have the scope to explore at length the implications of Decker's analysis.

[91] Doane. "Film and the Masquerade". 133.

And to be sure, her insight seems to apply to *Revenge* as well. When the camera dwells on sexualized areas of Jen's body, it treats Jen as an image rather than an agent. She is, in this view, a good cast for the viewing audience's consumption and pleasure. Such a view of Jen is woefully incomplete, though. As we have seen, *Revenge* humanizes and empowers Jen. So too, I argue, does it begin to associate Jen with the filmic image's depths rather than merely its surface.

To demonstrate this, let us contrast two images from *Revenge*. First, we have the aforementioned image of the men standing at the edge of the lake. Second, we have the film's parting image of Jen looking back over her shoulder at the camera. The shots share their high levels of depth. But they also begin to demonstrate one of the film's key moments (indeed one of the rape-revenge texts' key moments): the disempowerment of the men and simultaneous empowerment of the women.

Because *Revenge* repeatedly connects Jen and her strength to the natural world, the lake's prominence in the first shot's foreground necessarily robs the men of their power. Their power, in essence, flows away from them into the lake's sapping waters, waters which then feed that power to Jen when she kills Dmitri. In the second shot, that final image, Jen looks back at the camera, looking back at the 3 dead men and Richard's house. Symbolically, she is leaving behind her definition via the male gaze;[92] she has triumphed, if momentarily, over the male bourgeoises. Furthermore, Jen is the shot's focus, and she is positioned not at the fore (the surface) but in the depths, visually suggesting her importance. No longer is she the proverbial cover girl, the image for male consumption. Instead, she is the owner of the image.

To augment this shot's importance, we can consider Teresa de Lauretis's observation that, in film, women represent narrative closure, the fulfillment of narrative promise.[93] On the one hand, this sort of fulfillment relies on the female character's place as a prize for the male protagonist to win. On the other, however, *Revenge*'s narrative hereby offers us a different way of construing how heroines can represent narrative closure. The promise of *Revenge*'s narrative does not lie with any male character winning Jen. It lies with Jen winning. Here, the image of the heroine offers not the promise of heterosexual fulfillment but instead the promise of female empowerment and triumph over these sorts of systems. And, thus, *Revenge* disrupts this aspect of conventional feminist film analysis.[94]

---

[92] Creed. *Return of the Monstrous-Feminine.* 17.

[93] de Lauretis 88.

[94] Or, at least, it disrupts the conventions of classical cinema.

Here, though, I reach an important point: whether a particular rape-revenge work (or any rape-revenge work) proves effective for an audience member is an intensely personal question. It is a question that maps not onto the logical centers of the brain but rather, as Bruun Vaage suggests, onto our emotional core.[95] On this note, Stephen King observes that horror films operate as "nerve-music rather than head-music," meaning the texts this volume considers connect with audiences on a deeply emotional level.[96] Worse yet, the emotions they connect to are perhaps the most intensely personal that one can feel. Fictional depictions of sexual assault invariably unveil the traumatic repressed memories of audience members who (like me) are the survivors of sexual violence and abuse.

These films are, therefore, as King asserts: "nerve-music."[97] But the cord they strike is one many audiences would rather leave mute and forgotten. And even those audience members for whom forgetting is not an option may well find themselves (as I frequently do) unsettled at displays of fictionalized sexual violence. Unfortunately, sexual violence is at once a common crime and an intensely traumatic one, with rape survivors experiencing high rates of post-traumatic stress disorder.[98] A war rages in the psyche of the sexual assault survivor, and these fictions are an uncomfortable reminder that for some and for Western society, that battle seems never-ending.

---

[95] Bruun Vaage 421.

[96] Stephen King, "What's Scary," foreword in *Danse Macabre*. (New York: Gallery Books, 2010), xxvi.

[97] Ibid.

[98] *The Relationships Between Military Sexual Assault, Post-Traumatic Stress Disorder and Suicide, and on Department of Defense and Department of Veterans Affairs Medical Treatment and Management of Victims of Sexual Trauma*: Hearing before the Subcommittee on Personnel of the Committee on Armed Services, United States Senate, One Hundred Thirteenth Congress, Second Session, February 26, 2014. U.S. Government Printing Office, 2014. Per Senator Gillibrand's statements in the report, female veterans of the United States military who experienced sexual assault during their time in the armed forces experience post traumatic stress disorder (PTSD) at rates far exceeding those of veterans who did not experience sexual assault while in the military. Rape and sexual violence therefore correlate to higher rates of PTSD than combat does; the Department of Veteran Affairs' own research on the issue buttresses this observation, noting that soldiers who experience sexual assault while serving are more likely to suffer from PTSD than are their fellow soldiers who do not experience sexual assault while serving. See: https://www.ptsd.va.gov/professional/treat/type/sexual_trauma_military. asp#three. See, also: https://mainweb-v.musc.edu/vawprevention/research/mental impact.shtml

This is not to assert sexual assault survivors cannot derive pleasure from these narratives, however, as anecdotal evidence suggests they do.[99] And so the important fact emerges that these stories' efficacy is ultimately (at least partially) a subjective question open to personal interpretation and, more importantly, personal experience.[100] My analyses of these texts, ergo, reveals when these narratives fall short and when they succeed aesthetically and philosophically. It does not (and cannot) rob these films of their cathartic role if and when they have one. Nevertheless, I believe the weight of the textual evidence has distinguished *Revenge* as particularly successful in communicating an anti-rape message. No amount of analysis, however, can overwrite (or de-legitimize) an emotional revulsion to the contrary. Such is the power of disgust.

---

[99] Heller-Nicholas. 2nd edition. 5-6.

[100] King writes: "...I believe that horror does not horrify unless the reader or viewer has been personally touched..." (*Danse Macabre* 12).

Conclusion:
Post-Catharsis: How Rape-Revenge Works Show Protagonists Moving On

Throughout this volume, I have identified the cathartic role rape-revenge works fulfill, including their ability to help real-life survivors of sexual violence.[1] Within the texts, then, revenge sometimes comes across as a moment of triumph for protagonists. After all, as we have seen, many rape-revenge stories end with the completion of the revenge. The heroine or heroines kill their assailant(s), and the credits roll. That quick transition from revenge to ending suggests a sense of finality. The heroine(s) won; so what remains for the films to show?

Other texts answer this question by positing, as we have seen, revenge as unfulfilling. In *I Spit* (2010), Jennifer hardly seems to exult in her vengeance. Rather, she sits stock still, a thousand-yard stare affixed on her face. Looking at neither her assailants nor the camera, she is lost in her trauma, trauma that her revenge has done little to override. Unfortunately, here *I Spit* (2010) and its sequel *I Spit III*, reflect real-life scholarship of trauma. Indeed, in her seminal work *Trama and Recovery*, Judith Herman reports how trauma in adulthood "erodes the structure of the personality already formed."[2] Put another way, trauma attacks and reshapes the very construct of the self, and so it is only logical that a survivor like Jennifer would find herself changed after suffering sexual assault.

After the cathartic moments of revenge and disgust, therefore, we find the moment of rumination, in which the films leave characters and audience members alike to ponder the implications of their actions. The protagonists question the ethics of their revenge as well as the futility of it for erasing their trauma; the audience questions, perhaps, the ethics of consuming such fiction. This haunting quality, whereby rape-revenge works stay with their audiences far beyond their endings, may be rape-revenge's greatest strength. When we watch such a film or read such a work of literature, we are aware we are engaging with disturbing, distressing material. We are aware, too, perhaps, that these works will stay with us, far beyond the moment of narrative catharsis, the purgation of disgust. Like the heroines, we will walk through life in the moment

---

[1] Heller-Nicholas. 2nd edition. 5-6.
[2] Judith Lewis Herman, *Trauma and Recovery*. (BasicBooks, 1992), 96.

post-catharsis, searching for answers to tough ethical and narrative questions which remain, so far as I can tell, unresolved.

This moment warrants further attention, as it opens yet another can of worms for these challenging texts. Throughout this volume, I have argued that rape-revenge texts are difficult to interpret, offering as they do a number of moral ambivalences (ambivalences whose roots grow from the paradox of disgust). Part of the issue lies with the very problem of ever thinking we can separate images of femininity from their cultural and ideological baggage.[3] But I think the problem not only persists but goes further. The fact is, these texts are often unsatisfying in the long-term, and we should investigate why this is, overdetermined, though it may be.

One of the reasons these texts can be so hard to arrive at definitive readings of is their engagement with questions that have proved slippery in real life. Herbert, for instance, writes that rape myths "are peculiarly resistant to debunking."[4] And so those auteurs who tell these stories for specifically anti-rape ends find themselves fighting the tide. Writing about horror's enduring appeal, Cowan observes that horror broaches questions we audiences find compelling but for which we and the horror genre lack enduring answers.[5] The relief/pleasure we may feel from a rape-revenge work and its entailed disgust cannot last, meaning we keep returning to these works.[6]

And so we return yet again to the question of disgust. Kolnai observes that destroying disgusting objects will not necessarily remove the feeling of disgust.[7] Purging, therefore, has its limits. Not only may it not last, but it may not work to begin with. We see this in the rape-revenge texts themselves. Whereas Freeland argues rape-revenge shows revenge as psychologically satisfying,[8] we have seen this is not always the case. For her part, Williams observes how fantasies prolong desire, not solve it.[9]

---

[3] Doane. "Woman's Stake". 96.

[4] Herbert 37.
For the prevalence of belief in rape myths among rapists, see: Johnson, Larissa Gabrielle and Anthony Beech. "Rape myth acceptance in convicted rapists: A systematic review of the literature." *Aggression and Violent Behavior*, Volume 34, 2017, 20-34.

[5] Cowan. *The Forbidden Body*. 5.

[6] Sobchack. "The Violent Dance". 117. By "we" I am only addressing those of us who have watched and continue to watch and engage with these texts. Many audiences, I am sure, avoid them as a matter of course, and I do not presume to lump them into this category alongside myself.

[7] Kolnai. "On Disgust". 58.

[8] Freeland 509.

[9] Williams 277.

And even in real life, the problem is not so clear-cut. Though we may turn to fiction for escapist fantasies, stories do not always set out to satisfy this desire. In the real world, rape survivors often find violent revenge fantasies helpful in the short term, but such daydreams rarely help in the long-term.[10] After all, rape survivors often find it takes years to rebuild,[11] not the condensed, fantastical timeframes these stories tend to offer. And so rape-revenge texts often operate as fantasies, fantasies which must end in at least partial failure.[12] Thus, in futile attempts to remedy that failure, we continue the rhythmic returning, hoping to find sustaining pleasure.[13]

While I believe my analysis has helped identify some of the difficulties in discussing rape-revenge texts, and while I believe I have made some progress in untangling part of this Gordian Knot, the fact remains that problems persist, and questions linger. One of the problems lies in catharsis, which I have identified as one of the pleasures this disgusting sub-genre offers. When I set out to write this volume, catharsis was, in fact, my goal. I wanted to purge myself of these texts and their vexing questions. My own research process, however, revealed the limits of catharsis. Namely, even as I put the final words into this book, I know I am nowhere near the relieved destination I sought. Far from the summit, I have but reached the foot of the mountain. As such, I will keep working, no longer in search, necessarily, of a destination, but rather for the sake of the trek. I have more questions about these texts that I have shelved for the sake of keeping my argument more cohesive and my task manageable. And so, like a horror film monster, I shall return.

-Brandon West, May 2024

---

[10] Henry. "Challenging". 134.

[11] Bowdler 128.

[12] Williams 277.

[13] Nanay 13. I have argued elsewhere in this volume that the aesthetic of disgust can, in fact, offer sustaining pleasure, meaning this point is not necessarily always true.

Bibliography

Primary Sources

Alone. Directed by John Hyams, performance by Jules Wilcox, Magnet Releasing, 2020.

Avenged. Directed by Michael S. Ojeda, performance by Amanda Adrienne, Raven Banner Entertainment, 2013.

Beaumont, Francis and John Fletcher. "The Maid's Tragedy." 2002. *English Renaissance Drama: A Norton Anthology*. Ed. David M. Bevington et al. New York: W.W. Norton, 2002, 1147-1212.

Black Rock. Directed by Katie Aselton, performance by Katie Aselton and Lake Bell, LD Entertainment, 2012.

Bound to Vengeance. Directed by José Manuel Cravioto, performance by Tina Ivlev, IFC Midnight and Scream Factory, 2015.

Death Proof. Directed by Quentin Tarantino, performance by Rosario Dawson, Dimension Films, 2007.

Deeper: The Retribution of Beth. Directed by Jeffrey Andersen, performance by Elise Gatien and Matthew Kevin Anderson, Fat Lemonade, 2015.

Even Lambs Have Teeth. Directed by Terry Miles, performance by Kirsten Prout and Tiera Skovbye, Backup Media, 2015.

Hard Candy. Directed by David Slade, performance by Elliot Page, Lionsgate, 2005.

Irréversible. Directed by Gaspar Noé, performance by Monica Bellucci, StudioCanal, 2002.

I Spit on Your Grave. Directed by Meir Zarchi, performance by Camille Keaton. Cinemagic Pictures, 1978.

I Spit on Your Grave. Directed by Steven R. Monroe, performance by Sarah Butler, Anchor Bay Entertainment, 2010.

I Spit on Your Grave II. Directed by Steven R. Monroe, performance by Jemma Dallender, Anchor Bay Entertainment, 2013.

I Spit on Your Grave III: Vengeance is Mine. Directed by R.D. Braunstein, performance by Sarah Butler, Anchor Bay Films, 2015.

I Spit on Your Grave: Déjà Vu. Directed by Meir Zarchi, Performance by Camille Keaton and Jamie Bernadette, Déjà Vu LLC, 2019.

John Wick. Directed by Chad Stahelski, performance by Keanu Reeves, Lionsgate, 2014.

King, Stephen. "That Feeling, You Can Only Say What It Is in French." In *Everything's Eventual*, Scribner, 1998.

Lady Snowblood. Directed by Toshiya Fujita, performance by Meiko Kaji, Toho, 1973.

The Last House on the Left. Directed by Wes Craven, performance by Sandra Peabody, American International Pictures, 1972.

Ms .45. Directed by Abel Ferrara, performance by Zoë Lund, Rochelle Films, 1981.

Rashomon (羅生門). Directed by Akira Kurosawa, performance by Machiko Kyō, Daiei Films, 1950.

Revenge. Directed by Coralie Fargeat, performance by Matilda Lutz, Rézo Films, 2017.

Richardson, Samuel. *Clarissa, or, The History of a Young Lady*. St. Ives, United Kingdom, Penguin Group, 1985.

Rust Creek. Directed by Jen McGowan, performance by Hermione Corfield, IFC Films, 2019.

Straw Dogs. Directed by Sam Peckinpah, performance by Susan George, 20th Century Fox, 1971.

Teeth. Directed by Mitchell Lichtenstein, performance by Jess Weixler, Roadside Attractions, 2007.

Thelma & Louise. Directed by Ridley Scott, performance by Geena Davis, MGM, 1991.

You're Next. Directed by Adam Wingard, performance by Sharni Vinson, Lionsgate, 2011.

Secondary Sources

Abraham, HD and AB Joseph. "Bulimia vomiting alters pain tolerance and mood." *International Journal of Psychiatry in Medicine*, 16(4), 1986, 311-316. https://pubmed.ncbi.nlm.nih.gov/3030947/. https://doi.org/10.2190/QG04-4 2KU-MKVR-CRHT.

Airaksinen, Timo. *The Philosophy of H.P. Lovecraft: The Route to Horror*. Peter Lang, Inc., 1999.

Altman, Rick. *Film/Genre*. British Film Institute, 1999. https://doi.org/10. 5040/9781838710491.

Bailey, John. "Bang Bang Bang Bang, Ad Naseum [sic]." In *Screening Violence*, edited by Stephen Prince, Rutgers University Press, 2000, 79-85.

Bakhtin, Mikhail. *Problems of Dostoevsky's Poetics*. 1929.

Ballard, Finn. "No Trespassing: The post-millennial road-horror movie." *The Irish Journal of Gothic and Horror Studies*, 4, 2008. https://irishgothicjournal. net/wp-content/uploads/2018/03/finn-ballard.pdf.

Bamford, Karen. *Sexual Violence on the Jacobean Stage*. New York: St. Martin's, 2000.

Bettelheim, Bruno. *The Uses of Enchantment: The Meaning and Importance of Fairy Tales*. New York: Vintage Books, 1989.

Bottigheimer, Ruth B. *Grimms' Bad Girls and Bold Boys: the Moral and Social Vision of the Tales*. Yale University Press, 1987.

Botting, Fred. *Limits of Horror: Technology, Bodies, Gothic*. Manchester: Manchester University Press, 2008.

Boulanger, Ghislaine. *Wounded by Reality: Understanding and Treating Adult Onset Trauma*. Mahwah, NJ: Analytic, 2007. Psychoanalysis in a New Key Book Ser.; v. 6. https://doi.org/10.1037/e490102008-001.

"Bound to Vengeance." Rotten Tomatoes. https://www.rottentomatoes.com/m/bound_to_vengeance.

Bowdler, Michelle. *Is Rape a Crime? A Memoir, an Investigation, and a Manifesto.* Flatiron Books, 2020.

Brinkema, Eugenie. "The Lady Van(qu)ishes: Interiority, Abjection, and the Function of Rape in Horror Films." *Paradoxa: Studies in World Literary Genres* 20, 2006, 33-65. https://doi.org/10.1215/02705346-20-1_58-33.

Brooks, Peter. *Reading for the Plot: Design and Intention in Narrative.* Harvard University Press, 1984.

Brownmiller, Susan. *Against Our Will: Men, Women, and Rape.* New York, Fawcett Columbine, 1975.

Brunvand, Jan Harold. *The Vanishing Hitchhiker: American Urban Legends & Their Meanings.* New York: W.W. Norton and Company, 1981.

Bruun Vaage, Margrethe. "On the Repulsive Rapist and the Difference Between Morality in Fiction and Real Life." In *The Oxford Handbook of Cognitive Literary Studies.* Ed. Lisa Zunshine. 1st ed. Oxford University Press, 2015, 421-439.

Carroll, Noël. *The Philosophy of Horror.* New York: Routledge, 1989.

---. "Why Horror?" In *Horror, The Film Reader*, edited by Mark Jancovich, Routledge, 2002, 33-46.

Catty, Jocelyn. *Writing Rape, Writing Women in Early Modern England: Unbridled Speech.* Houndmills, Basingstoke, Hampshire: Macmillan, 1999.

Celeghin, Alessia, et al. "Basic Emotions in Human Neuroscience: Neuroimaging and Beyond." *Frontiers in Psychology*, 24 August 2017, doi: 10.3389/fpsyg.2017.01432. https://www.ncbi.nlm.nih.gov/pmc/articles/PMC5573709/.

Chaber, Lois A. "Christian Form and Anti-Feminism in *Clarissa.*" *Eighteenth-Century Fiction*, 15(3-4), 2003. https://doi.org/10.1353/ecf.2003.0023.

Cherry, Brigid. "Refusing to refuse to look: Female viewers of the horror film." In *Horror, The Film Reader*, edited by Mark Jancovich, Routledge, 2002, 169-178.

Citron, et al. "Women and Film: A Discussion of Feminist Aesthetics." In *Feminist Film Theory: A Reader*, edited by Sue Thornham, Edinburgh University Press, 1999, 115-121. https://doi.org/10.1515/9781474473224-015.

Clemens, Valdine. *The Return of the Repressed: Gothic Horror from the Castle of Otranto to Alien.* State University of New York Press, 1999.

Clover, Carol J. *Men Women and Chainsaws: Gender in the Modern Horror Film.* London: BFI, 1992.

Cowan, Douglas E. *The Forbidden Body: Sex, Horror, and the Religious Imagination.* New York: New York University Press, 2022. https://doi.org/10.18574/nyu/9781479803132.001.0001.

---. *Sacred Terror: Religion and Horror on the Silver Screen.* Waco, Texas: Baylor University Press, 2008.

Cowie, Elizabeth. "Woman as Sign." In *Feminism and Film*, edited by E. Ann Kaplan, Oxford University Press, 2000, 48-65.

Creed, Barbara. *The Monstrous-Feminine: Film, Feminism, Psychoanalysis.* New York, Routledge, 1993. https://doi.org/10.4324/9781003036654.

---. *Return of the Monstrous-Feminine: Feminist New Wave Cinema*. Routledge, 2022.

"Criminal Justice System Statistics." RAINN. https://www.rainn.org/statistics/criminal-justice-system.

Damrongpiwat, Pichaya. "Fictions of Materiality in Clarissa." *The Eighteenth Century*, 62(1), 2021, 43-62. https://doi.org/10.1353/ecy.2021.0002.

Decker, Lindsey. "The Transnational Gaze in *A Girl Walks Home Alone at Night*." In *Women Make Horror: Filmmaking, Feminism, Genre*, edited by Alison Peirse, Rutgers University Press, 2020, 170-182. https://doi.org/10.36019/9781978805156-014.

de Lauretis, Teresa. "Oedipus Interruptus." In *Feminist Film Theory: A Reader*, edited by Sue Thornham, Edinburgh University Press, 1999, 83-96. https://doi.org/10.1515/9781474473224-011.

Derrida, Jacques and Avital Ronell. "The Law of Genre." *Critical Inquiry*, 7(1), 1980, 55-81. https://doi.org/10.1086/448088.

Derry, Charles. *Dark Dreams 2.0 : a Psychological History of the Modern Horror Film from the 1950s to the 21st Century*. McFarland & Co., 2009.

Doane, Mary Ann. "*Caught* and *Rebecca*: The Inscription of Femininity as Absence." In *Feminist Film Theory: A Reader*, edited by Sue Thornham, Edinburgh University Press, 1999, 70-82. https://doi.org/10.1515/9781474473224-010.

---. "Film and the Masquerade: Theorising the Female Spectator." In *Feminist Film Theory: A Reader*, edited by Sue Thornham, Edinburgh University Press, 1999, 131-145. https://doi.org/10.1515/9781474473224-017.

---. "Woman's Stake: Filming the Female Body." In *Feminism and Film*, edited by E. Ann Kaplan, Oxford University Press, 2000, 86-99.

Doolittle, Robyn. *Had It Coming. Rape Culture Meets #MeToo: Now What?* Truth to Power, Steerforth Press, 2021.

Dunkley, Cara R. and Lori A. Brotto. "The Role of Consent in the Context of BDSM." *Sex Abuse*, 32(6), 657-678, https://pubmed.ncbi.nlm.nih.gov/31010393/. https://doi.org/10.1177/1079063219842847.

Dyer, Richard. *Lethal Repetition: Serial Killing in European Cinema*. Bloomsbury Publishing, 2019. https://doi.org/10.5040/9781838711825.

---. *Only Entertainment*. Routledge, 2002.

Ebert, Roger. "I Spit on Your Grave." 16 July 1980. https://www.rogerebert.com/reviews/i-spit-on-your-grave-1980.

---. "I Spit on Your Grave." 6 October 2010. https://www.rogerebert.com/reviews/i-spit-on-your-grave-2010.

Edelstein, David. "Irreversible Errors: Gaspar Noé's cinematic rape." *Slate*. March 3, 2007. https://slate.com/culture/2003/03/irreversible-a-cinematic-rape.html.

Erickson, Steve. " 'Enter the Void' Director Gaspar Noé Talks Sex, Drugs and Narrative Cinema." *Wall Street Journal*, September 21, 2010. https://www.wsj.com/articles/BL-SEB-46231.

Evans, Walter. "Monster Movies and Rites of Initiation." *Journal of Popular Film and Television*, 4, 1975, 124-142. https://doi.org/10.1080/00472719.1975.10661766.

"Femicides in France are up – despite attempts to quell the problem." *Euronews*, 2023. https://www.euronews.com/2023/09/02/femicides-in-france-are-up-despite-attempts-to-quell-the-problem#:~:text=Femicides%20in%20France%20are%20up%20%2D%20despite%20attempts%20to%20quell%20the%20problem,-A%20protest%20at&text=A%20new%20study%20has%20found,La%20croix%20de%20la%20Rochette.

Fernandez, Jay A. "Katie Aselton to Star in and Direct Thriller 'Black Rock' (Cannes)." *The Hollywood Reporter*. May 11, 2011. https://www.hollywoodreporter.com/movies/movie-news/katie-aselton-star-direct-thriller-187336/.

Ferreday, Debra. "'Only the Bad Gyal could do this': Rihanna, rape-revenge narratives and the cultural politics of white feminism." *Feminist Theory*, 18(3), 2017, 263-280. https://doi.org/10.1177/1464700117721879.

The Found Footage Phenomenon. Directed by Sarah Appleton and Phillip Escott, Caprisar Productions, 2021.

Fox, Pat. "The Most Terrifying Film of All Time…*Come and See*." Film Hounds, 2022. https://filmhounds.co.uk/2022/06/the-most-terrifying-film-of-all-time-come-and-see/.

Fredriksson, Tea. "Avenger in distress: a semiotic study of Lisbeth Salander, rape-revenge and ideology." *Nordic Journal of Criminology*, 22(1), 2021, 58-71.

Freeland, Cynthia. "Feminist Frameworks for Horror Films." In *Film Theory & Discussion*. 8th edition, edited by Leo Braudy and Mashall Cohen, Oxford University Press, 2016, 563-579.

Fulkerson, Mary McClintock. "Sexism as Original Sin: Developing a Theacentric Discourse." *Journal of the American Academy of Religion*, vol. 59, no. 4, [Oxford University Press, American Academy of Religion], 1991, http://www.jstor.org/stable/1465528. https://doi.org/10.1093/jaarel/LIX.4.653.

Gledhill, Christine. "Pleasurable Negotiations." In *Feminist Film Theory: A Reader*, edited by Sue Thornham, Edinburgh University Press, 1999, 166-179. https://doi.org/10.1515/9781474473224-021.

Gonzalez, Ed. "Review: *Bound to Vengeance*." *Slant Magazine*. June 20, 2015. https://www.slantmagazine.com/film/bound-to-vengeance/.

Greenstadt, Amy. *Rape and the Rise of the Author: Gendering Intention in Early Modern England*. Farnham, England: Ashgate, 2009.

Greven, David. *Representations of Femininity in American Genre Cinema: The Woman's Film, Film Noir, and Modern Horror*. Palgrave Macmillan, 2011. https://doi.org/10.1057/9780230118836.

Groom, Nick. *The Gothic: A Very Short Introduction*. Oxford University Press, 2012. https://doi.org/10.1093/actrade/9780199586790.001.0001.

Halberstam, Judith. *Skin Shows: Gothic Horror and the Technology of Monsters*. Durham, NC: Duke University Press, 1995.

Hand, Richard J. *Terror on the Air!: Horror Radio in America, 1931-1952*. Jefferson, NC: McFarland, 2006.

Hanich, Julian. *Cinematic Emotion in Horror Films and Thrillers: The Aesthetic Paradox of Pleasurable Fear*. Routledge, 2010. https://doi.org/10.4324/9780203854587.

---. "Dis/Liking disgust: the revulsion experience at the movies." *New Review of Film and Television Studies*, 7(3), 293-309. https://doi.org/10.1080/174 00300903047052.

Hansen, Miriam. "Pleasure, Ambivalence, and Identification: Valentino and Male Spectatorship." In *Feminism and Film*, edited by E. Ann Kaplan, Oxford University Press, 2000, 226-252.

Haskell, Molly. *From Reverence to Rape: The Treatment of Women in the Movies.* [1st ed.], Holt, Rinehart and Winston, 1974.

Heller-Nicholas, Alexandra. *Rape-Revenge Films*. Jefferson, NC: McFarland, 2011.

---. *Rape-Revenge Films: A Critical Study* 2nd edition. Jefferson, NC: McFarland & Company, Inc., 2021.

Heller, Terry. *The Delights of Terror: an Aesthetics of the Tale of Terror*. University of Illinois Press, 1987.

Hendel, Hilary Jacobs, LCSW. "Disgust: A Natural Emotional Response to Abuse." *Psychology Today*. October 14, 2019. https://www.psychologytoday.com/us/blog/emotion-information/201910/disgust-natural-emotional-response-abuse.

Henry, Claire. "Challenging the boundaries of cinema's rape-revenge genre in *Katalin Varga* and *Twilight Portrait*." *Studies in European Cinema*, 10(2+3), 2013, 133-145. https://doi.org/10.1386/seci.10.2-3.133_1.

---. *Revisionist Rape-revenge Redefining a Film Genre*. Basingstoke: Palgrave Macmillan, 2014. https://doi.org/10.1057/9781137413956.

Herbert, T. Walter. *Sexual Violence and American Manhood.* Harvard University Press, 2002. https://doi.org/10.4159/9780674273641.

Herman, Judith Lewis. *Trauma and Recovery.* BasicBooks, 1992.

Hidden Clips, "Wes Craven Interview (screamography)," YouTube, May 26, 2015, https://www.youtube.com/watch?v=_zmo9fGtcVE&t=1203s.

Hill, Annette. *Shocking Entertainment: Viewer Response to Violent Movies.* Luton, Bedfordshire, U.K.: U of Luton, 1997.

Hoeveler, Diane Long. *Gothic Feminism: the Professionalization of Gender from Charlotte Smith to the Brontës*. Pennsylvania State University Press, 1998. https://doi.org/10.1515/9780271072449.

hooks, bell. "The Oppositional Gaze: Black Female Spectators." In *Feminist Film Theory: A Reader*, edited by Sue Thornham, Edinburgh University Press, 1999, 307-320. https://doi.org/10.1515/9781474473224-033.

Hutchings, Peter. *Historical Dictionary of Horror Cinema*. Lanham, MD: Scarecrow, 2008.

Irigaray, Luce. *This Sex Which Is Not One.* Ithaca, NY: Cornell UP, 1985.

"Irreversible." IMDB. https://www.imdb.com/title/tt0290673/.

"Irreversible." Rotten Tomatoes. https://www.rottentomatoes.com/m/irreversible.

"I Spit on Your Grave (1978)." IMDB. https://www.imdb.com/title/tt0077713/.

"I Spit on Your Grave (part 1) – Count Jackula Horror Review." Uploaded by The Count Jackula Show, *YouTube*, September 21, 2015, https://www.youtube.com/watch?v=CQcDLLnKuhM.

"I Spit on Your Grave (part 2) – Count Jackula Horror Review." Uploaded by The Count Jackula Show, *YouTube*, September 22, 2015, https://www.you tube.com/watch?v=ZRlbB-jDS5U.

"I Spit on Your Grave." Rotten Tomatoes. https://www.rottentomatoes.com/m/ i_spit_on_your_grave.

Jancovich, Mark. "Introduction." In *Horror, The Film Reader*, edited by Mark Jancovich, Routledge, 2002, 57-60. https://doi.org/10.4324/9780203204849.

Jauss, Hans Robert. *Toward an Aesthetic of Reception*. Translated by Timothy Bahti, University of Minnesota Press, 1982.

Johnson, Larissa Gabrielle and Anthony Beech. "Rape myth acceptance in convicted rapists: A systematic review of the literature." *Aggression and Violent Behavior*, Volume 34, 2017, 20-34. https://doi.org/10.1016/ j.avb.2017.03.004.

Johnston, Claire. "Women's Film as Counter-Cinema." In *Feminist Film Theory: A Reader*, edited by Sue Thornham, NYU Press, 1999, 31-40. https://doi. org/10.1515/9781474473224-005.

Jones, Darryl. *Horror: a Very Short Introduction*. Oxford University Press, 2021. https://doi.org/10.1093/actrade/9780198755562.001.0001.

Kaplan, E. Ann. "Is the Gaze Male?" In *Feminism and Film*, edited by E. Ann Kaplan, Oxford University Press, 2000, 119-138.

Keymer, Tom. *Richardson's Clarissa and the Eighteenth-Century Reader*. Cambridge University Press, 2009.

Kilpatrick, Dean G. "The Mental Health Impact of Rape." National Violence Against Women Prevent Research Center, Medical University of South Carolina, 2000. https://mainweb-v.musc.edu/vawprevention/research/men talimpact.shtml.

King, Stephen. *Danse Macabre*. New York: Gallery, 2010.

---. "What's Scary," foreword in *Danse Macabre*, xi-xxxi. New York: Gallery Books, 2010.

Kolnai, Aurel. "On Disgust." Edited by Barry Smith and Carolyn Korsmeyer, Open Court.

---. "The Standard Modes of Aversion: Fear, Disgust, and Hatred." Edited by Barry Smith and Carolyn Korsmeyer, Open Court.

Korsmeyer, Carolyn. "Disgust and Aesthetics." *Philosophy Compass*, 2012, 753-761. doi: 10.1111/j.1747-9991.2012.00522.x. https://doi.org/10.1111/j.1747-9991.2012.00522.x.

Kristeva, Julia. *Powers of Horror: An Essay on Abjection*. Translated by Leon S. Roudiez. New York: Columbia University Press, European Perspectives, 1980.

Lerner, Harriet G. *Women in Therapy*. Harper & Row, 1998.

Levin, Roy J. and Willy von Berlo. "Sexual arousal and orgasm in subjects who experience forced or non-consensual sexual stimulation—a review." *Journal of Clinical Forensic Medicine*, 11(2), April 2004, 82-88. https://pubmed. ncbi.nlm.nih.gov/15261004/. https://doi.org/10.1016/j.jcfm.2003.10.008.

Lowenstein, Adam. *Shocking Representation: Historical Trauma, National Cinema, and the Modern Horror Film*. New York: Columbia University Press, 2005.

"Making *Hard Candy*." Directed by David Slade. In *Hard Candy*. Lions Gate, 2006.

McGillvray, Maddi. "The Feminist Art-Horror of New French Extremity." In *Women Make Horror: Filmmaking, Feminism, Genre*, edited by Alison Peirse, Rutgers University Press, 2020, 122-132. https://doi.org/10.36019/978197 8805156-010.

Meagher, Michelle. "Jenny Saville and a Feminist Aesthetics of Disgust." *Hypatia*, vol. 18, no. 4, Fall 2003, 23-41. http://faculty.winthrop.edu/stockk/WOmen%20in%20art/Meagher%20saville%20disgust.pdf. https://doi.org/10.1353/hyp.2003.0085.

Mee, Laura. "The re-rape and revenge of Jennifer Hills: Gender and genre in *I Spit on Your Grave* (2010)." *Horror Studies*, 4(1), 2013, 75-89. https://doi.org/10.1386/host.4.1.75_1.

Meyers, Helene. *Femicidal Fears: Narratives of the Female Gothic Experience*. SUNY Press, 2001.

Morales, Andrea C., et al. "How Disgust Enhances the Effectiveness of Fear Appeals." *Journal of Marketing Research*, Vol. 49, No. 3, June 2012, 383-393. https://www.jstor.org/stable/41714433. https://doi.org/10.1509/jmr.07.0364.

Mosley, Matthew. "How 'Come and See' Avoids the Inherent Problem With Anti-War Films." Collider, 2022. https://collider.com/come-and-see-avoids-problems-with-anti-war-films/.

Mulvey, Laura. "Visual Pleasure and Narrative Cinema." In *Film Theory & Criticism* 8th ed. Edited by Leo Braudy and Marshall Cohen. Oxford University Press, 2016, 620-631.

Murphy, Bernice M. *The Highway Horror Film*. Palgrave Macmillan, 2014. https://doi.org/10.1057/9781137391209.

Nanay, Bence. *Aesthetics: A Very Short Introduction*. Oxford University Press, 2019. https://doi.org/10.1093/actrade/9780198826613.001.0001.

National Research Council. *Estimating the Incidence of Rape and Sexual Assault*. Washington, DC: The National Academies Press, 2013.

Ndalianis, Angela. *The Horror Sensorium: Media and the Senses*. Jefferson, NC: McFarland, 2012.

Neale, Steve. *Genre and Hollywood*. Routledge, 2005. https://doi.org/10.4324/9780203980781.

Paul, William. *Laughing Screaming: Modern Hollywood Horror and Comedy*. Columbia University Press, 1995.

Peirse, Alison. "Women Make (Write, Produce, Direct, Shoot, Edit, and Analyze) Horror." In *Women Make Horror: Filmmaking, Feminism, Genre*, edited by Alison Peirse, Rutgers University Press, 2020, 1-23. https://doi.org/10.36019/9781978805156-001.

"Perpetrators of Sexual Violence: Statistics." RAINN. https://www.rainn.org/statistics/perpetrators-sexual-violence. Accessed December 2021.

Phelan, Laurence. "Film Censorship: How moral panic led to a mass ban of 'video nasties'. *The Independent*. 13 July 2014. https://www.independent.co.uk/arts-entertainment/films/features/film-censorship-how-moral-panic-led-to-a-mass-ban-of-video-nasties-9600998.html.

Pinedo, Isabel Cristina. *Recreational Terror: Women and the Pleasures of Horror Film Viewing.* State University of New York Press, 1997.

Prince, Stephen. "Graphic Violence in the Cinema: Origins, Aesthetic Design, and Social Effects." In *Screening Violence*, edited by Stephen Prince, Rutgers University Press, 2000, 1-46.

Projansky, Sarah. *Watching Rape: Film and Television in Postfeminist Culture.* New York University Press, 2001.

Read, Jacinda. *The New Avengers: Feminism, Femininity, and the Rape-Revenge Cycle.* Manchester University Press, 2000.

The Relationships Between Military Sexual Assault, Post-Traumatic Stress Disorder and Suicide, and on Department of Defense and Department of Veterans Affairs Medical Treatment and Management of Victims of Sexual Trauma: Hearing before the Subcommittee on Personnel of the Committee on Armed Services, United States Senate, One Hundred Thirteenth Congress, Second Session, February 26, 2014. U.S. Government Printing Office, 2014.

"Revenge." IMDB. https://www.imdb.com/title/tt6738136/.

"Revenge." Rotten Tomatoes. https://www.rottentomatoes.com/m/revenge_2018.

"Revenge." Shudder. https://www.shudder.com/movies/watch/revenge/2cef63838af05b94. Accessed December 13, 2021.

"Self-Control and its Connection to Disordered Eating." *Eating Disorders Review*, vol. 27, no. 5, 2016. https://eatingdisordersreview.com/self-control-and-its-connection-to-disordered-eating/.

Silverman, Kaja. "Lost Objects and Mistaken Subjects." In *Feminist Film Theory: A Reader*, edited by Sue Thornham, NYU Press, 1999. https://doi.org/10.1515/9781474473224-012.

Simkin, Stevie. *Early Modern Tragedy and the Cinema of Violence.* Basingstoke: Palgrave Macmillan, 2006. https://doi.org/10.1057/9780230597112.

---. *Straw Dogs.* Palgrave Macmillan, 2011. https://doi.org/10.1007/978-0-230-34497-6.

Snider, Clifton. "Jungian Theory, Its Literary Application, and a Discussion of *The Member of the Wedding*." In *Psychological Perspectives on Literature: Freudian Dissidents and Non-Freudians: a Casebook*, edited by Joseph P. Natoli, Archon, 1984.

Sobchack, Vivian C. "The Violent Dance: A Personal Memoir of Death in the Movies." In *Screening Violence*, edited by Stephen Prince, Rutgers University Press, 2000, 110-124.

Spolsky, Ellen. *The Contracts of Fiction: Cognition, Culture, Community.* 2015. https://doi.org/10.1093/acprof:oso/9780190232146.001.0001.

Stacey, Jackie. "Desperately Seeking Difference." In *Feminism and Film*, edited by E. Ann Kaplan, Oxford University Press, 2000, 450-465.

Stidham, Daniel. *Cutprintfilm.* June 23, 2015. https://web.archive.org/web/20150625100050/http://www.cutprintfilm.com/reviews/bound-to-vengeance/.

Street, et al. "Military Sexual Trauma." PTSD: National Center for PTSD, U.S. Department of Veteran Affairs, 2022. https://www.ptsd.va.gov/professional/treat/type/sexual_trauma_military.asp#three.

Stubbe, Maria. *"Was that my misunderstanding?" Managing miscommunication and problematic talk at work.* 2010. Victoria University of Wellington, PhD thesis. https://core.ac.uk/download/pdf/41336781.pdf.

Tamborini, Ron and K. Salomonson. "Horror's Effect on Social Perceptions and Behaviors." In *Horror Films: Current Research on Audience Preferences and Reactions*, edited by James B. Weaver and Ron Tamborini, Routledge, 1996.

Tropp, Martin. *Images of Fear: How Horror Stories Helped Shape Modern Culture, 1818-1918.* McFarland & Co., 1990.

Tudor, Andrew. *Monsters And Mad Scientists: A Cultural History of the Horror Movie.* 1989.

Turner, Jonathan H., and Alexandra. Maryanski. *Incest: Origins of the Taboo.* Boulder, Colo.: Paradigm, 2005.

Van Dam, Andrew. "Less than 1% of rapes lead to felony convictions. At least 89% of victims face emotional and physical consequences." *The Washington Post.* October 6, 2018. https://www.washingtonpost.com/business/2018/10/06/less-than-percent-rapes-lead-felony-convictions-least-percent-victims-face-emotional-physical-consequences/.

Van Marter, Shirley. "Richardson's Revisions of 'Clarissa' in the Third and Fourth Editions." *Studies in Bibliography*, vol. 28, 1975, 119–152. JSTOR, www.jstor.org/stable/40371613.

West, Brandon. *At the Edge of Existence: Liminality in Horror Cinema Since the 1970s.* Jefferson, NC. McFarland & Company, Inc., 2022.

Williams, Linda. "Film Bodies: Gender, Genre, and Excess." In *Feminist Film Theory: A Reader*, edited by Sue Thornham, NYU Press, 1999. https://doi.org/10.1515/9781474473224-029.

Wilson, Laura. *Spectatorship, Embodiment and Physicality in the Contemporary Mutilation Film* (Illustrated ed.). Springer, 2015, 84–85. https://doi.org/10.1057/9781137444387.

Wisker, Gina. *Horror Fiction: an Introduction.* Continuum, 2005.

Wood, Robin. *Hollywood from Vietnam to Regan...And Beyond.* Columbia University Press, 2003.

Young, Alison. *The Scene of Violence: Cinema, Crime, Affect.* Abingdon: Routledge-Cavendish, 2010.

Zillman, D. and R. Gibson. "Evolution of the Horror Genre." In *Horror Films: Current Research on Audience Preferences and Reactions*, edited by James B. Weaver and Ron Tamborini, Routledge, 1996.

Index

A

Alone, 42, 43, 44, 135
Aselton, Katie, 23, 24, 25, 135, 139
At the Edge of Existence, 116, 144
Avenged, 29, 41, 135

B

Bamford, Karen, 6, 7, 17, 18, 48,
   136
Black Rock, 23, 24, 25, 26, 27, 30,
   31, 44, 135, 139
Bound to Vengeance, 24, 40, 47, 48,
   49, 50, 101, 106, 107, 108, 110,
   111, 112, 119, 135, 139
Brinkema, Eugenie, 4, 11, 15, 16,
   19, 137
Brownmiller, Susan, 137
Bruun Vaage, Margrethe, 54, 55,
   57, 58, 59, 60, 128, 137

C

Catty, Jocelyn, 17
Clarissa, 45, 54, 61, 62, 63, 64, 65,
   66, 67, 136, 144
Clover, Carol J., 4, 8, 9, 10, 12, 17,
   18, 46, 58, 60, 67, 68, 116, 123,
   126, 137
Creed, Barbara, 91, 123

D

Death Proof, 31, 32, 33, 34, 35, 36,
   38, 44, 135

disgust, ix, 3, 43, 44, 54, 55, 57, 59,
   60, 62, 66, 67, 68, 101, 108, 113,
   116, 118, 120, 140

E

Ebert, Roger, 46, 48, 49, 60, 64, 138
Even Lambs Have Teeth, 107, 135

G

gaze, 123, 126

H

Hard Candy, 36, 37, 38, 39, 40, 41,
   44, 135, 142
Haskell, Molly, 106, 140
Heller-Nicholas, Alexandra, ix, 2,
   24, 31, 32, 33, 34, 36, 46, 57, 58,
   59, 85, 86, 87, 88, 89, 90, 108,
   123, 129, 140
Henry, Claire, 15, 16, 24, 27

I

I Spit on Your Grave, 1, 2, 4, 6, 8, 9,
   10, 11, 13, 15, 18, 19, 24, 29, 30,
   33, 38, 43, 46, 47, 48, 50, 54, 56,
   58, 60, 61, 64, 66, 67, 92, 101,
   105, 106, 108, 110, 111, 112, 113,
   114, 117, 119, 122, 123, 135, 138,
   140, 141
incest, 91
Irigaray, Luce, 1
Irreversible, 38, 39, 43, 101, 113,
   114, 115, 116, 117, 118, 119, 138,
   140

www.ingramcontent.com/pod-product-compliance
Lightning Source LLC
Chambersburg PA
CBHW050520280326
41932CB00014B/2392